For Katharine
and
Edward

in memory of a happy day spent at
Mount Vernon. 1937.

from H.C.P.

MOUNT VERNON

MOUNT VERNON

Washington's Home and the Nation's Shrine

BY

PAUL WILSTACH

*Illustrations from Photographs
by Henry H. Saylor, and others*

BLUE RIBBON BOOKS, INC.
NEW YORK CITY

Printed and bound by The Cornwall Press, Inc., for
Blue Ribbon Books, Inc., 386 Fourth Ave., New York City

Printed in the United States of America

To
HARRISON HOWELL DODGE

MOUNT VERNON

No estate in United America is more pleasantly situated than this. It lies in a high, dry, and healthy country, 300 miles by water from the sea, and on one of the finest rivers in the world. Its margin is washed by more than ten miles of tide water. . . . It is situated in a latitude between the extremes of heat and cold, and is the same distance by land and water . . . from the Federal City, Alexandria, and Georgetown; distant from the first, twelve, from the second, nine, and from the last sixteen miles.—*George Washington.*

From beneath that humble roof went forth the intrepid and unselfish warrior—the magistrate who knew no glory but his country's good; to that he returned happiest when his work was done. There he lived in noble simplicity; there he died in glory and peace. While it stands the latest generations of the grateful children of America will make this pilgrimage to it as to a shrine, and when it shall fall, if fall it must, the memory and name of Washington shall shed an eternal glory on the spot.—*Edward Everett.*

Everything, every subject, every corner and step, seems to bring him close. . . . It is an exquisite and friendly serenity which bathes one's sense . . . that seems to be charged all through with some meaning or message of beneficence and reassurance but nothing that could be put in words. . . . You may spend an hour, you may spend a day, wandering, sitting, feeling the gentle power of the place; you may come back another time, it meets you, you cannot dispel it by familiarity. . . . And as you think of this you bless the devotion of those whose piety and care treasure the place and keep it sacred and beautiful.—*Owen Wister.*

TABLE OF CONTENTS

TABLE OF CONTENTS   xi

CHAPTER IX

CHAPTER X

CHAPTER XI

CHAPTER XII

CHAPTER XIII

CHAPTER XIV

CHAPTER XV

CHAPTER XVI

CHAPTER XXI

APPENDIX

A

B

C

D

ILLUSTRATIONS

PREFACE TO FOURTH EDITION

Every true lover of Mount Vernon, and every one who reveres the name of Washington and who fain would visualize him in the place he loved, and longed for when national affairs kept him absent from his home, should possess a copy of Mr. Wilstach's delightful book, *Mount Vernon, Washington's Home and the Nation's Shrine.*

To me it is invaluable. I keep it close at hand and find myself constantly referring to it, knowing that in its charmingly written pages I shall find the information I am seeking correctly stated; a point I wish to stress, for while this book makes no claim to being a history of General Washington, the account of the years he spent at Mount Vernon, years which he himself called "the happiest of my life," is accurately and truthfully presented in an interesting and sympathetic manner.

It is therefore a pleasure to recommend to intelligent and patriotic people this new edition of Mr. Wilstach's book, the latter part of which deals with The Mount Vernon Ladies' Association of the Union, of which I have the honor of being the Regent.

AUGUST 6TH, 1930.

Alice Haliburton Richards

Regent.

INTRODUCTION

To Dr. Johnson has been attributed the epigram,
"The most difficult thing in the world, sir, is to
get possession of a fact"; and to few perhaps does
this come home with more force than to those who undertake to extract the truth from the traditions and
glamour of romance that have grown around so much of
the life and customs of Colonial America. The gratification, perhaps the pride, engendered by the accounts
that have come down to us of the imposing dignity of
the lives of our Colonial ancestors and the elegance of
their homes has sometimes received a rude shock as we
have gazed for the first time on the "Mansions" in
which they lived; and while, on the one hand, this is
true; on the other, it is equally true that some of those
old worthies whose names are scarce remembered, and
who may perhaps "have sealed their letters with their
thumbs," are shown by careful research to have possessed homes as stately as any, and to have contributed
as prodigally to Virginia's reputation for hospitality
and heroism as did those whose names have gone sounding down the ages; and as it is the task of the faithful
historian to make "history as written accord with history as performed," so in the field he has chosen to
occupy, this is what Mr. Wilstach has endeavored to
accomplish, and I believe he has achieved it.

Much of what, in the past, has been said and written

about Mount Vernon has been based on tradition, and while Mr. Wilstach's careful investigation has confirmed many of these traditions, some of what has been believed has been found not entirely accurate, and his patient research has brought to light much that was not known. It was not an easy task, and those who feel an abiding interest in the home of the Father of his Country, and who appreciate faithful endeavor, will recognize the debt due the author for his patient labor of love.

Lawrence Washington

July, 1916.

CHAPTER I

Mount Vernon's Beginnings—The Doeg Indians—John Smith's Account of the Upper Tidewater Potomac—Leonard Calvert at Piscataway—Early Royal Grants of the Northern Neck—The English Washingtons—First Washingtons in Virginia—Washingtons and Fairfaxes Move Up the Potomac —Title to Hunting Creek Tract—The First Dwelling—The Fire—Lawrence Washington.

MOUNT VERNON, the home and last resting place of George Washington, is situated on the Virginia shore of the Potomac River, in Fairfax County, fourteen miles south of the Capital of the United States.

Its wide fame, the deep affection in which it is held, and the familiarity given it by written and painted history, make it difficult for the mind to erase the picture of Washington's home and think of its parked heights as virgin forest overlooking a sailless, undiscovered river. Yet less than one hundred and fifty years before it came into his hands, so far as is positively known, white man had never seen it.

In Mount Vernon's early history events punctuated long series of years. The first title holders to these hills and meadows were the Doeg Indians, a tribe of the Algonquin race. Their remains have been unearthed on the rising ground near the river in very recent years. Their possession was secure and undisputed, when one day, around the broad bend to the west, there appeared a strange sail on an open barge. As it drew nearer it re-

finest of all mortar made of the burnt oyster shells taken from the beds of the tidal "creeks," which give endless diversity to the shores of the lower Potomac. Later, when time has aged these mansions and the restorer comes to repair their century-old walls, he will find that it is more frequently the bricks which yield and crack under the pick and hammer than the oyster-shell mortar.

Until the early seventies the tracts along the west bank of the Potomac from Dogue's Creek to Little Hunting Creek were without recorded proprietors. Larger tracts of which this was a part were then granted, some say by the Crown and others say by the Royal Governor in Virginia. The recorders and later chroniclers seem to contribute much confusion. Perhaps they are right, and the seventeenth century state of Northern Neck titles was confusing.

Certain it is that Charles II in exile, without throne or crown, did grant to two tricky favorites, the Earl of Arlington and Lord Culpepper, "to be held by them for thirty-one years at a yearly rental of forty shillings," all the lands between the Rappahannock and the Potomac and known as the Northern Neck. Later this grant was withdrawn to be extended again on a larger scale to include "all that tract and territory, region and dominion of land and water commonly called Virginia."

Here was strong meat indeed for the stomach of freedmen. It would not digest and was one of the causes which begat Bacon's Rebellion. In spite of resentment their title seems to have been sustained, for Arlington conveyed his share of the proprietorship of Virginia to Culpepper, and the title deeds to Mount Vernon begin with a grant from Lord Culpepper "in the twenty seventh year of the reign of our Sovereigne Lord, King Charles ye Second, Anno Domini 1674," to Lieutenant Colonel John Washington and Colonel Nicholas Spencer, of five thousand acres "scituate, lying and being in the County of Stafford"—which county had been cut off from Westmoreland and from a part of which Prince William and Fairfax counties were later created—"in the ffreshes of the Pottomeek River and neare opposite to Piscataway, Indian towne of Mariland." This Washington, known as John the Emigrant, was the great-grandfather of George of Mount Vernon, and was the first of George Washington's forebears to cross from England to America.

The greatness of George Washington inflamed the imagination of his early biographers. If we cannot abide by their accuracy it is possible to be amused by their invention. One of them traces his line back through generations and centuries of noble and valiant ancestors, until he brings up at the throne of the hearty Scandinavian deity, Odin, "the god who gives victory." The name Washington is traced from de Wessynton, to Wessynton without the de, to Wasshington and Washington. As last written it early appeared as the name of a parish in the County of Durham in England. The forebears of our Washington trace in a direct line through their namesakes of Sulgrave Manor, Northamptonshire, to John Washington of Warton, Lancashire. Beyond him is conjecture. After him the line is authentic. His son, the grantee of Sulgrave, was named Lawrence, and his name, like his father's, reappears frequently in future generations. In the coat-of-arms engraved on this Lawrence's tomb in the church at Sulgrave is found the three spur rowels above the red bars on a white field, which appeared as early as 1360 in the seal of William de Wessyngton, and which are popularly regarded as having suggested the stars and stripes of the flag of the United States.

Lawrence of Sulgrave fell upon hard times and he was obliged to give up his manor house, whereupon his good friend and neighbor, Lord Spencer, in 1606 built him the house in the village of Little Brington where he lived during the remaining years of his life. As already indicated, the names of Washington and Spencer are to be joined again, in another transaction involving a home, but in Virginia next time, in title deeds on which is founded the proprietorship of Mount Vernon itself.

Washington House, as it has been known and pointed out to pilgrims these hundred years, was afterward occupied by Lawrence's brother Robert and his family. After Robert's death Lawrence's widow came again, and lived there until 1636, when she went into Essex to make her home with her son, another Lawrence, who was rector of Purleigh. This son, the Reverend Lawrence Washington, M.A., married Amphillis Rhodes and their issue was six sons and daughters, among whom was John the Emigrant, and his brother, third of the name of Lawrence, and a sister, who both followed him to America.

At this time England was in civil convulsion. Charles II was in banishment, and the Puritans of the eleven years' commonwealth were carrying government with a high hand. The Washington family were committed to the royalist cause, not merely by their holding of the Rectory of Purleigh, but by the traditional sympathies inbred by generations of devotion to the crown. Politics deprived the father of his parish in 1643, and, casting about for opportunity and ease from petty persecution, his son John, and later his son Lawrence and the young men's sister, crossed the seas to the colony of Virginia as recited above.

John reached Virginia about 1658. He did not come at once to the upper end of tidewater Potomac. His first plantation was in Westmoreland County between the Rappahannock and the Potomac, and it gave his name to the parish. Soon he married for his second wife Miss Ann Pope, and, where Bridges Creek meets the Potomac seventy miles down river from the present capital, he built a modest dwelling, later named Wakefield. Here were born their eldest son, Lawrence, and this Lawrence's eldest son, Augustine.

The name of Washington appeared continually in colonial chronicles both of Burgesses and vestry. John Washington, the Emigrant, was a member of the House of Burgesses, and the recurrence of his name in connection with the business of the Assembly indicates that he took no unimportant part in its work. This was at Williamsburg. On Westmoreland plantation, however, so far away from the gay little capital and so near the frontier, life during the last half of the seventeenth century was even and uneventful, save for brushes with the Indians and the struggle to force the forest back and make the good red clay yield its harvest.

The family evidently rose to some estate, for, after a little more than fifty years in Virginia, it is able to send Augustine, John's grandson, to England to be educated. On his return he married Jane, daughter of Caleb Butler, of Westmoreland, who bravely wrote "Esquire" after his name. They had four children, but of them only Lawrence and Augustine lived beyond childhood. Jane Washington died in 1728. In less than two years Augustine married again, this time Mary, youngest daughter of Colonel Joseph Ball. He brought her to his Bridges Creek plantation overlooking the lower Potomac, and soon the first blessing of this union was recorded in the old quaint quarto Bible, now among the treasures at Mount Vernon, in these terms:

George Washington Son to Augustine & Mary his Wife was born. y. 11th Day of February 1731½ about 10 in the Morning & was Baptiz'd the 5th of April following Mr. Beverly Whiting & Capt. Christopher Brooks Godfathers and Mrs. Mildred Gregory Godmother *

It was a fruitful union. George's younger brothers were Samuel, John Augustine, and Charles, and his sisters were Elisabeth, who appears later as Betty, and Mildred, who died in childhood.

Other lands than Wakefield had come into the hands of the great-grandfather of Lawrence and his half-brother George, as already noted in the grant from Lord Culpepper, the crown grantee. This five-thousand-acre holding of John Washington and Nicholas Spencer was not divided until 1690. Meantime John died and in his will bequeathed his half of this tract to his son Lawrence. The division thirteen years later gave him the eastern half, facing Little Hunting Creek, and the Spencer family took the western half, facing Dogue Run.

This Lawrence in his will bequeathed "all my land in

*Washington was born February 11 old style, February 22 new style. See page 217.

Stafford County, lying upon Hunting Creek . . . by estimation 2,500 acres," to his daughter Mildred. It has been stated that "Mildred died in infancy, and the Hunting Creek estate became the joint possession of the widow and two sons, until it fell to the survivor of them all, Augustine, about the year 1730." Another historian dismisses this transfer with the comfortable though indefinite remark that "we find. Augustine Washington . . . in possession of one half of the above 5,000 acres in 1740."

The transfer from Mildred to Augustine is definitely accounted for by a deed of May 26, 1726, from Mildred and her husband, Roger Gregory, to Augustine Washington, "her brother," for "a moietie or half of five thousand acres formerly Lay'd Out for Collo Nicholas Spencer and the father of Capt Lawrence Washington Bounded as follows Begining by the River Side at the Mouth of Little Hunting Creek and Extending up the said Creek according to the several courses and Meanders thereof nine hundred Eighty and Six Poles to a mark'd A Corner Tree standing on the West side of the South Branch being the main branch of said Hunting Creek From there by a lyne of Mark'd trees west eighteen Degrees South across a Woods to the Dividing Lyne as formerly made Between Madam Francis Spencer and Captain Lawrence Washington and from hence W by the said Lyne to ye River and with the River and all the Courses and Meanders of the said River to the Mouth of the Creek afor'sd."

Augustine Washington moved up river and established his family on his Hunting Creek lands within a short time after George's birth, for Augustine's name appears as vestryman of Truro Parish in 1735. Accompanying the Washingtons came their friend William Fairfax, colonial agent of his cousin Lord Fairfax in England, on whose lands he settled, nearby his friends.

The Fairfax estate was a long peninsula of nearly three thousand acres on the west side of Dogue Creek, and it was one of the finest set estates on the river. Its waterfront measured, by all its "corses and meanders," nearly ten miles. The high front jutted out into the deepest point of the river channel, and the creeks, which flanked it east and west, made it possible to enclose the entire acreage with little more than one mile of fence on its western side. On the glorious promontory overlooking the river William Fairfax built Belvoir, a great house destined to be the scene of much that was significant in the lives of both Lawrence Washington and his young brother George.

Augustine's Hunting Creek plantation, derived originally from Lord Culpepper, is described in his father's bequest of 1697 as "the land where Mrs. Eliza Minton and Mrs. Williams now live." These are the earliest recorded dwellers on the lands later to become so famous. It is a strange prank of the chronicles to call attention to two women dwelling in the wilderness, pioneers by nearly half a century of the next known resident. Where were their cabins—at the head of the creek secluded from the curiosity of river rovers, or standing boldly forth on the mount by the river, with a free sweep for miles above and below?

From 1735, when Augustine Washington and Mary his wife came to this estate, it was continually owned and occupied by a Washington for one hundred and twenty-three years, when the fame of the spot and the overwhelming rush of pilgrims grew beyond the endurance of private ownership and it passed into the hands of the association of patriotic women who care for it now.

With Augustine and Mary were their children George, Elisabeth, and Samuel, and possibly John Augustine, though he may have been born here. If Lawrence and Augustine, the elder half-brothers of these children, came to the new home it was for only a short time, for they soon went to England and entered the school at Appleby, up near the Scottish border, in the County of Westmoreland, for which their own native county in Virginia had been named. While living on the upper Potomac the family had been increased by the birth of a daughter, christened Mildred, who died in infancy.

There seems to be no conclusive evidence to determine where Augustine built the first house on this tract. Some historians have accepted the conjecture that he cleared a homestead site and built a house alongside the mill which so long survived him, where the trickling branch met the tidal Dogue Creek. This use of the word creek for bay or inlet is common on all shores of the Chesapeake and its tributary rivers. The running feeder of the creek is more often called the run or branch. It was so in colonial days and it is the same to-day.

Other chroniclers incline to the theory that Augustine reared his house on or near the site of the present mansion. A third theory places it on the site of the greenhouse. Wherever it stood, the first home of the Washingtons on this site was short-lived. It burned to the ground in 1739. There is no record that it was rebuilt. If

we could see the letters that had been passing between
Virginia and the Virginian schoolboys in English Westmoreland it would perhaps be easier to understand
why the father now gathered his young family about
him again and moved to yet another Washington property, on the Rappahannock, near Fredericksburg.

This thriving little city was no mean centre at this
time. It was second in importance only to the capital
at Williamsburg. It had no gold-laced governor, no
busy burgesses, and no university, but it was a flourish-
ing focus of trade and travel, at the junction of all the
roads from the South with the Kingshighway which
led to the northern colonies; not a bad place to keep in
touch with the world.

Augustine did not return to Westmoreland, because
his second son and namesake was then home from England, or on his way, to marry rich Miss Aylett, and
that property was intended for him. The Hunting
Creek tract and the mill nearby he had in mind for his
eldest boy, Lawrence, and to him he deeded it in 1740,
at the same time confirming the gift in his will.

This Lawrence, the third of the name in America,
becomes of particular interest to this narrative, for his
is the first name definitely identified, as owner and
occupant, with the historic mansion which overlooks
the Potomac to-day.

CHAPTER II

What Lawrence Found on His Tract—Pioneer Buildings—Abandons His Estate for Military Service in the West Indies Under Admiral Vernon—Returns and Marries Anne Fairfax—Career of Lawrence Washington—Arrival of George to Make His Home at Mount Vernon—Parson Weems—Influences on George's Young Character at Mount Vernon and at Belvoir—The Original House—Who Built It?—The Cornerstone.

WHEN Lawrence took possession of his estate "in the ffreshes of the Pottomeek river and neare opposite to Piscataway, Indian town of Mariland," there is no assurance that he found more than two important buildings. Of cabins for the slaves and shelter for the animals there was probably a plenty of some kind, but the enduring "improvements" were the mill back at the head of Dogue Creek and probably the old brick barn on the mount overlooking the river.

The mill ground flour for over a century, and the ancients of the neighborhood can still remember it standing before the Civil War. Eventually it succumbed to abandonment, though even to-day one traces its dimensions in the rounded banks left on the site of its foundations, which were pilfered piecemeal to help support many a younger house in the neighborhood. The mill is worth bearing in mind, for it will have its part to play in this story, and will be the last place on the estate visited by its chief personage before he died. The barn has fared better than the mill. It stands to-

15

day stout and strong, the proud veteran of the village
of buildings on either side of the bowling green.

There are various scraps of tradition about other
pioneer buildings. Lossing speaks of "the original
cottage" where hung "the dingy iron lantern" which
during George's occupancy of the mansion lighted the
hall. The lantern was taken to Arlington after Mrs.
Washington's death, and after a long interval at the
National Museum in the Capital City is again in the
hall at Mount Vernon. There is a tradition in the
Washington family that the lantern was given to Lawrence by Admiral Vernon. Where "the original cottage" stood or what became of it Lossing did not say.
Moncure D. Conway says "an old house stood where
Washington built his greenhouses in which probably
the four years of his childhood there were passed,"
and asserts with certainty that Lawrence built Mount
Vernon house.

Whatever Lawrence found on his estate when he
came into possession, he seems to have had other ideas
than settling down to the life of a planter. At twenty-
two the heel is spry. Besides, the call had gone forth
from the mother country for a quota of troops from her
American colonies to reinforce General Wentworth and
Admiral Vernon, who were disciplining the West Indian
Spanish.

Lawrence received a captain's commission, departed
with the colonial troops, fought at Carthagena, survived the fever scourge which swept away many times
more than Spanish marksmanship, and returned to his
Potomac estate in the autumn of 1742.

What of his land in the interval? Did it await its

master's coming untenanted and abandoned, or are we privileged to think of it still humanized by the presence of the aged but undaunted Amazons of the frontier, Mrs. Minton and Mrs. Williams?

His sympathy with a military career and his affection for his commanders, Vernon and Wentworth, were so strong that he displayed some restlessness on his return to Virginia and considered going to England and joining his regiment. But another and stronger affection had taken root in his heart, one that bound him to Virginia and his own neighborhood with tender but unyielding bonds.

At the neighboring mansion of Belvoir there was more than a neighbor's welcome for him. William Fairfax had two daughters, and Lawrence spent the winter after his return in the most absorbing of all adventures, that of winning a wife. In the spring of 1743 he and Anne Fairfax, the elder of the two sisters, were to be married, when he was summoned down to the farm near Fredericksburg, by the illness and death of his father, and he became the head of the family in America. He was an executor of his father's will and devoted himself to his father's bequests. In July he went over to Belvoir, claimed his bride, and brought her to their home on the heights which, in remembrance of his admired commander, he named Mount Vernon.

Nature is constant, and to-day the same outlook charms the eye from the Mount Vernon doorway that greeted Lawrence and Anne. Before them the river extended nearly a mile from the Virginia to the Maryland shore. To the left it seemed to sweep toward

them through a break in a high ridge. Already the
Digges family had reared Warburton Manor on the
opposite point, where now rises Fort Washington, and
at its foot broad Piscataway Creek, joining the Potomac, lay revealed along its more than two miles of
length. The low Maryland shore opposite accented
the height of Mount Vernon. To the right the river
swept majestically to the southwest, passed the high
green point of Belvoir, and was abruptly bended toward
the south by the distant shore of Mason's Neck, where,
back on the highland, was soon to rise George Mason's
Gunston Hall. The panorama embraced nearly twelve
miles of water.

Mount Vernon stands on what is literally a mount,
though to the casual observer the house appears to
stand merely on a high bank, a part of a continuous
shore-line elevation. The land in fact slopes away in all
directions. On the west it descends to the first river
bottom elevation, which extends the mile and a quarter
to Dogue's Creek. On the east it falls away to the
water at its boundary, Little Hunting Creek, and on
this side of the estate the west bank of the Potomac
does not rise again to the same level until it reaches
the highlands at Georgetown. On the north and west
the elevation drops away to the broad valley through
which runs the historic Kingshighway.

Lawrence was twenty-five years old at the time of his
marriage, and during the next ten years he developed
into one of the important men of the colony. His
marriage had united him to one of the great families
of Virginia, for Anne was a cousin of Thomas Lord
Fairfax, and her half-brother, Bryan, succeeded to the

title though he did not assume it. His landed possessions exceeded twenty-five hundred acres, for to his hereditary tract he added at least two hundred acres near the mill. The royal governor appointed him adjutant of his military district, with the rank of major, though with a salary of only one hundred and fifty pounds a year, and he repeatedly represented his county in the House of Burgesses at Williamsburg. In 1750 he was made president of the Ohio Company, formed the year before to colonize the great wilderness of the Ohio Valley, under a royal grant of five hundred thousand acres.

In his effort to carry out the work of the company of which he found himself the president he proposed introducing German immigrants from the colony of Pennsylvania. Being dissenters, they ran into a net of double taxation by moving into the jurisdiction of Virginia, which was the occasion for Lawrence Washington, in the face of the state establishment, to deliver what is one of the first, if not the first, appeals for religious tolerance in the history of the colony of Virginia.

"It has ever been my opinion and I hope it ever will be," he said, "that restraints on conscience are cruel in regard to those on whom they are imposed, and injurious to the country imposing them."

Lawrence left no journals and few letters. There is little on which to found a picture of life at Mount Vernon while he was master. It could scarcely have been gay. Anne bore him four children, but not one lived beyond babyhood.

To break their loneliness Lawrence's young brother George often came to visit them, sometimes sailing up river from Westmoreland, oftener on horseback over the road from his mother's place at Fredericksburg. These visits meant much to both brothers, for the affection which existed between them is often attested.

Though George was merely in his mid-teens, he was Lawrence's eldest unmarried brother and the prospective head of the family. A real intimacy existed between Lawrence of twenty-nine and George of fifteen, and it disclosed the boy's promise to the elder's shrewd observation.

Such accounts of George's youth as have come down to us languish under the doubts of the historians. However, that which cannot be proven need not be despised. Conway calls it "Washington Mythology, a folklore such as must always invest the founders of nations or the man of the people. Washington is entitled to his Washington-lore, by which, indeed, he is rather draped than disguised."

Lawrence saw him through no such illumination. He was doubtless not less amused than edified by the boy's first literary product, the astonishing Rules of Civility and Conduct, written when he was fourteen. If he left his brief schooling "a bad speller and a still worse grammarian," Lawrence knew him for a good cipherer, a skilful horseman, and a young man of firm grasp and sound judgment, of normal appetites, willingness, application, endurance, and thoroughness in work and play.

There came a day in the autumn of 1747 when George arrived, not to visit merely. He came to make Mount Vernon his home. It had in reality been familiar to him from his earliest recollection. His father had moved up river from Westmoreland when George was only three years old, too young to have left behind any permanent impressions, but old enough to enjoy his environment. It was the waters of Hunting Creek and Dogue Creek and the fields and woods between which were the background of his first boyhood experiences.

Here "in his sixth year," according to Parson Weems, he acted the immortal scene of the cherry-tree and the hatchet, a piece of boyish heroism it is pleasant to see growing again into some standing as history after the long reaction against its acceptance. Parson Weems was a victim of his own florid, extravagant style. The incidents he related very probably did not happen as he related them, but stripped of the halo of romantic morality he gave them, in merely following a literary fashion of his time, there is little reason to discredit them. The writer had excellent opportunity to gather the facts of George's boyhood at first, or, at most, second hand. He knew him, man and boy, well. For a time he officiated at Pohick Church, which the Mount Vernon family attended and which he erroneously, but with an eye to the main chance, called "Mount Vernon Parish" on his title page. Moreover, he was an intimate of Washington's intimates and married Fanny Ewell, of Belle Aire, whose mother was a near relative of Washington's. Perhaps she was the anonymous lady from whom he acknowledges having received the cherry-tree story.

Until he returned to Mount Vernon to live George had four homes among which he divided his time. The schooldays were spent at his mother's house on the Rappahannock. The earlier vacation days he spent at his birthplace, Wakefield, down on the Westmoreland shore of the Potomac, visiting his half-brother, Augustine, whom he called Austin. His mother's home was somewhat austere. There was another kind of life at Wakefield, kept up by his rich sister-in-law's money.

It was at Belvoir and Mount Vernon, however, that he found the stimulating and refining influences which reacted on his character. Lawrence was a far-travelled man. He had been to school in England and had fought in the West Indies. In the adventures he recounted there was fuel indeed for a hungry boyish curiosity. Vessels of His Majesty's navy came up the river and anchored off Mount Vernon, and the officers, among whom were some with whom Lawrence had fought at Carthagena, came ashore. Over the punch and toddy, through the haze of smoke rolling from the long church-wardens, while the candles burned bright, there was brave talk enough, of campaigns and strategy, to fire the imagination of the listening lad of fifteen.

At Belvoir he came under another influence, that of a polished English household, no negligible substitute for that trip abroad which he was never privileged to take. At his mother's there was the discipline and the sound, simple morality which strengthened the root and branch of his character, but at Mount Vernon and Belvoir he found an outlook on a broader world of experience and culture which produced the bloom thereon.

The Mount Vernon that young George came to was far from being the extensive mansion which he left fifty years later and which the pilgrim finds to-day. There was no spreading village of outbuildings. The big brick barn and only a few frail sheds and cabins for the slaves stood detached from the house. There were no colonnades flung from the ends, no lofty portico on the river front, and the house itself was only a portion of the mansion into which it later expanded.

The history of the house is easily read in the evidence in the building itself, and George Washington's letters confirm the conjectures of the architectural archeologist. Detach the present banquet hall on the north and the library on the south, together with the second story thereof, and the developments of the third story, and the original house remains. Then, as to-day, there was the central hall extending from western front to river front, but divided at that time by a partition midway between the two doors on each of the sides. On each side of the hall were two rooms. The same stairway wound gracefully to the second floor, where the small upper hall opened into the four large bedrooms over the four large rooms below, and a small room matched the space at the east end of the hall. It was not accounted a large house for a colonial country gentleman of family.

The foundations were of sandstone. The cellar extended the full length and breadth of the house, with partition walls of brick held by oyster-shell mortar. This stone is showing age in a way that might be translated into an argument for the theory that they held up Augustine Washington's house which burned in 1739. Years and whitewash have destroyed all charred traces, if there were any. But the damp, which creeps into the cool cellar in the hot summer and is evaporated by the artificial heat introduced over the past twenty winters, is having a curious pulverizing effect which the severe baking in an early fire might explain.

Midway of the central north and south alley there was found in the west wall, years ago, a carefully engraved stone called "the corner stone." It may be seen to-day under glass in the relic house near the mansion, whither it has been removed out of danger of the disintegrating effects of the damp and heat. A copy, cut to scale, has been inserted in the place of the original in the cellar wall. The stone is twenty-three inches long, by seventeen and one-half inches high, by six inches thick. In the centre of the carved face are two crossed battle-axes in whose angle is engraved a heart. On either side of the axes are the initials of Lawrence Washington, "L. W." It adds to the enigma of the original builder, for apparently only he himself would have put his initials on the cornerstone. Those who advance his father, Augustine, as the builder of Mount Vernon say that he intended the house for this son and they claim the initialled stone as evidence of their theory.

In one corner of the original cellars, the one to the southwest, there is a well opening filled up but clearly defined. A curious place to put a well, it would seem, but conditions at the time explain. It is said to have been the custom in the colonies, at least for houses in the new country on the frontier not far from the receding Indians, to dig a well under the house, so that in case of barricade against attack or in case the women of the family wanted water in the absence of the menfolk, there would be a protected supply in reach without risk.

The original hand-hewn oak beams are apparently as

strong to-day as when laid in.   There, too, are the stout
oak pins with which they were put together.   Nails
were not admitted to the larger timbers of the colonial
house.   It is only in the lighter pieces of the trim and in
the broad planked floors that nails appear.   They were
handwrought, in a forge on the place as a rule, and their
heads were long and exceeding thin.

There is nothing to gainsay the belief that George
saw these cellars dug and walled; the huge oaks felled
and hewn and pinned in place; the walls reared and
roofed and the whole put under the protection of the
coats of white lead and oil, for the house was a part of all
his life.

CHAPTER III

Lawrence Plans George's Career—Letter of Uncle Joseph Ball—
Fox Hunting with Lord Fairfax—Absent Surveying in The
Valley—Sentimental Manifestations—Military Tutors at
Mount Vernon—Lawrence Ill—Lawrence and George Sail
for Barbadoes—Return and Death and Will of Lawrence—
George Master of Mount Vernon.

A PROPER career for George was one of the topics
much discussed at Mount Vernon at this time.
His two advisers were Lawrence and Lord Fairfax, who had come to Virginia and made his home with
his cousin William nearby at Belvoir.

Lawrence had fancied a career at sea, hoping that,
after some experience before the mast, some influence
might be controlled to secure a commission in the
Royal Navy. George yielded to the romance of this
idea. His father is said to have followed the sea in
earlier days. His trunk was packed, and there is said
to have been a vessel anchored below the house on
which he was to have shipped. His mother, however,
was of another mind. When the project was first
broached she wrote to her brother, a London lawyer,
and from all accounts she arrived at Mount Vernon
with his reply at the last moment before her boy's
departure.

The letter, carefully considered, dissipates the myth
that Lawrence had actually secured a midshipman's
commission in the navy. Moreover, it gives some

gauge of the Washington family's sphere and influence; and of George's expectations; and is sound, direct, vigorous, and refreshing:

"I understand that you are advised and have some thoughts of putting your son George to sea. I think he had better be apprenticed to a tinker, for a common sailor before the mast has by no means the common liberty of the subject; for they will press him from a ship where he has fifty shillings a month and make him take twenty-three, and cut, and slash, and use him like a negro, or rather like a dog. And, as to any considerable preferment in the navy, it is not to be expected, as there are always so many gaping for it here who have interest, and he has none. And if he should get to be master of a Virginia ship (which it is very difficult to do), a planter that has three or four hundred acres of land and three or four slaves, if he be industrious, may live more comfortably, and leave his family in better bread, than such a master of a ship can. . . . He must not be too hasty to be rich, but go on gently and with patience, as things will naturally go. This method, without aiming at being a fine gentleman before his time, will carry a man more comfortably and surely through the world than going to sea, unless it be a great chance indeed. I pray God keep you and yours.

"Your loving brother,
"JOSEPH BALL."

This cleared the air. George remained at home and devoted himself to his studies, among which mathematics was the most congenial; to sports; somewhat to sentimental matters; and a great deal to the companionship of his elders at home and at the mansion across Dogue Creek.

The fox, like the Indian, and certain other aborigines mentioned by John Smith, has been pushed westward. He still furnishes sport in the hills and in certain parts of The Valley, but he is no longer enough in evidence in Fairfax to maintain fox-hunting in its place in the country gentleman's life that it held in Washington's youth. It was in fact the boy's favorite sport. Lord Fairfax was equally fond of the chase, and together they hunted Reynard over the hills and meadows, through fields and woods, for days at a time. The climate of Virginia and the country life of the period invited to the open air.

It was in the saddles that these two boon companions became best acquainted, Washington silent and attentive, his lordship sharing with him the treasures of a rare mind well stocked with rare experience. Lord Fairfax was a graduate of Oxford, his family gave him easy access to the best society of London, and he had been a contributor to Mr. Addison's *Spectator*. It is said that he was jilted on his wedding day for a higher title. His disappointment and chagrin seemed to change his whole outlook on society. Journeying to Virginia to see his vast land holdings, administered by William of Belvoir, he was so delighted with what he saw that he later took up his home on his estate in the lower Shenandoah Valley, where he lived into his ninetieth year.

The companionship and interest of such a patron was the most fortunate substitute for the university education and sojourn abroad, so much affected by other young colonial gentlemen, that could have come to an open and serious mind of Washington's years.

It was at Lord Fairfax's suggestion that he took up surveying as a career. After charting Mount Vernon and Belvoir, he set out to survey his lordship's thousands of acres in The Valley.

He left Mount Vernon early in March, 1748, and was absent a month and two days. The journal of this trip is not without its amusing passages. Of the 15th and 16th of March he writes:

"We got our suppers & was Lighted into a Room & I not being so good a woodsman as ye rest of my company, striped myself very orderly and went into ye Bed, as they calld it, when to my surprize, I found it to be nothing but a little straw matted together without sheets or anything else, but only one thread bear blanket with double its weight of vermin, such as Lice, Fleas, &c. I was glad to get up (as soon as ye Light was carried from us.) I put on my cloths & lay as my companions. Had we not been very tired, I am sure we would not have slep'd much that night. I made a Promise not to sleep so from that time forward, chusing rather to sleep in ye open air before a fire, as will appear hereafter.

"Wednesday 16th. We got out early & finish'd about one o'clock & then travelled up to Frederick Town, where our Baggage came to us. We cleaned ourselves (to get Rid of ye Game we had catched ye night before). I took a Review of ye Town & then re-turn'd to our Lodgings where we had a good Dinner prepared for us. Wine & Rum Punch in plenty, & a good Feather Bed with clean sheets, which was a very agreeable regale."

One day's journey from home, on his return, he did "this day see a Rattled snake, ye first we had seen in all our journey." No doubt he was better acquainted with the black snakes and moccasins of Fairfax. On the 13th of April, he notes: "Mr. Fairfax got safe home and I Myself to my Brothers, which concludes my journal."

One of two letters written on this trip shows his interest growing in another direction:

"DEAR FRIEND ROBIN,

"As it's the greatest mark of friendship and esteem, absent friends can show each other, in writing and often communicating their thoughts, to his fellow companions, I make one endeavor to signalize myself in acquainting you, from time to time, and at all times, my situation and employments of life, and could wish you would take half the pains of contriving me a letter by any opportunity, as you may be well assured of its meeting with a very welcome reception. My place of residence is at present at his Lordship's, where I might, was my heart disengaged, pass my time very pleasantly as there's a very agreeable young lady lives in the same house, (Colonel George Fairfax's wife's sister.) But as that's only adding fuel to fire, it makes me the more uneasy, for by often, and unavoidably, being in company with her revives my former passion for your Lowland beauty; whereas, was I to live more retired from young women, I might in some measure eliviate

MOUNT VERNON MANSION

LAWRENCE WASHINGTON

Half-brother of George and reputed builder of Mount Vernon. From a painting
in the possession of Mrs. Lawrence Washington

my sorrows, by burying that chaste and troublesome passion in the grave of oblivion or etarnall forgetfulness, for as I am very well assured, that's the only antidote or remedy, that I shall ever be relieved by or only recess that can administer any cure or help to me, as I am well convinced, was I ever to attempt any thing, I should only get a denial which would be only adding grief to uneasiness."

From which it seems George did not take seriously Lord Fairfax's warnings about women, of whom, as has been seen, his lordship's early experience had made him as suspicious and bitter as later on Tony Weller was of "vidders."

At Mount Vernon these were quiet and uneventful years. In this the life on the estate only reflected the calm of the colony. There was no war on at the time with French or Indian, no trouble with colonial governor, and not yet any acute trouble with the mother country. There was peace, plenty, and growth. Lawrence devoted himself to his estate and to his public offices as adjutant of the militia, member of the House of Burgesses, and president of the Ohio Company.

George, though still in his nonage, pursued his career as surveyor in earnest. It is said that he had an office in the small but important city of Alexandria, on the Potomac six miles above Mount Vernon, and that he rode back and forth over the rolling country on horseback. In the summer of 1749 he was appointed surveyor of the County of Culpepper, just west of Fredericksburg. His surveyor's tripod may be seen in the library at Mount Vernon.

At this time every day's absence must have been an anxiety, for his brother, who had been to him friend and father as well, began to develop the weakness of the lungs which was his eventual undoing. The winters of 1750 and 1751 were full of foreboding for those at Mount Vernon. In the spring Lawrence felt obliged to resign his commission as adjutant and succeeded in having George appointed in his stead.

So at nineteen and at Mount Vernon began his military career. "He now set about preparing himself, with his usual method and assiduity," says Washington Irving, "for his new duties. Virginia had among its floating population some military relics of the late Spanish war. Among them was a certain Adjutant Muse, a Westmoreland volunteer, who had served with Lawrence Washington in the campaigns in the West Indies, and had been with him in the attack on Carthagena. He now undertook to instruct George in the arts of war, lent him treatises on military tactics, put him through the manual exercises, and gave him some idea of evolutions in the field. Another of Lawrence's campaigning comrades was Jacob Van Bramm, a Dutchman by birth, a soldier of fortune of the Delgatty order; who had been in the British army, but was now out of service, and, professing to be a complete master of fence, recruited his purse in this time of military excitement, by giving the Virginian youth lessons in the sword exercise. Under the instructions of these veterans, Mount Vernon, from being a quiet rural retreat, where Washington, three years previously, had indited love ditties to his 'lowland beauty,' was suddenly transformed into a school of arms, as he practised

the manual exercise with Adjutant Muse, or took lessons
on the broadsword with Van Bramm."

Lawrence remained at home during the warm Virginia summer, but, as the autumn approached, he was
advised to seek a change. Barbadoes, the most easterly
of all the West Indies, was selected as a healthy and
agreeable resort, and thither he sailed the middle of
September. His wife had a baby less than a year old in
her arms, and in her stead George accompanied his
brother on the stout sailing vessel which carried them
the length of the Spanish Main, consuming, in the
leisurely fashion of wind-driven travel, over six weeks
from the Potomac to Barbadoes.

This was not the first time a Washington set foot on
this island. Another of this name, some say John, the
Emigrant, great-grandfather of the two young travellers,
stopped here on his way from England to Virginia, nearly
a hundred years before, in 1658. This, however, was
the only time that George Washington went outside the
confines of his own country.

The two brothers were apparently much missed at
Mount Vernon, and Lawrence felt keenly the separation
from his wife. He decided to remove to Bermuda for the
spring and dispatched George home to get Mrs. Washington and bring her to him there. George "embarked on
the *Industry*, Captn Saunders," for Virginia on December 12th, only a few days after his release from the
quarantine imposed on him by an attack of smallpox.
He reached home through pounding seas on the 1st of
February.

For some reason Lawrence's wife did not leave home.
It was a trying springtime at Mount Vernon. George

had not brought encouraging news from the invalid. Soon significant letters came from Bermuda, tempering the edge of their surprise when Lawrence hurried home "in time to die under his own roof, surrounded by his family and friends," the 26th of July, 1752.

This was the first poignant sorrow of George's life. He had been really too young to realize his loss when his father died, and Lawrence meant more to his sum of happiness, experience, and advancement than any other member of the family. George looked up to him with affection and confidence. His brother's death was, indeed, one of the crucial events of his life. It placed him in a position of independence and responsibility. Henceforward he walked alone. It marked his transition from boyhood to manhood.

They laid Lawrence by the side of his three infant children in the family burying ground on the estate. He seems, however, to have felt the need of something more ambitious and permanent, for in his will he directed "that a proper vault, for interment, may be made on my home plantation, wherein my remains together with my three children may be decently placed; and to serve for my wife, and such other members of my family as may desire it."

As executor of his brother's will, George faithfully fulfilled this wish. He built the vault on the brow of the hill about two hundred yards south of the house and in plain view of the south windows. It was built of brick and sandstone and survives to-day, with its arched entrance over oak doors. It sinks into the green bank in such a way that it seems a part of the hillside. There Lawrence and his children were laid, and it received and held the remains of the family who died at Mount Vernon for nearly one hundred years.

The disposition of Mount Vernon was partially provided for in the will of Augustine, father of Lawrence and George, in this:

"Item Forasmuch as my several children in this my will . . . cannot inherit from one another in order to make a proper Provision ag.ᵗ their dying without Issue, It is my will and desire that in Case my son Lawrence should dye without heirs of his body Lawfully begotten that then the Land and the Mill given him by this my Will lying in the County of Prince William shall go & remain to my son George and his heirs."

Lawrence in his will expressed his "will and desire" that his wife should have the "benefits and profits" of Mount Vernon estate during her lifetime. To his daughter Sarah, who at the time of his death was less than a year old, he did "give and bequeath" all his real and personal estate in Virginia and Maryland "not otherwise disposed of," which included Mount Vernon. But in case his daughter died without issue he gave "unto my loving brother George Washington" all his lands in Fairfax (formerly a part of Prince William) County.

Little Sarah died in September. Anne was welcome in the house which now virtually belonged to her brother-in-law, but it had been a home of disappointment, suffering, and grief, and she preferred to return to Belvoir. She seems to have enjoyed the "benefits and profits" of Mount Vernon, for, soon after this, having

married George Lee, the uncle of Charles and Richard
Lee, her husband joined her in a deed to George which
indicates that her young brother-in-law bought her life
interest:

"We the parties of the first part grant to the party of
the second part the life interest of Ann Lee, widow of
Lawrence Washington, in two parcels of land, one
situated on Little Hunting Creek, the other on Dogue
Creek in Fairfax, of which Lawrence Washington died
seized, also one Water Grist Mill, also certain Slaves—in
consideration that Geo Washington during the natural
life of Ann Lee, do each year pay to her husband, Geo
Lee—on the 25th of December, the sum or quantity of
fifteen thousand pounds of tobacco in fifteen hogsheads,
to be delivered at one or some of the Warehouses in the
Co of Fairfax, or as much current money of Virginia in
lieu thereoff as will be equal thereto at twelve (12)
shillings & six pence current money, for every hundred
weight of tobacco."

Thus George, heir to Mount Vernon and executor of
his brother's will, at twenty, wisely completed his title
to his estate.

CHAPTER IV

Absences from Home—Military Expeditions to the Ohio—Mary
Washington's Last Visit to Mount Vernon—Organizing the
Household—Political Aspirations—John Augustine Wash-
ington the First Manager—Off to the West with Braddock—
Military Career Unremunerative—Home with Extended
Fame, General Braddock's Battle Charger and Bishop—Wo-
men Who Might Have Been Mistress of Mount Vernon—
Washington Made Commander of All Virginia Troops—A
Winter's Illness at Mount Vernon, Not Without Compensa-
tion.

THE story of Mount Vernon during the next
seven years is not notably eventful. Its new
master was a bachelor, the leading strings of
his developing career drew him easily away from his
home, and he has not left in his letters evidence that he
was even preparing to organize his estate into anything
approaching the perfected condition which it reached
later and which became the wonder and the admiration,
and in some degree perhaps the despair, of those who ap-
preciated what he overcame in meagre resources and
service.

He was a constant visitor to the Fairfaxes at Belvoir,
to George Mason's family at Gunston Hall, and to the
Ewells of Belle Aire, where he often stopped on his way
to see his mother and sister Betty at Fredericksburg and
to keep in touch with others of the family thereabouts.
On the 4th of November, 1752, he was initiated into the
secrets of Masonry at Fredericksburg, though later he

affiliated with the lodge at Alexandria, so much more conveniently near his home.

A mistress for Mount Vernon was continually in his thoughts. Women had a great attraction for him from his earliest youth. His early diaries and letters are full of sentimental confidences.

Perhaps at this time his attack of "pleurise" had passed and he continued on down to the lower tidewater home of Betsy Fauntleroy, as he promised her father in this letter of the previous May:

"Sir: I should have been down long before this, but my business in Frederick detained me somewhat longer than I expected, and immediately upon my return from thence I was taken with a violent pleurise, which has reduced me very low; but purpose, as soon as I recover my strength, to wait on Miss Betsy, in hopes of a revocation of the former cruel sentence, and see if I can meet with any alteration in my favor. I have enclosed a letter to her, which should be much obliged to you for the delivery of it. I have nothing to add but my best respects to your good lady and family."

Betsy, however, seems to have been unwilling to revoke her "former cruel sentence," and so his detached domestic situation made it easier to accept Governor Dinwiddie's difficult commission to bear his protest to the encroaching French on the far western frontier of the Ohio. It may almost be believed that for the next two years he made no effort to keep Mount Vernon in commission as a place of residence, for he frequently passed it by on his way between Alexandria and Fredericksburg without mention of visiting his estate, though the highroad ran near his western boundary.

In his diary of the Ohio expedition in 1753 he begins by noting: "I arrived [November 1st] at *Fredericksburg* and engaged Mr. *Jacob Vanbramm*, to be my *French* interpreter; and proceeded with him to *Alexandria*, where we provided Necessaries. From thence we went to *Winchester*." This diary of his two months' absence draws to a close with this note, of January, 1754: "On the 11th I got to Belvoir: where I stopped one Day to take necessary Rest; and then set out and arrived in Williamsburg the 16th."

On these occasions he was within two miles of his own house. Yet it is scarcely to be believed that he crossed over even while stopping the day at Belvoir, for in mid-January boating on tidewater Potomac is made treacherous by cold high winds sweeping down the "creeks" when the river is not actually impassable by reason of the ice which sometimes grips its entire surface.

Soon after his return from the West he was commissioned Lieutenant Colonel and ordered to return to the Ohio in command of a military expedition which Governor Dinwiddie sent at the end of March "to aid Captain Trench in building Forts and in defending the Possessions of his Majesty against the attempts and hostilities of the French." It was the beginning of the Seven Years' War.

"It was strange that in a savage forest of Pennsylvania," says Thackeray in "The Virginians," "a young Virginian officer should fire a shot and waken up a war which was to last for sixty years, which was to cover his

own country and pass into Europe, to cost France her
American colonies, to sever ours from us, and create
the great Western Republic; to rage over the Old
World when extinguished in the New; and, of all the
myriads engaged in the vast contest, to leave the prize
of the greatest fame with him who struck the first
blow!"

Washington fought through the summer in the West,
but a military order from Dinwiddie made it impossible
for him to serve longer with self-respect. He resigned
his commission and returned to Mount Vernon, where
he arrived in October, remaining almost continuously
until March.

Whatever his other occupations during the winter,
he seems not to have been free of his chronic entangle-
ment of the heart, for a friend, one of the officers at
Williamsburg, wrote him:

"I imagine you by this time plung'd in the midst of
delight heaven can afford and enchanted By Charmes
even Stranger to the Cyprian Dame." (Mrs. Neil.)

The arrival of the spring of 1755 seems to have found
some sort of menage established in the house, for, having been invited by General Braddock to accompany his
expedition to the West, he writes from home, in a letter
to Orme, the General's Aide-de-Camp:

"The arrival of a good deal of company (among
whom is my mother, alarmed at the report of my intentions to attend your fortunes) prevents me the
pleasure of waiting on you to-day, as I had intended."

This was Mary Washington's last appearance at Mount Vernon. She retired to Fredericksburg, where she spent the rest of her days, at first at her farm across the Rappahannock but, later, near her daughter Betty Lewis' "Kenmore," in the centre of the little city, in a house which her son George bought for her. He visited her whenever he passed through Fredericksburg and wrote to her always with high but somewhat formal affection.

Though this visit to Mount Vernon, to persuade her son to keep out of the military service, was her last appearance there, it was not her last protest on this same score. In August she besought him again not to endanger his life in farther armed exploits. He replied from Mount Vernon:

"Honored Madam,

"If it is in my power to avoid going to the Ohio again, I shall; but if the command is pressed upon me, by the general *voice* of the country, and offered upon such terms as cannot be objected against, it would reflect dishonor upon me to refuse; and *that*, I am sure, must or *ought* to give you greater uneasiness, than my going in an honorable command, for upon no other terms will I accept of it. At present I have no proposals made to me, nor have I any advice of such an intention, except from private hands."

In the letter to Orme quoted above he said of the domestic situation at his home:

"I find myself much embarassed with my affairs, having no person in whom I can confide, to entrust the management of them with. Notwithstanding, I am determined to do myself the honor of accompanying you, upon this proviso, that the General will be kind enough to permit my return, as soon as the active part of the campaign is at an end, if it is desired; or, if there should be a space of inaction, long enough to admit a visit to my home, that I may be indulged in coming to it."

Orme replied:

"The General orders me to give his compliments, and to assure you his wishes are to make it agreeable to yourself and consistant with your affairs, and, therefore, desires you will so settle your business at home, as to join him at Will's Creek, if more convenient for you; and, whenever you find it necessary to return, he begs you will look upon yourself as entire master, and judge what is proper to be done."

Free to return as necessity might compel, he prepared to turn his back again on the comforts and interests of his estate. Three days before setting out to accompany Braddock he wrote from Mount Vernon, under date of May 25, 1755, to William Byrd, whose fame survives, not merely as master of Westover on the James, where he gathered the finest library in the colony, but as "the great Virginia wit and author of the century":

"I am sorry it was not in my power to wait upon you at Westover last Christmas. I enjoyed much satisfaction in the thought of doing it, when an unexpected accident put it entirely out of my power to comply either with my promise or inclination, both of which prompted me to make the visit.

"I am now preparing for, and shall in a few days set off, to serve in the ensuing campaign, with different views, however, from those I had before. For here, if I gain any credit, or if I am entitled to the least countenance or esteem, it must be from serving my country without fee or reward; for I can truly say, I have no expectation of either. To merit its esteem, and the good will of my friends, is the sum of my ambition, having no prospect of attaining a commission, being well assured it is not in Gen'l. Braddock's power to give such an one as I would accept of. The command of a Company is the highest commission vested in his gift. He was so obliging as to desire my company this campaign, has honored me with particular marks of his esteem, and kindly invited me into his family—a circumstance which will ease me of expenses that otherwise must have accrued in furnishing stores, camp equipage, &c, whereas the cost will now be easy (comparitively speaking) as baggage, horses, tents, and some other necessaries, will constitute the whole of the charge.

"Yet to have a family just settling, and in the confusion and disorder mine is at present, is not a pleasing thing and may be hurtful. Be this as it may, it shall be no hindrance to my making *this* campaign."

The "family just settling" was that of his younger and favorite brother, John Augustine, father of the next owner of Mount Vernon. He wrote his brother frequently during his absence, usually subscribing himself, "Dear Jack, your most affectionate Brother."

In an early letter George expresses the hope that his brother "will have frequent opportunities to particularize the state of my affairs, which will administer much satisfaction to a person in my situation."

In another he indicates his first interest in politics:

"As I understand the County of Fairfax is to be divided, and that Mr. Alexander intends to decline serving it. I should be glad if you would come to Colo. Fairfax's intentions, and let me know whether he purposes to offer himself as a candidate. If he does not, I should be glad to take a poll, if I thought my chances tolerably good.

"Majr. Carlyle mentioned it to me in Williamsburg in a bantering way, and asked how I would like it, saying, at the same time, he did not know but they might send me, when I might know nothing of the matter, for one or t'other of the counties. I must confess I should like to go for either in that manner, but more particularly for Fairfax, as I am a resident there."

His reply to John Augustine, on receiving the report of his own death, is one of the evidences that he was not without a healthy humor when he chose to disclose it: "As I have heard, since my arrival at this place, a circumstantial account of my death and dying speech, I take this early opportunity of contradicting the first, and of assuring you, that I have not as yet composed the latter."

The fruit of the sacrifices he made in his absences from Mount Vernon, during the three years since it became his, he sums up vigorously to his half-brother, Augustine, on his return from the Braddock campaign at the end of July:

"I was employed to go on a journey in the winter (when, I believe, few or none would have undertaken it), and what did I get by it? My expenses borne! I then was appointed, with trifling pay, to conduct a handful of men to the Ohio. What did I get by *this?* Why, after putting myself to a considerable expense, in equipping and providing necessaries for the campaign, I went out, was soundly beaten, lost them all!—came in and had my commission taken from me, or, in other words, my *command* reduced, under *pretence* of an order from *home!* I then went out a volunteer with General Braddock, and lost all my horses and many other things; but this being a *voluntary* act, I ought not to have mentioned *this;* nor should I have done it, was it not to show that I have been upon the losing order ever since I entered the service, which is now near two years. So that I think I cannot be blamed, should I, if I leave my family again, endeavor to do it upon terms as to prevent suffering; (to *gain* by it being the least of my expectation)."

Futile and tragic as had been Braddock's whole campaign, Washington came out of it with added distinction. An amusing and intimate proof of this is found in a note which was brought to Mount Vernon the day after his arrival. The master of Belvoir wrote begging his appearance at his house on Sunday, intimating that if he did not come, "the Lady's will try to get Horses to equip our Chair or attempt their strength on Foot to Salute you, so desirous are they with loving Speed to have an occular Demonstration of your being the same Identical Gent—that lately departed to defend his Country's Cause."

With this arrived the following appeal signed by Sally Fairfax, Ann Spearing, and Elizabeth Dent:

"DEAR SIR: After thanking Heaven for your safe return I must accuse you of great unkindness in refusing us the pleasure of seeing you this night. I do assure you that nothing but our being satisfied that our company would be disagreeable should prevent us from trying if our Legs would carry us to Mount Vernon this night, but if you will not come to us to-morrow morning very early we shall be at Mount Vernon."

There was another Sally Fairfax besides the signer of the Belvoir round-robin. She was born Cary and was the wife of George's friend, George William Fairfax. If George had had his way she would have succeeded Ann as chatelaine of Mount Vernon. However, he was a persevering lover and is said to have proposed at varying times to Mary Cary, who afterward married Edward Ambler; to Lucy Grymes, who later became Mrs. Henry Lee, mother of "Lighthorse Harry"; and to Mary Philipse, a New York Tory who fled to England on the outbreak of hostilities with the mother country.

Accompanying Washington to Mount Vernon on his return from the Braddock expedition was a servant who deserves some introduction, for he henceforth be-

THE CORNER STONE OF MOUNT VERNON

The original stone was found in the walls of the cellar in a crumbling condition.
To prevent further disintegration it was removed, a duplicate was inserted
in its place, and the original stone is preserved among the historic
relics at Mount Vernon. It is here reproduced for the first time

THE KITCHEN FIREPLACE

In the small building connected with the Mansion by the west colonnade. The
most interesting feature of the great kitchen fireplace is the smoke-jack—a
slender belt chain operating from a circular fan in the chimney that turns
the spit. The chain runs over a flanged wheel at the end of the
spit, and the draft from the fire keeps the fan in motion

came a figure in his master's life and one of the historic characters of his home.

His name was Bishop. He was an English soldier who accompanied Braddock to America. The General observed superior qualities in the man and made him his military servant. When Braddock fell he made some effort to repair his neglect of the young Virginia Colonel's sound advice. The dying soldier presented his battle charger to Washington, the only one of four he rode in the fatal battle of the Monongahela to survive, and he commended to his service and care the faithful Bishop. The two rode together across the mountains to Mount Vernon and only once afterward did Bishop leave the neighborhood except to accompany his master.

A proof of the colony's appreciation of Colonel Washington's performance under Braddock came within a few months when there arrived at Mount Vernon his commission as commander of all the Virginia forces. He was soon off, and during the two years following he was rarely at home.

In August of the next year, 1756, however, he petitioned the Governor for leave to return to the Potomac, "As a general meeting of all the persons concerned in the estate of my deceased brother is appointed to be held at Alexandria about the middle of September next, for making a final settlement of all his affairs; and as I am deeply interested, not only as an executor and heir to part of his estate, but also in a very important dispute, subsisting between Colonel Lee, who married the widow, and my brothers and self, concerning advice in the will which brings the whole personal

estate in question." The trip was in vain, "the Assembly having called away the principal persons concerned."

After another year on the frontier he hurried back
again the next September, 1757, to attend the funeral of
"Col. Fairfax." It is not surprising he should have
made this long trip, under necessity of hurrying directly
back, for it was William Fairfax he came to bury,
father of Anne, the first mistress of Mount Vernon,
the friend of his earliest recollections when the two
families came up river to Dogue Creek neighborhood
together.

His friends found him somewhat changed under
the stress of his long military campaigns. Soon after
his return to his service duties he was stricken with
an illness which obliged him to return home again,
where he arrived in November. He was attended by
his friend, Charles Green, doctor at once of physic and
divinity, the Mount Vernon family physician and rector
of their parish Church of Pohick. Instead of abating,
the disorder became so aggravated that early in the
new year Washington wrote that he had "too much
reason to apprehend an approaching decay." But good
Doctor Green had him up and on his feet and off again
before April.

Much of significance in the story of his home was to
happen before Mount Vernon saw him again. In May
he hurried to Williamsburg with his report on affairs in
the West. He was accompanied by the now inseparable
Bishop. On his way to the capital, in crossing the ferry
over the Pamunkey River, the south branch of the
York, he most miraculously fell in with "one Mr.

Chamberlayne, who lived in the neighborhood," and insisted on the traveller resting at his house as his guest. Colonel Washington submitted amiably to being captured and led off, but before the day was done he had been twice captured.

CHAPTER V

A Chapter Wholly Away from Mount Vernon—Most Significant to Its History—Bishop's Vigil—Dinner at Mr. Chamberlayne's—Martha Dandridge Custis—Her Family—Early Life —George Washington and Martha Custis Betrothed—Off to the West—Letters—Restoring Mount Vernon in Its Master's Absence—The Wedding—Honeymoon at the Six-chimney House in Williamsburg—Washington in the House of Burgesses—Bringing the Bride to Mount Vernon— Curiosity of the Neighbors and Retainers—The Arrival—Martha Washington Mistress of Mount Vernon.

THERE is only one account of that significant day in the life of Washington and the future mistress of Mount Vernon. It is handed down by the grandson of "the charming widow":

"The colonel was introduced to various guests (for when was a Virginian domicil of the olden time without guests?), and above all, to the charming widow. Tradition relates that they were mutually pleased on this their first interview, nor is it remarkable; they were of an age when impressions are strongest. The lady was fair to behold, of fascinating manners, and splendidly endowed with worldly benefits. The hero, fresh from his early fields, redolent of fame, and with a form on which 'every god did seem to set his seal, to give the world assurance of a man.' The morning passed pleasantly away. Evening came, with Bishop, true to his orders and firm at his post, holding his favorite charger with one hand, while the other was waiting to offer the ready stirrup. The sun sank in the horizon, and yet the colonel appeared not. And then the old soldier marvelled at his chief's delay . . . for he was the most punctual of all men. Meantime, the host enjoyed the scene of the veteran at the gate, while the colonel was so agreeably employed in the parlor; and proclaiming that no guest ever left his house after sunset, his military visitor was, without much difficulty, persuaded to order Bishop to put up the horses for the night. The sun rode high in the heavens the ensuing day, when the enamored soldier pressed with his spur his charger's side, and speeded on his way to the seat of government."

The remarkable lady whose attractions captivated the marvel of punctuality and caused his servant a vain vigil was Mrs. Martha Dandridge Custis. Though this is represented as her "first interview" with Washington, it is hardly to be believed that they were unknown to each other. Her town and country houses were respectively in and near Williamsburg. Washington was in the capital at least twice every year between October, 1753, and November, 1756, in all on six different occasions. His growing fame and the official nature of his visits to Williamsburg made him a conspicuous figure even now in his twenty-sixth year. In this instance introduction was a shallow formality.

Martha Custis was one of the most admired young matrons in lower tidewater. She was Washington's junior by a few months. Her girlhood home was in New Kent at the head of the York River. The social life of the young women of that time began at an age almost inconceivable now, so it is small wonder to read that, when according to modern ideas she should have been in the nursery, or at most in the school-room, she was "presented" in Williamsburg "during the administration of Governor Gooch." There's a whole panorama in the phrase, for in the picturesqueness of brocade and laces, jewels and smallswords, powdered coiffures and tie-back wigs, indeed in all the formality of manner and observance, the Royal Governors in the Colony of Virginia held a veritable court.

When sixteen Martha Dandridge engaged the attentions of Daniel Parke Custis, in point of antecedents and personal character one of the most desirable bachelors in their neighborhood, in the large sense of the far-flung neighborhood of those days. At seventeen she became his bride. They were married one June day in 1749, at St. Peter's Church, near the White House, their home in New Kent. Vaughan Kester, in "The Prodigal Judge," hints amusingly at the tradition that the titles of the old-time Southern planters might be read in the number of chimneys on their houses. If, as his Yancy said they did, two chimneys breveted a man colonel and four raised him to the rank of general, what shall be said of the magnificent rank of a man whose house stood supported by six chimneys? The Williamsburg house of the Custises was known as the Six-chimney House. Between the two homes they spent the eight years of their married life. Two children, John Parke and Martha, survived their father. Their mother, widowed at the age of twenty-five, was in her own right one of the rich women of the colony.

The day after her first meeting with Washington he rode gayly forward to the Capital and represented "the fortunes of our officers at Winchester" with all possible speed, for there was a strong lure in his heart and he hastened his return overland to the White House on the Pamunkey for his second meeting with pretty Mrs. Custis. His entire stay in the East was brief; not more than a fortnight, it is said. But when he turned his horse's head westward early in June and began his journey back to the mountains, he took with him the promise which insured Mount Vernon a mistress as soon as he could conclude his military service and come and bear her away to his home at the head of tidewater Potomac.

The mails in those days were irregular and uncertain, even over the well-travelled coastwise highways. The carriage of letters to and from the frontier, as anything beyond the Shenandoah Valley was called at that time, must have been quite irresponsible enough to try the two lovers' souls. Yet what messages passed between them then or afterward was made a secret forever when later Martha destroyed the letters she had from George. By some chance at least one escaped and is preserved. It is of this period of their engagement, and was sent her as he was putting added miles of uncertain wilderness between them. Self-possession was characteristic of Washington, as boy and as man, but there is a gravity in this letter which, coupled with its tenderness, indicates apprehension for his issue from this military expedition:

"We have begun our march for the Ohio. A courier is starting for Williamsburg, and I embrace the opportunity to send a few words to one whose life is now inseparable from mine. Since that happy hour when we made our pledges to each other, my thoughts have been continually going to you as another Self. That an all-powerful Providence may keep us both in safety is the prayer of your ever faithful and affectionate friend."

An entire other mood is reflected in the letter written James Wood about the same time, when Washington heard that he was elected to the House of Burgesses:

"If thanks flowing from a heart replete with joy and Gratitude can in any Measure compensate for the fatigue, anxiety and Pain you had at my Election, be assured you have them; 'tis a poor, but I am convinced, welcome tribute to a generous Mind. Such, I believe yours to be. How shall I thank Mrs. Wood for her favorable Wishes, and how acknowledge my sense of obligations to the People in general for their choice of me, I am at a loss to resolve on. But why? Can I do it more effectually than by making their Interest (as it really is) my own, and doing everything that lyes in my little Power for the Honor and welfare of the Country? I think not; and my best endeavors they may always command. I promise this now, when promises may be regarded, before they might pass as words of course."

Washington's great-grandfather, John the Emigrant, his own father and his half-brother Lawrence, sat in the lower house of the Assembly at Williamsburg.

It has been seen how three years before he wrote his brother John at Mount Vernon of his willingness to put his name up for election to represent his home county of Fairfax, if his chances were "tolerably good." When the call did come it was not from Fairfax but from Frederick, his headquarters during many months of his military service on the frontier. From this time he held his seat as Burgess consecutively for nearly fifteen years. Until 1765 he represented Frederick County, and after that until the outbreak of the Revolution he was returned by Fairfax County.

One of Washington's first thoughts after the happy conclusion of his sentimental errand to the White House was of the future home of the bride. Mount Vernon in 1758 was substantially as when built except that it was the worse for fifteen or more years of wear. Though absent on the frontier, Washington wrote directions for a thorough renovation of the villa, as it was called at the time.

His brother John had moved from the estate. The house was empty. Reports of the progress of the improvements sent him from Mount Vernon show that Humphrey Knight was in charge of the farms, William Poole operated the mill when there was water in the branch to turn the wheel, and the rebuilding of the house was pushed forward by John Patterson. From time to time George William Fairfax came over from Belvoir, overlooked the work of Patterson and the carpenters, supplied hewed and sawed lumber from his stock when Washington's was delayed in coming from other directions, and wrote him frequent neighborly letters about the details of the rebuilding project.

The house seems not to have been enlarged at this time, but it was thoroughly rebuilt, inside and out. Fifteen thousand bricks were burned on the place, the house was raised on its foundations and new foundations were placed under it. New weather-boarding, newly painted, freshened up the outside; the windows were all reglazed; and new sheathing and shingles went on to the roof. Inside there was a deal of ripping out of old plaster and laying on of new, closets were built in, and the floors upstairs and the stairway into the attic gave Colonel Fairfax and Patterson much concern.

"For with regard to the Garrett Stairs," wrote Col. Fairfax, "I am at a loss unless I know whether you intend that for Lodging Apartments for Serv^{ts}. If not the Stairs may be carried from the left hand room, which you design for Lumber, without making it publick." Considering the dilemma of whether to plane down the old floors or to lay new ones, Patterson wrote with an indication of honesty: "Its just ye Nail holes of ye latter, looks but indifferent, but ye Joynts makes amends for that; & in me would be base to take it up, when I am confident, its not in my power to lay a better one, ye Stuff of it being dry, & when playnd over will have much a better look." But in spite of this Colonel Fairfax decided on new floors and the planks were sent over from Belvoir.

Two new small houses were built at this time. In the absence of any written evidence of where they stood, it is easy to locate them by regular and identical submerged foundations, below the present turf, at equal distances from the west front, and equidistant from the front door. The little houses were razed when later the additions were made to the villa and the curved colonnades were flung out at either end. The submerged foundations define the little houses of this time as having stood just west of the extreme ends of the present enlarged mansion. They were probably connected with the villa by some architectural device—wall, lattice, or colonnade.

No doubt when winter closed in and the villa and its complementary little houses were completed they presented a neat and comfortable appearance. In whatever he did Washington's taste did not err at either end of parsimony or extravagance.

There were letters from others at Mount Vernon, one in particular which the Colonel must have passed about for the amusement of his staff. Those were days of irresponsible spelling and use of capital letters. But William Poole the miller in addressing his "honourabel Cornal," disclosed real imagination in the use of these tools of expression. Punctuation he ignored altogether. Here is Poole's phonetic masterpiece:

"Most honourabel Cornal this with Great Submishon and i hope with out a fens and i hope your honour is in good health, i have hear made Bold to let you no the Qualatys of your mill i have in gande now gaind 604 Barels of Corn and Sixteen Barels of wheat and have in gaind a Great Deal of Custum from meariland as well as heare and now She fails for want of water By reason of a good Deel of Dry weather which makes me Sorry that i cant grind faster for your Custumers and by havein so Cloes in ploy with the mill the

fore part of the year it has hind ard me from tendin
the ground which i was to have and by M⨪ John Washingtons Desiers i throd up the ground to humphry
Knight and M⨪ John washington told me he would
be bound your honour would Sattis fy me for it in which i
make no Dout of your honours goodness as i am reaDy
to obay and have in a Large famalea to maintane i must
in Deaver for a maintaneance for them in which i hope
youre honour wont tak it amiss and that you will
bepleast to let me no in time if i am to minde the mill
agane and upon what tirms as i Can maintane my
famalea i be in very willin to serv your honour with out
hurtin my Self the hors which your Brother put here
Dyᵈ with a Distemper which is a great Dis a pointment to the meariland Custumars and now Sur i must
begg a line ar to from your honour that i ma no what
i have to Doo up on which i Shall rely. and so to Con-
clud from your humbel Servant at Command

WILLIᴬM POOLE miller

July yᵉ 9 : 1758

To
The Honourabel Curnal George
    Washington — att Win Chester or
    Elsewheare
        This.

The end of the campaign in the West terminated the
frontier troubles with the French, and Washington was
free to fulfil with honor his earlier purpose to resign his
commission. This he did on his return to Williamsburg
in December, 1758. He did not again take up his sword
until the Colonies called him from his retirement at

Mount Vernon, nearly seventeen years later, to lead their army in the War of Independence.

The termination of the war with the French meant more to Washington than merely his return to civil life. It brought the consummation of those promises exchanged the previous spring. He and Martha Custis were married in January, 1759.

There is so little that is definite and authentic about this event, so important in this story, that it is not easy to reconstruct a detailed picture of the interesting occasion. The Rev. Mr. Mosson, rector of St. Peter's, performed the ceremony. The exact date was lost for nearly a hundred years, when it was picked out of a letter written by Mrs. Bache to her father, Benjamin Franklin, and dated January, 1779. She wrote: "I have lately been several times invited abroad with the general and Mrs. Washington. He always inquires after you, in a most affectionate manner, and speaks of you highly. We danced at Mrs. Powell's on your birthday, or night, I should say, in company together, and he told me it was the anniversary of his marriage; it was just twenty years that night."

Dr. Franklin was born on the seventeenth of January by the new calendar in vogue at the date of his daughter's letter. Washington was married when the old calendar was still generally in vogue which fixes his wedding day on the sixth of January.

The place where they were married is still undetermined. Washington Irving, Bishop Meade, and Benson J. Lossing say at Mrs. Custis' residence, the White House on the Pamunkey. Worthington Ford and Henry Cabot Lodge say at Saint Peter's Church. The

bride's own grandson avoided the controversy. As all
the accounts of the festivities at the White House that day
are based on tradition, his recital is apt to be as depend-
able as any. And much had he heard of that marriage,
he said, "from gray-haired domestics who waited at the
board where love made the feast and Washington was
the guest. And rare and high was the revelry, at that
palmy period of Virginia's festal age; for many were
gathered to that marriage, of the good, the great, the
gifted, and the gay, while Virginia, with joyous ac-
clamation, hailed in her youthful hero a prosperous and
happy bridegroom. 'And so you remember when
Colonel Washington came a courting of your mistress?'
said the biographer to old Cully, in his hundredth year.
'Ay, master, that I do,' replied the ancient family
servant, who had lived to see five generations; 'great
times, sir, great times! Shall never see the like again!'
'And Washington looked something like a man, a
proper man; hey, Cully?' 'Never seed the like, sir;
never the likes of him, tho' I have seen many in my day;
so tall, so straight! and then he sat a horse and rode
with such an air! Ah, sir; he was like no one else!
Many of the grandest gentlemen in their gold lace were
at the wedding, but none looked like the man himself!'"

Mrs. Pryor, in her life of the mother of Washington,
says Martha's wedding gown "was thus described by one
of the guests: a white satin quilt, over which a heavy white
silk, interwoven with threads of silver, was looped back
with white satin ribbons, richly brocaded in a leaf pattern. Her bodice was of plain satin, and the brocade was
fastened on the bust with a stiff butterfly bow of the
ribbon. Delicate lace finished the low, square neck.

There were close elbow sleeves revealing a puff and frill of lace. Strings of pearls were woven in and out of her powdered hair. Her high-heeled slippers were of white satin, with brilliant buckles."

There is at Mount Vernon one surviving link between that event and what can be conjectured of it. It is preserved at this writing in the cabinet in one of the upper chambers, known as the Green Room, a quaint old pincushion made of a piece of Martha Custis' wedding dress, and from it may be confirmed at least that portion of the anonymous guest's description which says that it was brocaded satin and was white and was threaded with silver.

The honeymoon was spent in Williamsburg. To-day the old town is a diminishing echo of the sprightly capital of the middle of the eighteenth century. The venerable buildings of William and Mary rise in proud consciousness that it is the second oldest college in the country. The Raleigh Tavern, where the "dissolved" Burgesses met in defiance of their Royal Governor, still stands and nearby is old Bruton Church shepherding its yard of colonial notables. But gone is the House of Burgesses where Washington sat a part of every one of fifteen consecutive years. Gone is the Governor's palace, scene of so much viceregal splendor, social and official. Gone are the old mansions where the worthies lived and made the capital so gay; among them Martha Custis' Six-chimney House. Near the place where it was stands a yew tree, and the visitor is told that it was planted by her own hand. In the days of this story the Six-chimney House stood bravely forth one of the handsome mansions of the little capital. Here the young couple spent the first months of their honeymoon. Martha had never been to Mount Vernon, and keen as was her curiosity to see her new home it had to wait on the readjustment of her affairs and her husband's attendance upon his first session of the House as a Burgess.

Already a man of extended land possessions, Washington, by his marriage, found himself a well-provided man in other respects. Besides the extensive acreage, along the Potomac, which made up his home estate of Mount Vernon, he owned thousands of acres beyond the mountains, part of the bounty land which the colony paid its soldiers. His wife's estate was described by her lawyer as "large and very extensive," and he had urged her to engage a steward, but "none except a very able man though he should require very large wages." Her grandson estimated that, "independently of extensive and valuable landed estates," she received fifteen thousand pounds from Mr. Custis. Elsewhere the widow's third is described as equalling "fifteen thousand acres of land, a good part of it adjoining the city of Williamsburg; several lots in the said city; beween two and three hundred negroes; and about eight or ten thousand pounds upon bond."

If he found the partnership of material advantage, so did she. He was one of the ablest administrators of his time, and how devoted he was as husband to her and as father to her children and grandchildren will be seen.

Not less engrossing than the Colonel's readjustment of her business affairs were Mrs. Washington's preparations in closing one and opening another domestic period in her life. The old houses were to be abandoned, and she was preparing to settle her family in a new and distant home. Those were the days of water travel. The boats were loaded at the landing near the mansion with the furniture and bulkier baggage, and sailed out of the York and up the Potomac. No such leisurely conveyance for the master and mistress. Time was valuable to them. Only the speediest form of travel would satisfy. As soon as the Burgesses rose, the Colonel, his bride, and her two children, with their attendants and light luggage, flew across country in their own coach, behind four galloping thoroughbreds, whips cracking and dust clouds rolling, faster and faster, but not so fast as their eagerness to reach the house of his promise and her hope.

Mount Vernon and its neighborhood were on their part in a high state of expectancy. First the engagement and then the wedding had supplanted every other topic and curiosity fed on the dire poverty of information about the bride. To those on the estate she was an entire stranger whom they were nevertheless eager to welcome on their trust in the master's choice. It was long before the day when a photograph might have satisfied the curious. Even Daguerre was fifty years in the future with his sensitized silver plates. The only acquaintance they had with her was built from bits out of letters of varying dates to numerous people. She was "plump," of "medium height," with "hazel eyes and brown hair," "hot tempered," "over-fond, possessed of many amiable beauties of disposition."

When the wedding day was announced it was believed at Mount Vernon that they would come there at once. But when the Assembly was pleaded for a delay in the South, it was seen to be fortunate that she

was not to have her first homecoming over the bottom-
less clay of January roads, and arrive amid the desola-
tion of leafless, shivering winter into an unwomaned
house. Expectation was willingly transferred to May,
when the birds, the blossoms, and the balmy days and
nights of spring would create a more fitting atmosphere
for the bride.

That was the incomparable month when Martha first
knew Mount Vernon. Advance riders with the small luggage brought word that the great coach was on the way.
Another courier hurried ahead from Fredericksburg with
the detailed directions for every trifle of preparation, as
was Washington's wont, while he remained long enough
to rest the bride at Sister Betty's Kenmore House in the
centre of town and then take her across the Rappahannock to his mother's farm that she might know her new
daughter. On the last lap of the trip Belle Aire invited
a stop with a welcome from the Ewells and Graysons.
Then forward again, across the head of Belmont Bay on
Colchester Ferry, over the highlands past the old parish
church, down Michael Reagen's hill, through another
valley with two or three branches to ford, up the long
hill at the west end of Colonel Fairfax's lands, and, as
the road descends again, with the Potomac in sight at
the right, an interminable valley on the left, its long
reach lost in the purple haze of the distant hills, and
before them the glistening white villa on the high horizon three miles to the east, they came on to their own
domain. They were home again, and for forty years
neither knew any other place by that hallowed name
except Mount Vernon.

CHAPTER VI

Settling in Mount Vernon—Development of the Domestic Life on the Plantation—Martha Washington as a Housekeeper—Mount Vernon Grows into a Village—The Spinning House—The Laundry—The Dairy—The Smokehouse—The Kitchen—Shopping in London by Way of the Tobacco Ships—Washington's Taste—Daily Routine—The Beginnings of Sixteen Years of Home Life and the Upbuilding of the Estate.

W ITH the arrival of the master and the new mistress life at Mount Vernon took on a new aspect. During the previous seven years the mansion had been occupied only occasionally, there seems to have been no ordered life on the place, and none of the development under which it soon blossomed into one of the first estates of the colony. During these seven years the master was absent almost continuously on the western frontier. Even the extensive repairs, which he planned in anticipation of bringing home his bride, had been made in his absence.

Mount Vernon now became a house of life and gayety. The estate was developed and enlarged. The sixteen years following the arrival of Martha in the spring of 1759, until the outbreak of the Revolution in 1775, was the longest period of the Washingtons' uninterrupted life at home.

Writing to England in the year of his marriage, Washington said: "I am now I believe fixd at this seat with an agreable Consort for Life. And I hope to find more happiness in retirement than I ever experienced amidst a wide and bustling World." He would like to have visited the land of his ancestors and the capital of the mother country, but he admitted the restraint on his further freedom: "I am now tied by the leg and must set Inclination aside."

Mrs. Washington had brought with her to Mount Vernon the two children of her former marriage: Martha and John Parke Custis. Washington became their guardian. His home was their home, and by all the ties except blood there was an affectionate union between them which went a long way to compensate him for his childless marriage.

These four were the nucleus of a busy and extensive life on the estate. The gradual accumulation of shoemakers, tailors, smiths, carpenters, wheelwrights, masons, charcoal burners, farmers, millers, hostlers, house and outside servants, and overseers, all with their families, constituted an army of several hundred. Everything and everybody that had no relation to the "big house," as the master's dwelling on a Virginia estate has always been called, fell under the direct jurisdiction of Colonel Washington. This phase of life at Mount Vernon will be considered later in its detail and development. The house servants and all those connected with the domestic side of life in the big house were the responsibility of Mrs. Washington.

She was a woman of methodical habits, with real love for domestic management, and a native energy which kept her hands busy at all times. Even when she sat down to visit or rest the knitting needles danced under her chubby fingers.

Her grandson gives this brief sketch of her domestic life: "In her dress though plain, she was so scrupulously neat, that ladies often wondered how Mrs. Washington could wear a gown for a week, go through her kitchen and laundries, and all the varieties of places in the routine of domestic management, and yet the gown retained its snow-like whiteness, unsullied by a single speck. In her conduct to her servants, her discipline was prompt, yet humane, and her household was remarkable for the excellence of its domestics."

Near the big house grew up little houses for all sorts of domestic offices and manufacture. In one the shuttle bobbed back and forth through the great loom, in another buzzed a whole battery of spinning-wheels. In one year at Mount Vernon one man and four girls wove "eight hundred and fifteen and three quarters yards of linen, three hundred and sixty five and one quarter yards of woollen, one hundred and forty four yards of linsey, and forty yards of cotton, or a total of thirteen hundred and sixty five and one half yards." Later, when other hands were added, the list of manufactured cloths included: "Stripped woolen, woolen plaided, cotton striped, linen, wool-birdseye, cotton filled with wool, linsey, M.'s & O's, cotton-India dimity, cotton jump stripe, linen filled with tow, cotton striped with silk, Roman M., Janes twilled, huccabac, broadcloth, counterpain, birdseye diaper, Kirsey wool, barragon, fustian, bed-ticking, herring-box, and shalloon."

Across the lawn in another of the little white houses stood the suddy, steaming tubs. There was no appointed "washday" on the plantation. Every day the laundry rang with the music of washboard and mangle, beaten clothes and hissing steam. Its neighbor, the dairy, was scarcely less active with the gallons of milk to skim, the butter to churn, and the cheese to prepare. A nearby smokehouse, lined with sides, legs, and shoulders hanging on crude forked hooks of natural wood, was the one quiet house in the little group.

After the fashion of most old Virginia homes, the kitchen was in a detached house next to the big house, and processions of pickaninnies carried the heaped dishes across the lawn in to the family dining-room. The modern or even the now old-fashioned cook-stove was unknown. The altar of this temple was a great fireplace with an opening which would accommodate half a dozen grown persons. Here andirons held wood cut to cord size, and often oak logs which strained a brace of black backs to lift into place. Cranes of iron, wrought over the hill in the blacksmith shop, swung steaming kettles over the glowing coals. Quarters of beef, young suckling pigs, and rows of fowl, game and domestic, were roasted on spits. Corn pone and sweet potatoes nestled in the ashes. The plantation cooks knew the nice properties of all the woods, and were particular to have sassafras or beech-nut, red or white oak, hickory, pine, or gum, according as they needed a slow fire or fast, or as the epicure demanded each wood's own smoky aroma.

Mrs. Washington refurnished Mount Vernon throughout. Some things she brought up from her former homes in the York country and she retained a few things in the house which survived the days of Lawrence and Anne. Among the latter were the painting of the

English fleet before Carthagena and the old lantern in the hall, sent Lawrence by Admiral Vernon, and the brass window cornices and curtain bands in the west parlor, all of which have survived the changes of years and are to-day preserved in their accustomed places.

In the main Mount Vernon was refurnished by order on London. The Virginia colonial dame of means shopped almost exclusively by mail order on England, though in point of time she was then more distant from the London market than is Japan to-day.

Robert Cary & Company were Washington's London correspondents at this time. Immediately the Colonel and his bride reached home they made an invoice of needed furnishings and sent a long order, which included:

"1 Tester Bedstead 7½ feet pitch with fashionable bleu or blue and white curtains to suit a Room laid w yl Ireld. paper.—

"Window curtains of the same for two windows; with either Papier Maché Cornish to them, or Cornish covered with the Cloth.

"1 fine Bed Coverlid to match the Curtains. 4 Chair bottoms of the same; that is, as much covering suited to the above furniture as will go over the seats of 4 Chairs (which I have by me) in order to make the whole furniture of this Room uniformly handsome and genteel.

"1. Fashionable sett of Desert Glasses and Stands for Sweet meats Jellys &c—together with Wash Glasses and a proper Stand for these also.—

"2 Setts of Chamber, or Bed Carpets—Wilton.

"4. Fashionable China Branches & Stands for Candles.

"2 Neat fire Screens—

"50 lbs Spirma Citi Candles—

"6 Carving Knives and Forks—handles of Stained Ivory and bound with Silver.

"1 Large neat and Easy Couch for a Passage.

"50 yards of best Floor Matting.—

"Order from the best House in Madeira a Pipe of the best Old Wine, and let it be secured from Pilferers."

This order further included hosiery of cotton and silk; half a dozen pairs of shoes "to be made by one Didsbury, on Colo. Baylor's Last—but a little larger than his—& to have high heels"; riding gloves; a "Suit of Cloaths of the finest Cloth & fashionable colour"; a "large assortment of grass seeds"; "the newest and most approvd Treatise of Agriculture"; also "a New System of Agriculture, or a Speedy Way to grow Rich," and "Six Bottles of Greenhows Tincture."

This was dispatched in May, 1759. In September Washington forwarded an order of about two hundred and fifty items, nearly all from two to six pairs or dozens of the articles itemized. Activities were extending on a large scale on the estate, but the orders assumed such wholesale character because they were sent to the English agents only twice a year.

"From this time," he writes, "it will be requisite, that you should raise three accounts; one for me, another for the estate, and a third for Miss Patty Custis; or, if you think it more eligible (as I believe it will be), make me debtor on my own account for John Parke Custis, and for Miss Martha Parke Custis, as each will have their part of the estate assigned to them this fall, and the whole will remain under my management, whose particular care it shall be to distinguish always, either by letter or invoice, from whom tobbacos are shipped, and for whose use goods are imported, in order to prevent any mistakes arising."

Quaint items arrest the eye all along these lists.

There are "a light summer suit made of Duroy, 2 plain Beaver Hats, a Salmon-covered Tabby, Calamanco shoes, 6m Minnikin Pins, 30 yards Red Shalloon, 6 castor Hats, 2 Postilion Caps, one dozen pairs coarse shoe and knee buckles, 450 ells Osnabergs." In an order "for Miss Custis, 4 years old," were "2 Caps, 2 pairs Ruffles, 2 Tuckers, Bibs, and Aprons, if fashionable, 2 fans, 2 Masks, 2 Bonnetts," a "stiffened Coat of Fashionable silk, made to pack-thread stays," one fashionable dressed baby 10s. For "Master Custis, 6 years old," he ordered "1 piece black Hair Ribbon, 1 pair handsome silver Shoe and Knee Buckles, 10s. worth of toys, 6 little books for children beginning to read, and 1 light duffel Cloak with silver frogs."

Other interesting articles in the early lists are some two hundred carpenter's tools, an extensive provision for the pharmacopœia, "all liquids in double flint bottles," and these art objects for the adornment of his rooms listed under "Directions for the Busts":

"4. One of Alexander the Great; another of Julius Cæsar; another of Charles XII. of Sweden; and a fourth of the King of Prussia.

"N. B. These are not to exceed fifteen inches in height, nor ten in width.

"2 Other busts, of Prince Eugene and the Duke of Marlborough, somewhat smaller.

"2 Wild Beasts, not to exceed twelve inches in height, nor eighteen in length.

"Sundry small ornaments for chimney-piece."

These objects have been described as having actually been a part of the furnishings of Mount Vernon. Un-

fortunately, Washington was disappointed in expecting
these. Indeed, when the vessel brought the other goods
ordered, the invoice had these entries instead of the art
objects requested:

"A Groupe of Aeneas carrying his Father out of Troy,
with four statues, viz. his Father Anchises, his wife Creusa
and his son Ascanius, neatly finisht and bronzed with copper £ 3.3
 Two Groupes, with two statues each of Bacchus & Flora
finisht neat, & bronzed with copper £2.2 each 4.4
 Two ornamented vases with Faces and Festoons of Grapes
and vine Leaves, finished neat & bronzed with copper . . . 2.2
            The above for ye Chimney Piece.
Two Lyons after the antique Lyons in Italy, finished neat
and bronzed with copper, £1.5 each 2.10
 These is the best ornaments I could possibly make for the
chimney piece. And of all the wild beasts as coud be made, there
is none better than the Lyons. The manner of placing them on
ye chimney piece should be thus:
 A groupe of——Vase——Aeneas——Vase——Groupe of
    Flora   Bacchus
 There is no Busts of Alexander ye Great, (none at all of Charles
12th of Sweden,) Julius Cæsar, King of Prussia, Prince Eugene,
nor the Duke of Marlborough, of the size desired; and to make
models would be very expensive—at least 4 guineas each."

However, William Cheere, the London art dealer,
offered to make "Busts exactly to the size wrote for (15
inches) and very good ones, at the rate of 16/ each: of
Homer, Virgil, Horace, Cicero, Plato, Aristotle, Seneca,
Galens, Vestall, Virgin Faustina, Chaucer, Spencer,
Johnson, Shakespear, Beaumont, Fletcher, Milton,
Prior, Pope, Congreve, Swift, Addison, Drydon, Locke,
Newton."

Although bills were itemized in pounds, shillings, and pence, they were paid in tobacco. This plant was at once a crop and currency. Washington, like other great planters, shipped his tobacco to London and drew against it in orders for merchandise.

The orders which were sent from Mount Vernon to London show as clearly as any other surviving evidence the taste of the master which he stamped on the life there. He did not believe in a false economy. There is rarely a question of price. But throughout the orders appear the three requisites: good, neat, and fashionable. Always fashionable, but never ostentatious. In one letter he asks for the "finest cloth and fashionable colour"; again for a "genteel suit of cloaths made of superfine broadcloth, handsomely chosen"; but, he writes, "I want neither lace or embroidery. Plain clothes, with a gold or silver button (if worn in genteel dress), are all I desire." This excellence, neatness, and fashionableness in his personal attire was reflected in his house and its furnishings.

The domestic life at Mount Vernon was simple and methodical. One of Washington's sense of order and organization could endure nothing else. Martha, either natively or by cultivation, supplemented him exactly. "Everywhere order, method, punctuality, economy reigned," said his adopted son. "His household . . . was always upon a liberal scale, and was conducted with a regard to economy and usefulness."

They both were early risers, though breakfast was not early for all the household. Washington in winter often made his own fire in his library and there, over his correspondence and accounts, did an immense amount of work in a few hours. Mrs. Washington rose when he did and directed the beginning of the day's domestic duties into easy and ordered channels. After breakfast he rode out on one of his horses to overlook the laborers on the various farms into which he divided Mount Vernon estate, and returned, according to Custis, "Punctual as the hand of a clock, at a quarter to three . . . and retired to his room to dress, as was his custom." Mrs. Washington chose the first hour for religious devotion in her own room, an unfailing custom her life long. Dinner was a mid-afternoon meal after the Southern tradition. Washington rarely ate any supper, though it was always spread for his household and guests. When at Mount Vernon it was his habit to retire at nine o'clock.

Washington was already an important figure, one of the most important in the colony. But in the sixteen years of his married life at Mount Vernon before the Revolution he led a life of comparative retirement, and of real freedom and ease, devoting himself to the amenities of family life and the development of his estate. It was the life of his choice. He never planned and he had no ambition for any career elsewhere than on his own acres. Mount Vernon was the shrine of his greatest happiness. He was rarely far from his home during these sixteen years. When later he did consent to absent himself it was at the call of his country in the public service. It was only patriotic duty that made the long absences endurable, and he wrote and spoke of Mount Vernon always in terms of affection and homesickness.

If during this period the estate did not reach in every

aspect the maturity, expansion, and beauty of later
years, nevertheless, under his able administration, it
grew steadily in acreage and productiveness, until even
at this time it became one of the largest and best-
ordered plantations in the colonies. It was the scene of
an easy, graceful social life, based on an opulent hospitality for which the villa eventually grew too small and
compelled the additions which give the mansion its
familiar outlines. These years were freer of care and
more buoyant in happiness than any that followed,
when leadership imposed its burden of responsibility and
fame robbed him of his treasured retirement.

CHAPTER VII

Washington as a Planter—Extending the Boundaries of the
Estate—The Five Farms—Farm Organization—Virginia
Methods—Agricultural Experiments—Horses and Cattle
—The Old Mill—The Distillery—The Ovens—Fish and
Fishing—Charity—Making Ends Meet.

WASHINGTON'S ambitions when he settled in
retirement at Mount Vernon with his "agreable Consort" did not extend beyond a
desire "to pursue the arts of agriculture, increase his
fortune, cultivate the social virtues, fulfill his duties as a
citizen, and sustain in its elevated dignity the character
of a country gentleman."

But so thorough was he in all he undertook, that of
his pursuit of but one item of this program, the science
of farming, he made a career less notable only than his
public services to his country. He found "much more
delightful to an undebauched mind the task of making
improvements on the earth, than all the vain glory that
can be acquired by ravaging it by the most uninterrupted career of conquests." He expressed the belief that "the life of the husbandman of all others is the
most delectable. . . . To see plants rise from the
earth and flourish by the superior skill of the laborer fills
a contemplative mind with ideas which are more easy to
be conceived than expressed."

When he was settled his first thought was to extend
the boundaries of his estate. Washington seemed to

have possessed a passion for land, though he treated his purchases lightly and declared there was "in truth more fancy than judgment" in them. His eagerness to add to his home lands may for all that have been based on his foresight. He had seen about him overmuch of the habit of farming which planted one or at most two crops in repetition until it exhausted the ground and compelled the planter to turn to a virgin field for new production. Spreading acres gave the Virginian colonist more than a sense of domain. An abundance of new land eased his situation when repeated tobacco or wheat and corn crops destroyed the fertility of the overworked ground.

His first addition to Mount Vernon was the Clifton tract across the original Little Hunting Creek boundary, thus extending his river-front to the east. From Thomas Hanson Marshall, of Marshall Hall across the Potomac but in sight of Mount Vernon, and from his kindly but unfortunate neighbor, Captain John Posey, and from others he added land to the westward which in a measure completed the original Spencer-Washington tract bounded by Little Hunting Creek and Dogue Creek. Other lands were acquired which carried the estate northwestward over the hills at the head of the latter inlet. This gave him ferry landing a mile west of the Mansion, where he often crossed to the Maryland side and cut across country to Port Tobacco and thence ferried to the Virginia side only a short distance from his brother Augustine's in Westmoreland, where he sometimes visited on his way to the dower lands in New Kent and to Williamsburg. The purchase likewise added to his possession at the same point one of the notable "fishing shores" of the upper Potomac. In a few years the ferry proved unable to support the boats. On Washington's petition to the Assembly it was closed by law, but the fishing shore retains its ancient prestige to-day.

Washington was from the first a scientific farmer. He had all the respectable authorities he could obtain in his library. He organized and prosecuted the work with that masterly executive faculty which he displayed later in mustering and manipulating the raw colonial troops.

He divided Mount Vernon into five farms: the Mansion House Farm on which stood the big house and the village of surrounding buildings; the River Farm which lay across Little Hunting Creek to the east; Muddy Hole Farm on the low meadows to the north; Union Farm next west of Mansion House Farm along the river and Dogue Creek; and Dogue Run Farm which extended up the valley of the north branch of the run feeding Dogue Creek. About half of all Mount Vernon estate was in woodland.

Each farm was a separate establishment with its own overseer, hands, quarters for the slaves, farm buildings, and stock. Over all the farms was a general steward or overseer, who was responsible directly and only to Washington. He called this man his manager. Once a week, on Saturday, reports were made to the manager. These were set in order and passed on to the master. Washington transcribed the data in these reports with scrupulous exactness into note-books, diaries, and account books, as those which survive attest in his own handwriting. They recited in detail the work undertaken and accomplished; the labor performed by each hand; the place, time, and conditions of sowing, harvest, and sales. Though each farm was run separately Washington directed them all on an interdependent system.

He has described the mode of farming which prevailed in Virginia: "There is, perhaps, scarcely any part of America where farming has been less attended to than in this State. The cultivation of tobacco has been almost the sole object with men of landed property, and consequently a regular course of crops have never been in view. The general custom has been, first to raise a crop of Indian corn (maise) which, according to the mode of cultivation, is a good preparation for wheat; then a crop of wheat; after which the ground is respited (except from weeds, and every trash that can contribute to its foulness) for about eighteen months; and so on, alternately, without any dressing, till the land is exhausted; when it is turned out, without being sown with grass-seeds, or any method taken to restore it; and another piece is ruined in the same manner. No more cattle is raised than can be supported by lowland meadows, swamps, &c., and the tops and blades of Indian corn; as very few persons have attended to sewing grasses, and connecting cattle with their crops. The Indian corn is the chief support of the laborers and horses. Our lands, . . . were originally very good; but use, and abuse, have made them quite otherwise."

For the prevailing conditions he gradually studied out a substitute on the basis of stimulating and resting instead of taxing and exhausting the land. He finally drew up for his manager this rotation table, covering six years, as best for Mount Vernon farms:

"1ˢᵗ. . . . Indian Corn, with intermediate rows of Potatoes, or any root more certain or useful (if such there be) that will not impede the plough, hoe or harrow in the cultivation of the Corn.

2ᵈ. . . . Wheat, Rye or Winter Barley at the option of the Tenant—sown as usual when the Corn receives its last working.

3ᵈ. . . . Buckwheat, Peas or Pulse; or Vegetables of any sort, or partly of all; or anything else, except grain (that is corn crops)—for which this is preparatory.

4ᵗʰ. . . . Oats, or Summer barley, at the discretion of the Tenant, with Clover, if and when the ground is in condition to bear it.—

5. . . . To remain in Clover for cutting, for feeding, or for both—or if Clover should not be sown— or if sown should not succeed;—then and in that case the field may be filled with any kind of Vetch, pulse or Vegetables.

6. . . . To lie uncultivated in pasture, and for the purpose of manuring, for the same round of crops again."

From the time that he settled at Mount Vernon Washington conducted experiments in combinations of soil, fertilizers, and seeds. None is more interesting than one of his earliest set out in his diary, "Where, how, and with whom my time is Spent," for April 14, 1760; an example in theory and practice:

"Mix'd my compost in a box with ten apartments, in the following manner, viz:—in No 1. is three pecks of the earth brought from below the hill out of the 46 acre field without any mixture;—in No. 2—is two pecks of the same earth and one of marle taken out of the said field, which marle seem'd a little inclinable to sand.

"3. Has—2 Pecks of said earth, and 1 of river side sand.

"4. Has a peck of horse dung.

"5. Has mud taken out of the creek.

"6. Has cow dung.

"7. Marle from the gulleys on the Hill side which seem'd to be purer than the other.

"8. Sheep Dung.—

"9. Black mould taken out of the Pocoson on the creek side.

"10. Clay got just below the garden.

"All mix'd with the same quantity and sort of earth in the most effectual manner by reducing the whole to a tolerable degree of fineness and jabling them well together in a Cloth.

"In each of these divisions were planted three grains of wheat, 3 of oats, and as many of barley—all at equal distance in rows, and of equal depth (done by a machine made for the purpose).

"The wheat rows are next the number'd side, the oats in the middle, and the barley on that side next the upper part of the garden.—

"Two or three hours after sowing in this manner, and about an hour before Sunset I water'd them all equally alike with water that had been standing in a tub about two hours exposed to the Sun."

Later he made this proposal for the feeding of cattle:

"I think it would be no unsatisfactory experiment to fat one bullock altogether with Potatoes;—another.

altogether with Indian meal;—and a third with a mixture of both:—keeping an exact account of the time they are fatting, and what is eaten of each, and of hay, by the different steers; that a judgement may be formed of the best, and least expensive mode of stall feeding beef for market, or for my own use."

Another kind of experiment which was always going forward was the testing of foreign seeds in Mount Vernon's soil. Washington's fame as a farmer after some years spread to England and a lively correspondence grew up with English farming enthusiasts and experts. Mount Vernon became a kind of experimental station for the growth of the sample grains and seeds which they continually sent him.

Thorough in everything, he said: "I had rather hear it [grain] was delayed than that it should be sown before everything was in perfect order for it; for it is a *fixed* principle with me, that whatever *is done* should be *well done.*"

Indeed his thoroughness must have been the despair of his managers and farmers. His study in detail extended to the count of the number of honey locust seeds in a quart, and he found: "a (large) quart contains 4,000 seed; this, allowing ten Seed to a foot, would sow, or plant, four rows of 100 feet each."

His experiments were not all to circumvent the perversity of soil and seed. He had to contend with much perverse human nature. In plain terms the overseers of the various farms stole and sold the seed allotted to them to plant. To prevent this his manager was directed to "mix in a bushel of well dried earth as many pints of seed as you allow to an acre, and let it be sown in this manner. Two valuable purposes are answered thereby—1st in this State, the seed is rendered unsaleable; 2dly a person not skilled in sowing small seeds, will do it more regularly when thus mixed."

Tobacco was the purchase crop of the colony, in a sense the legal tender, and as such every planter was obliged to raise it. Washington began his farming at Mount Vernon with large acreages of the leaf, but he very soon discontinued it, and said: "I make no more of that article than barely serves to furnish me with goods." Eventually the estate raised large crops of wheat, corn, oats, hay, flax, buckwheat, potatoes, clover, hemp, saintfoin, and barley.

His attention to the advisability of growing other crops was, perhaps, not wholly on account of the vital tax tobacco laid upon the land. It may have been in discouragement as well with the parasites which destroyed his plants, for he wrote a friend that this crop "is assailed by every villainous worm that has had an existence since the days of Noah (how unkind it was of Noah, now that I have mentioned his name, to suffer such a brood of Vermin to get a birth in the Ark) but perhaps you may be as well of as we are—that is, have no Tobacco for them to eat, and there I think we nicked the Dogs."

In addition to selected breeds of plough and draft horses, Samson, Magnolia, Leonidas, Traveller, and other stallions "covered" mares on the place "with pastureage and a guarantee of foal." The roads on and about Mount Vernon were familiar with the leisurely progress of yoked oxen which were driven until their eighth year, when they were fattened for the market. The meadows took a decorative effect from the flocks of sheep and from the grazing beef cattle which were branded on the right shoulder with their owner's initials "G. W."

Washington kept before himself and his overseers always the intrinsic and permanent improvement of his property rather than the temporary gain from a transient crop: "Hedging, ditching, and putting my Meadows in prime order, would be infinitely more agreeable to me, and ultimately more profitable, than an attempt to encrease my crops of grain."

Coupled with his broad outlook on the scientific side of farming was a liberal policy of expenditure. "I shall begrudge no reasonable expence that will contribute to the improvement and neatness of my Farms," he told an overseer about to begin his stewardship; "for nothing pleases me better than to see them in good order, and everything trim, handsome and thriving about them;—nor nothing hurts me more than to find them otherwise."

Mount Vernon maintained a small army of men, women, and children, black and white. The farm work was done by native labor, for the most part slaves, but the more finished work like gardening and building was done almost entirely by imported and frequently indentured workmen. To support them all and to bring the land up taxed Washington's science and skill in economy to the utmost. Every resource of the place was utilized, for he knew how to squeeze out the by-products. The great work which went forward on the place was farming, but there were many affiliated establishments.

The old mill, which Augustine Washington built, was improved and turned out a quality of flour so well approved that the Mount Vernon label on the barrel was sufficient for the English officials to exempt it from examination as to grade. His diary (April 8, 1760) tells of word coming to the big house that, as a result of a heavy night rain, the mill was "in great danger of blowing." He hurried off with all hands and got there "just in time to give her a reprieve for this time by wheeling dirt into the place which the water had wash'd." A thunder-shower held him at the mill and he experimented on "what time the mill requir'd to grind a bushel of corn, and to my Surprize found she was within 5 minutes of an hour about this. Old Anthony attributed to the low head of water, but whether it was so or not I can't say—her works [being] all decayed and out of Order, which I rather take to be the cause.

" This bushel of corn when ground measurd near a peck more Meal."

He rebuilt the mill in 1770 and reconstructed the mill race in 1795. Time and neglect have since destroyed both, and the creek has so filled since that ships can no longer come within hundreds of yards of the old landing. During the last century the ruin was known as Jack's Mill from the name of the last miller Washington established there. Like Gray, who gave his name to Gray's Hill on the heights on the west, he was one of Washington's legion, a recommendation which never failed to reach the heart and interest of the commander.

A distillery was set up on the place and furnished

liquor for the hands at harvest time or when malaria gripped them. When a deposit of stone was found it was quarried and supplemented the brick-kilns in furnishing foundations for the buildings. Another institution was a huge oven, although this may have been at his other mill above Mount Vernon on Four Mile Run. When the price of wheat and flour was down they were turned into biscuit. One of the old contracts survives, signed by Washington, and provides for his delivery "at his mill on Potomack one thousand Barrels of fine barr flour & ———— Barrels of good well baked biscuit for a long Voyage. . . . It is agreed by Geo: Washington to lend his Boat to assist in getting the Flour from the Mill door to the Ship at the Mouth of the Creek."

Second only to the productiveness of the soil was the yield of the waters of the Potomac. The diaries often refer to the fishing shore, his seins and his schooner built on the place in 1765. One entry reads: "The white fish ran plentifully at my Sein landing having catch'd abt. 300 in one Hawl." At another time "the Herrings run in great abundance." Herring was the staple fish, but the Potomac has always been rich in a large variety of salt water fish, especially sturgeon, shad, cat, perch, and rock. The herring brought "five shillings per thousand" and the shad "twelve shillings per hundred." When the herring were abundant they were salted down in barrels for use on the place or for winter market at an advanced price. "A sufficiency of fish for the use of my own people" was secured from "the first that comes." There were repeated orders to the managers to send presents of fish from Mount Vernon to friends inland and

at Alexandria, and of the generosity in both fish and corn
which went forth from the place, Peake, a manager,
gives this testimony:

"I had orders from Gen. Washington to fill a corn
house every year, for the sole use of the poor in my
neighborhood, to whom it was a most seasonable and
precious relief, saving numbers of poor women and
children from extreme want, and blessing them with
plenty. . . . He owned several fishing stations
on the Potomac, at which excellent herring were caught,
and which, when salted, proved an important article of
food to the poor. For their accomodation he ap-
propriated a station—one of the best he had—and
furnished it with all the necessary apparatus for taking
herring. Here the honest poor might fish free of expense, at any time, by only an application to the overseer; and if at any time unequal to the labor of hauling
the seine, assistance was rendered by order of the
General."

Writing of his affairs four years after his marriage,
Washington gave this somewhat pessimistic review: "I
doubt not but you will be surprized at the badness of
their condition unless you will consider under what
terrible management and disadvantages I found my
estate when I retired from the publick service of this
Colony; and that besides some purchases of Lands
and Negroes I was necessitated to make adjoining me
(in order to support the expenses of a large family), I
had Provisions of all kinds to buy for the first two or
three years; and my Plantation to stock in short with

every thing;—buildings to make and other matters
which swallowed up before I well knew where I was, all
the money I got by marriage, nay more, brought me in
debt, and I believe I may appeal to your own knowledge
of my circumstances before."

Mount Vernon was eventually brought to high productiveness, but the scale of life there was such that
rarely did the farms show a balance wholly on the right
side of the ledger. Washington had to look to his
estate for other assets than appeared in the physical
valuation of its produce.   He found its true and largest
asset in the fulfilled ideal of private life; in solving the
interesting problems of the planter; in mental health
and physical strength; and in the enjoyment of the easy
and graceful social life of the colonial country gentleman, of which Mount Vernon became a veritable example.

CHAPTER VIII

Social Life—Processions of Guests—Dinner Parties—English
Naval Officers—Neighborhood Life—The Mansions on Both
Sides of the Potomac—To Annapolis for the Races—Captain
John Posey's Letter—Alexandria Associations—The Bread
and Butter Ball—Fox Hunting—Nearby Race Tracks—
Lotteries—Duelling—Mrs. Washington's Children, John and
Martha Custis—Dancing Classes.

BEFORE the Revolution Mount Vernon bore its
share of the open-handed hospitality which
distinguished Virginia colonial life. The brief
call of visitors whose home base is near by was practically unknown. Distances were great, travellers came
with their own coach and horses and servants, and an
arrival meant additional places at the master's table
and in the servants' hall, additional beds, and stabling
and feed for from six to twelve horses. It was part of
the flexible, cordial social system, and the hospitality
and provision was on a large scale. Every one was
welcome: brothers and sisters, nephews and nieces,
and cousins to remote degrees; friends passing north and
south, crossing from Maryland to lower Virginia, or
only on their way to the plantation next beyond. Not
least welcome were strangers, with and often without
letters. Washington is several times at a loss, in his
diary, to recall the names of visitors in his house. But
without distinction the horses were sent to the stables,
the servants to quarters, and the visitors were welcomed
to all the big house afforded.

Not less true of this period than a little later was De Chastellux's description of the guests' reception at Mount Vernon: "Your apartments were your house; the servants of the house were yours; and, while every inducement was held out to bring you into the general society of the drawing-room, or at the table, it rested with yourself to be served or not with everything in your own chamber."

The family were so rarely alone that when they were it was a matter of surprised comment and record. Day after day, year after year, the diary details the seemingly never-ending procession of guests. Here is a week in August, 1769, which is not unlike other weeks in other years:

10 Mr. Barclay dined with us again as did Mr. Power, and Mr. Geo. Thornton—

11 Lord Fairfax & Colo. Geo. Fairfax dined with us—

12 Mr. Barclay dined with us this day also

13 We dined with Lord Fairfax—

14 Colo. Loyd, Mr. Cadwallader & Lady, Mrs. Dalton & Daughter & Miss Terrett dind with us

15 Had my horses brought in to carry Colo. Loyd as far as Hedges on his return home & rid with him as far as Sleepy Creek—returned to Dinner & had Mr. Barclay & a Mr. Brown to dine with me—

16 Horses returnd from carrying Colo. Loyd— Mr. Barclay, Mr. Goldsbury, Mr. Hardwick, Mr. Jno. Lewis & Mr. Wr. Washington Junr. dined here—

17 Mr. Jno. Lewis, & Mr. W. Washington Junr. dined here— We drank Tea with My Lord—

18 Mr. Barclay, Mr. Woodrow & Mr. Wood dined here—My Lord ye two Colo. Fx's & others drank Tea here

The dining-room was not large and one wonders how it held them all, for in addition to those enumerated

there were Colonel and Mrs. Washington, Jack and
Patty Custis, and relatives and house guests. The week
quoted above shows only continual entertainment. The
numbers there given were indeed comparatively small.
On one occasion Washington reached home from Williamsburg and "found Mrs. Bushrod, Mrs. W. Washington and
their families here—also Mr. Boucher Mr. Addison Mr.
Magowan & Doctr Rumney." At another time he
enters: "The 4 Mr. Digges came to dinner also Colo.
Fairfax, Colo. Burwell. Messrs. Tilghman, Brown,
Piper, Adam, Muir, Herbert, Peake, and Dr. Rumney
all of whom stayd all night except Mr. Peake."

When British ships of war appeared in the Potomac
and ascended to Mount Vernon there was a general
exchange of courtesy between house and ship. A
characteristic entry in the diary is that in July, 1770,
when an English frigate anchored in the stream: "Sir
Thomas Adams and Mr. Glassford his first Lieutt
Breakfasted here— Sir Thos returnd after it; but
Mr. Glassford dined here as did the 2d Lieutt. Mr.
Sartell Mr. Johnston of Marines Mr. Norris & Mr.
Richmore—two Midshipmen."

Mount Vernon was the centre of a neighborhood
life of much activity. "Neighborhood" is a relative
term. Virginia country gentlemen of colonial days
called any man their neighbor who lived within a day's
ride. Separated from Washington's home only by
Dogue's Creek was Belvoir, the seat of his lifelong
friends the Fairfaxes. They were his nearest neighbors, but by water Belvoir was a barge ride of two miles
and on land it was a ride of about eight miles around
the head of the creek. Next beyond Belvoir, and

separated from it only by Gunston Cove, was Gunston
Hall, home of George Mason, an active planter on a
large scale and a philosophic statesman of the first
order. His son Thomson Mason's house, Hollin Hall,
was a few miles to the north of Mount Vernon, beyond
the River Farm and on the well-travelled road to
Alexandria. At a somewhat greater distance, but still
in the wide colonial latitude of neighborhood, was
Belle Aire, of which Gunston Hall was in many features a replica, high on the hills of Neabsco, the home of
the Ewells, cousins of the Washingtons, and a family
connected by marriage with William Grayson, Virginia's first Senator; Parson Weems, one of Washington's
early if not most reliable biographers, and Doctor James
Craik, Mount Vernon family surgeon and later Surgeon
General of the Revolutionary Army.

Like many other colonial country houses Mount
Vernon, Gunston Hall, and Belle Aire are all set iden-
tically the same in relation to the compass, with each
corner pointing to one of the cardinal points. In this
way each side of the house admits the sunlight at some
time during the day.

Across the Potomac to the eastward, where now rises
Fort Washington, was the estate of the Digges family
and their seat Warburton Manor. Washington and
Digges had a code of signals between Mount Vernon
and Warburton, and when the signal went up that there
were guests on the way the handsome barges which
each house maintained shot out from the shores, driven
by the oars of gayly liveried black men, and met in
midstream to transfer the visitors.

At Warburton the Washingtons met not only the

extensive connection of the Digges family but Governor
Eden, Major Fleming, Mr. Boucher, who tutored John
Parke Custis, the Calverts, Daniel of Saint Thomas
Jenifer, and other Maryland notables. At times the
whole party would cross the river for a hunt and dinner
at Mount Vernon, spend the night there, and next day
press on in a body to Belvoir for further entertainment,
and even on to Gunston Hall and Belle Aire, picking
up recruits to the merry party enroute, and on their leisurely return dropping them at their homes after partak-
ing of renewed hospitality.

The races at Annapolis always drew the family from
Mount Vernon. The visit to the Maryland Capital
gave country life a touch of urbanity. On these occasions the great coach, the horses, the coachman,
footmen, and postilions were sent across the river the
day before, to be in readiness without delay, for the
arrival of the master and mistress next morning for an
early start. The trip was broken by stops in Marlboro
and at Mount Airy, home of the Calverts, who were
later to be connected with the family at Mount Vernon
by the marriage of Miss Eleanor Calvert and John
Parke Custis.

Washington's pastors and friends at Pohick Church
were frequent and welcome visitors at his home, among
them Dr. Green, the Rev. Lee Massey, Captain Daniel
McCarty of Cedar Grove on Accotink Creek, Col.
Alexander Henderson, Dr. Peter Wagener, Col. William
Grayson, Mr. George Johnston, and Mr. Martin Cock-
burn of Springfield, near Gunston Hall.

Two other neighbors within sight of the villa were
Thomas Hanson Marshall of Marshall Hall on the Mary-

land shore about two miles to the south, and John Posey of Rover's Delight, the sentimental name he gave his house on the Dogue Creek tract later added to Mount Vernon. As revealed in their letters to Washington they were as definitely opposite types as could well be imagined. Marshall was precise, unyielding, self-sufficient, and admirable. Dear old Posey was easy-going, dependent, timid, irresolute, and delightful. Indeed a single passage from one of Posey's letters sent up to his friend Colonel Washington gives his character in a paragraph:

"I could [have] been able to [have] Satisfied all my old Arrears, Some months AGoe, by marrying [an] old widow woman in this County, She has Large soms [of] cash by her, and Prittey good Est — She is as thick, as she is high—And gits drunk at Least three or foure [times] a weak—which is Disagreable to me—has Viliant Sperrit when Drunk—its been [a] Great Dispute in my mind what to Doe,—I believe I shu'd Run all Resk's—if my Last wife, had been [an] Even temper'd woman, but her Sperrit, has Given me such [a] Shock—that I am afraid to Run the Resk Again, when I see the object before my Ey[e]s [it] is Disagreable."*

The Mount Vernon coach and horses were nowhere more familiar than on the road to Alexandria. The little city eight miles up river was the background of a large part of Washington's life and of some of the most important events of his career. Here at one time he is said to have had his office as surveyor; it was the base of

*"Letters to Washington" (Edited by Stanislaus Murray Hamilton), published by the Society of the Colonial Dames of America, Volume IV, page 66.

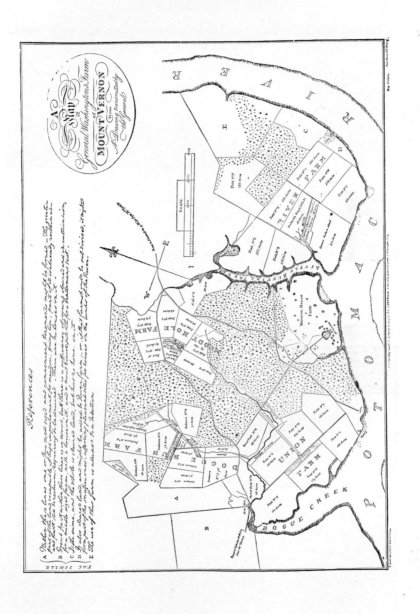

THE WEST LODGE GATES

Seen from the Mansion across the Bowling Green and the intervening meadows.
Through these gates Washington drove whenever leaving or returning home

THE RIVER SHORE

From the wharf. The high point of land in the distance is Belvoir. The lower
shore-line beyond is Gunston

his departure on his trips westward on surveying bound
and later to fight in the wars with the French, he represented it in the House of Burgesses, he surveyed its
streets, he was a member of the town council, here he cast
his votes, here later in life he worshipped at Christ
Church, and here he held his last review. Alexandria
was warehouse and market town for the products of
Mount Vernon farms, its physicians attended the family
in illness, and not only did the Washingtons enter fully
into the social life of the little city, but their friends
there were in an intimate sense their neighbors, and
stood out conspicuously in the picture of social life at
Mount Vernon.

The assemblies at Alexandria were a never-failing
lure to Washington. One of the first to which he took
Mrs. Washington after their marriage was thus recorded in the diary:

"Went to a ball at Alexandria, where Musick and
dancing was the chief Entertainment however in a
convenient room detached for the purpose abounded
great plenty of bread and butter, some biscuits, with
tea and coffee, which the drinkers of could not distinguish from hot water sweet'ned—

"Be it remembered that pocket handkerchiefs servd
the purposes of Table cloths & Napkins and that no
apologies were made for either. I shall therefore
distinguish this ball by the stile and title of the Bread
& Butter Ball."

Repeated like the responses in a litany are these
entries of Herberts, Alexanders, Carlyles, Ramsays,

Rumney, Laurie, and other Alexandrians at Mount Vernon, gathered at random from a few months of the diary in 1760 and 1768:

"Just as we were going to Dinnr. Capt. Walter Stuart appeared with Doctr. Laurie," who attended all Washington's people by contract for £15 a year; "Doctr. Craik left this for Alexandria"; "Doctr Laurie dined here"; "Returned home receiving an invitation to Mrs. Chew's Ball on Monday night next-first"; "Colo. Carlyle dind here"; "Return'd home, Mrs. Carlyle accompanying us, the day being exceeding fine"; "Mr. Carlyle (who came here from Port Tobo. Court last night) and Mrs. Carlyle were confin'd here all day"; "Mr. Carlyle and his wife returnd home"; "Doctr Laurie came here, I may say drunk"; "Mrs. Washington was blooded by Doctr Laurie"; "Sent Tom and Mike to Alexandria in my boat for 20 or 25 bushels of oats. Went up myself there to Court"; "At home with Doctr. Rumney"; "Confined by rain with Mr. Fairfax and Mr. Alexander"—the city was named after the Alexanders who were great landholders on its site and in its vicinity; "In the afternoon went up to Mr. Robt. Alexander's in order to meet Mr. B. Fairfax & others a fox Huntg"; "Returnd home, much disordered by a Lax, Griping & violent straining"; "Sent for Doctr. Rumney, who came in ye afternoon"; "Doctr still here—& Mr. Ramsay came down to see me"; "Went with Colo. Carlyle and our Families to Belvoir"; "Went to Court," at Alexandria; "Colo. Carlyle & Family also went up. Mr. Stedlar stay'd & Sally Carlyle"; "We (together wt. Miss Betey Ramsay) went to Alexa. to a Ball"; "Went to church at

Dulaney and his brother, and Messrs. Chichester, Wagener, Tilghman, Posey, Peake, and others.

There was a famous pack of hounds at Mount Vernon, in the kennels down on the western slope leading to the wharf. Their names ring across the years fresh and inspiring: Pilot, Musick, Countess, Truelove, Lawlor, Forrister, Singer, Ringwood, Mopsey, Cloe, Dutchess, Chaunter, Drunkard and, doubtless his son, Tipsy. From a stable full of thoroughbred mounts the names of Blueskin, Valiant, Ajax, and Chinkling are preserved.

The races in Fairfax or neighboring counties in Virginia and Maryland were potent in drawing forth the squire of Mount Vernon. He contributed liberally, entered horses from his stables, and occasionally laid a wager on the result. Washington was a steward of the Alexandria Jockey Club. Nearer Mount Vernon was Bogg's Race Track in the meadow below and to the west of Pohick Church, but the reader is left to wonder where might have been the track referred to in the brief entry: "Went up to a Race by Mr. Beckwith's & lodgd at Mr. Edwd. Paynes."

Rainy days or the early winter evenings were devoted to cards. Washington's account books indicate that playing cards were quickly used up. The profit and loss columns record his winnings and losses, which at times mounted to nine pounds at a sitting. It was a liberal age. Not only was gambling on a moderate scale considered a fashionable diversion, but the family at Mount Vernon patronized the lotteries on various occasions. These institutions were under distinguished social and even, in one instance, ecclesiastical patronage. Among the many lotteries in which Washington bought

ing country dances or the formal minuet. When the afternoon had been danced away and candles were brought, Mr. Christian retired, and the young people romped at "Button to get Pauns for Redemption" or "Break the Pope's Neck." The fun was carried on with "sprightliness and Decency," but the "Pauns" were potent to wring "kisses from the Ladies."

Washington was fond of dancing and he took an interest in the dancing classes and the after sport of the children. Though his manner was gentle and kindly, his presence was so imposing that young people as well as their elders were inclined to become reserved when with him. The reminiscence of an old Virginia lady of ninety-one, who in her twelfth year romped under the eyes of Colonel and Mrs. Washington, is a likely one: "Often, when at their games in the drawing-room at night—perhaps romping, dancing and noisey—they [the children] would see the General watching their movements at some side door, enjoying their sport, and if at any time his presence seemed to check them, he would beg them not to mind him, but go on just as before, encouraging them in every possible way to continue their amusement to their hearts' content."

The little family kept together until 1768, when the Reverend Walter Magowan, of lottery fame, who had been tutoring the Custis children, left for England. The education of girls was not a serious matter in those days, and Miss Patty was considered sufficiently accomplished in Mr. Magowan's rudiments and the graces Mr. Christian had given her. With a man it was different. He had to be educated. So in the same year Jack went over to Annapolis under the care of Reverend Jonathan

Alexandria and Dined at Colo Carlyle's"; "Went up to Alexandria to meet the Attorney-General & returned with him, his Lady and Daughter, Miss Corbin & Majr. Jenifer"; "At home with the above Company. Colo. Fairfax, his Lady & Miss Nicholas, Colo. West & his wife, & Colo. Carlyle, Captn. Dalton & Mr. Piper— the three last of whom stayd at night"; "Went to Alexandria & bought a Brick layer from Mr. Piper & returnd to Dinner. In the afternoon Mr. R. Alexander come"; "Miss Manly dind here, and Mr. Alexander came in the evening"; "Mr. Alexander & Miss Manly went away"; "Went to a Ball in Alexandria"; "Went to a Purse Race at Accotinck & returnd with Messrs. Robt. and George Alexander"; "Miss Sally Carlyle came here"; "Went to Alexandria to see a ship launched, but was dissapointed and came home"; "Went up again, saw the ship Launched, stayd all night to a Ball"; and so on.

One of the great attractions at Mount Vernon for Washington's friends was the hunting. Though the Potomac has always been famous for duck and fish, Washington only occasionally went gunning, and less often did he try his skill with hook and line. The latter sport was little in evidence on this river where fishing has always been done on a wholesale scale by seines and nets and traps.

His prime outdoor diversion was fox hunting. The pursuit of Brer Fox seems sometimes to have been less an object in itself than an excuse to be in the saddle and to ride afield, for he loved to feel a horse under him, and he rode with famous skill. He loved the yelp of the pack and the excitement of a galloping group of horsemen, and the hard ride for hours at a time "across a country that was only for those who dared." They justified the day whatever its end. It is inevitable that he was "fashionably" dressed for the hunt. His stepson says he "was always superbly mounted, in true sporting costume, of blue coat, scarlet waistcoat, buckskin breeches, top boots, velvet cap, and whip with long thong."

Some notion of the out-of-door life at Mount Vernon, as well as the relative number of days devoted to ducking and fox hunting may be gathered from these quotations from the diary for the months of January and February, 1769:

"Jan. 4, Fox hunting; 10, Fox hunting; 11, Fox hunting; 12, Fox hunting; 16, Went a ducking; 17, Fox hunting; 18, Fox hunting; 19, Fox hunting; 20, Fox hunting; 21, Fox hunting; 25, Hunting below Accotinck; 28, Fox hunting; Feb. 3, Went a Gunning up the Creek; 9, Went a Ducking; 10, Went a shooting again; 11, Ducking till Dinner; 14, Fox hunting; 17, Rid out with my hounds; 18, Went a hunting with Doctr. Rumney Started a fox or rather 2 or 3 & catched none—Dogs mostly got after deer & never joind; 27, Fox hunting."

When in pursuit of the fox they not infrequently started deer or bear.

These parties seem generally to have drawn from these friends and relatives: the Fairfaxes, Colonel Bassett, Jack Custis, T. and Wm. Triplet, H. Manley, Philip and Robert Alexander, William Ramsay, Colonel Fielding Lewis, Dr. Rumney, Captain McCarty, Lloyd

Boucher, who had several other young gentlemen under his charge. During the next five years Jack was away from home much of the time, either at Annapolis or at King's College in New York.

Running parallel with Washington's private life at Mount Vernon, throughout the pre-Revolutionary period, was an active public life, for he met and recognized the responsibilities of citizenship always in full. The period of this public service was so much overshadowed by his earlier and later military career and by his supreme service under the new Republic, that it is easy to think of Mount Vernon at this time merely as a home of an industrious, pleasure-loving planter. Bound up in his home though he was, there emanated from Mount Vernon wider and more unselfish interests than those which were merely social and domestic.

CHAPTER IX

Washington in Colonial Public Life—Vestryman of Truro Parish
—Drawing the Parish Lines to Capture Mount Vernon—
Attendance at Pohick Church—As a Churchman—As Burgess
in the Assembly at Williamsburg—Trips Between Mount
Vernon and the Capital—Late Summers at Bath Springs—A
Trip to New York—Charles Willson Peale—The First Portrait.

BEFORE the Revolution Mount Vernon was
represented in the civic life of the neighborhood
and colony by Washington's long tenure as a
vestryman of Truro Parish and as a member of the
House of Burgesses at Williamsburg.

The Revolution divorced the Church and State, but
until that time the Episcopal Church was a civic establishment in the colony as well as in England. The
parish was created by the Assembly, and by its direction the parish was surveyed and the first vestry was
elected by the "freeholders and housekeepers" of the
county. Thereafter the vestry constituted a tight
little self-perpetuating corporation, by itself filling all
vacancies in its own body. But the vestry was unfailingly representative of the "ablest and most discreet"
citizens of the neighborhood. Under authority and
direction of the vestry deeds were recorded, the tithe
lists made up, the tithes collected, the poor cared for,
and the landmarks renewed by the process called "processioning." To the churchwardens fell "the duty of
binding orphans and other indigent children as Ap-

prentices," and the obligation of looking after the apprentices' morals, their education and their initiation into the "Art and mystery" of shoemaker, carpenter, cooper, etc.

The vestry of Truro Parish was probably the most distinguished in the colony. Of its members eleven sat in the House of Burgesses; two of them, the Fairfaxes, were of His Majesty's Council for Virginia; another member, George Mason, author of the Virginia Bill of Rights and the Constitution of the State of Virginia, was one of the most enlightened men in the colonies; and, finally and first, George Washington.

Pohick, the parish church of Truro Parish, was first situated on Michael Reagan's Hill on the road from Alexandria and the north to Colchester and the south, due west of Mount Vernon by a drive of about nine miles. When in 1767 the present surviving edifice was projected, it was built at a point selected by Washington two miles nearer his home.

Washington was first elected vestryman October 25, 1762. The family name was not new to the Truro Parish register, for his father, Augustine Washington, entered the same vestry in November, 1735. The date is valuable in connection with establishing the period when the family, including George at the age of three years, came first to Mount Vernon.

Some confusion has marked the various statements as to where Washington and his family worshipped and when and to what vestries he belonged. The confusion results from an interesting parish contest for the possession of Mount Vernon.

Truro Parish was divided by act of Assembly, in

February, 1765, creating the new parish of Fairfax. Dogue's Run was a part of the dividing line, and Mount Vernon found itself in the new parish, cut off from old Pohick. This act raised immediate and general protest from the parent parish. Mount Vernon was the bone of contention. Washington himself seems to have been averse to being legislated out of Pohick and out of his association with Colonel Fairfax, Colonel Mason, and his other neighbors of the vestry, for he was one of a committee of Burgesses who introduced the act, passed the following May, which moved the northern boundary of the parish from Dogue's Creek on the west side of Mount Vernon to a line running with Little Hunting Creek to the northeast of the mansion. Mount Vernon was thus restored to Pohick, where it has remained ever since.

Meanwhile, on its creation in May, 1765, the new parish of Fairfax had at once elected Washington a vestryman. On the realignment of the parishes four months later he resigned from Fairfax and was again elected to the vestry of Truro. Washington was continuously reëlected to the same vestry and attended Pohick Church with a high average of regularity until the Revolution took him away from home.

The Mount Vernon coach was in evidence at Pohick from 1759 to 1774, often accompanied by a chaise and by gentlemen on horseback, for Washington seems to have been persuasive in inducing his usually numerous house guests to accompany him and Mrs. Washington to church. At least one effort has been made to establish Washington's lukewarmness as a churchman. The author thereof cites an average of fifteen entries of

church attendance each year between 1760 and 1773.
He assumes that Washington never went to church
that he did not record it in his diary. Even so he
might have thought better of Washington's fifteen
annual trips to Pohick if he had experienced year after
year the condition of colonial Virginia roads and realized
the futility of trying to force a great chariot through a
round trip of from fourteen to eighteen miles of Fairfax
clay during wet and winter weather. In further justice
to Washington's practical interest in the church it is
fair to call attention to the fact that Pohick Church
was not open every Sunday of the year. The rector
"supplied" one and sometimes two other churches.
Moreover, Washington made additional trips to Pohick
Church to attend meetings of the vestry. "During
the eleven years of his active service from February,
1763, to February, 1774," says the parish historian,
"thirty one 'vestries' were held, at twenty three of
which he is recorded as being present. On the eight
occasions when he was absent, as we learn from his diary
or other sources, once he was sick in bed, twice the
House of Burgesses, of which he was a member, was
in session, and three other times certainly, and on the
two remaining occasions probably, he was out of the
County."

Washington bought pew twenty-eight, in the centre of
the church, before the Communion table, on the north
aisle. Lund Washington bought number twenty-nine,
next behind, but George Washington later bought it
from him. The Sunday attendance from Mount
Vernon required these two great square box-like pews,
which Washington kept all his life, even when the

parish fell upon neglected days and Pohick was without a regular rector, and he and his family worshipped at Christ Church, Alexandria.

Churchgoing really played a large part in the social side of Virginia colonial life. Philip Vickers Fithian, in his *Journal*, gives a graphic idea of this phase:

"There are three grand divisions of time at the church on Sundays; Viz: before Service giving and receiving letters of business, reading Advertisements, consulting about the price of Tobacco, Grain, &c, and settling either the lineage, Age or qualities of favorite Horses. 2. In the church at Service, prayers read over in haste, a Sermon, seldom under and never over twenty minutes, but always made up of sound morality, or deep-studied Metaphysicks. 3. After Service is over, three quarters of an hour spent in strolling round the church among the crowd in which time invitations are given by gentlemen to go home with them to dinner."

Which gives significance to a certain item in the specifications for the building of Pohick Church: "And the said Daniel French doth further agree to build two Horse-Blocks with each two flights of Steps; to fix six benches for the people to sit on under the trees; and to clear and remove all the rubbish and litter from off the Church Lott, so as to fix it for the Reception of the Congregation; and to have those additional works done by the time appointed for the finishing of the Church."

As already seen, Mount Vernon had to wait for its new mistress on its master's first appearance in the House of Burgesses. After that session in 1759 he was returned as Burgess every year until the Revolution made his attendance impossible; at first, as stated, by Frederick County, but from 1765 by Fairfax.

Washington did not exert his influence on the floor of the House as an orator. His first effort there at a speech was a fiasco, but justified its failure by producing the celebrated tribute from Mr. Speaker Robinson. When Washington rose to reply to the Speaker's profession of the colony's thanks for his distinguished military services in the West, he blushed, stammered, and was mute. Mr. Robinson came to his rescue with: "Sit down, Mr. Washington, your modesty equals your valour, and that surpasses the power of any language I possess."

His genius showed itself rather in leadership in committee, in sound advice, and especially in the drafting of legislative papers. When John Parke Custis, at this time a boy at Mount Vernon, was later elected to the Assembly, Washington wrote to him his own conception of the duty of the Burgess:

"I do not suppose that so young a senator as you are, little versed in political disquisitions, can yet have much influence in a popular assembly, composed of Gentln. of various talents and of different views. But it is in your power to be punctual in your attendance (and duty to the trust reposed in you exacts it of you), to hear dispassionately and determine coolly all great questions. To be disgusted at the decision of questions, because they are not consonant to your own ideas, and to withdraw ourselves from public assemblies, or to neglect our attendance at them, on suspicion that there is a party formed, who are inimical to our cause, and to the true interest of our country, is wrong, because these things may originate in a difference of opinion; but, supposing the fact is otherwise, and that our suspicions are well founded, it is the indespensable duty of every patriot to counteract them by the most steady and uniform opposition."

The sessions of the Burgesses were held in the spring after the roads had settled and in the fall before winter opened them again. The trips back and forth between Mount Vernon and Williamsburg were made by coach as a rule, especially when Mrs. Washington accompanied her husband; otherwise in his chaise or "chair," or on horseback, attended by his servants.

The distance was generally covered in four days. The diary sets forth the dates and the stoppages which indicate the routes followed; first in October, 1768:

19. Set of on my Journey to Williamsburg & reachd Colo. Henry Lees to Dinner.
20. Detaind there all day by Rain.
21. Reachd Fredericksburg, found Warren Washington & Ca. there.
22. Dined at Parkers Ordy. & lodgd at Mr. Benja. Hubbards, Colo. Lewis also.
23. Dined at the Causey & got to Colo. Bassetts.
24. Dined at Josh. Valentine's sent Chairs & Horses over James River, & lodged in Wms.burg ourselves.

and returning the early part of next month:

6. Left Williamsburg & dined & lodgd at Colo. Bassetts.
7. Set out for home with Betsy Dandridge. Dined at King Wm. Court Ho. & lodgd at Mr. Wm. Ayletts.
8. Dined at Parkers and lodgd at Fredericksburg.
9. Reached home in about 7 hours & an half, found Doctr. Rumy. and Miss Ramy. here.

THE WEST PARLOR

THE FAMILY DINING ROOM

THE MUSIC ROOM

In the foreground is the harpsichord which General Washington imported from London for Mrs. Washington's granddaughter, Nellie Custis

THE SITTING ROOM

Across the hall from the Music Room. Beyond the open door is the stairway between General Washington's Library and his Bedroom

The round trip another year, in 1774, was made in this fashion, starting in May:

12. Set off with Mrs. Washington for Williamsburg. Dined at Dumfries and lodged at Col. Lewis's in Fredericksburg.
13. At Fredericksburg all day. Dined at Col. Lewis's and spent the evening at Weedon's.
14. Dined at Roys Ordinary and lodged at Tods Bridge.
15. Breakfasted at Ruffins Ferry and dined and lodged at Col. Bassett's.
16. Came to Williamsburg, dined at the Governor's, and spent the evening at Mrs. Campbell's.

And returning in June:

18. Dined at Mrs. Dawson's and came up to Col. Bassetts in the afternoon.
19. At Colo. Bassett's all day.
20. Set off from thence on my return home. Dined at Todd's Bridge and lodged at Hubbard's.
21. Breakfasted at the Bolling Green, dined and lodged at Col. Lewis's in Fredericksburg.
22. Reached home to a late dinner, after breakfasting at Acquia.

Many more days were sometimes consumed, however, as in the spring of 1768, when Washington loitered on the journey homeward over twenty-five days. The diary furnishes a graphic sketch of Washington at play:

May
6. Rid to the Plantations near Williamsburg & dined at Mr. Valentine's.
7. Came up to Colo. Bassett's to Dinner.
8. Went to Church & returnd to Dinner.
9. Went a Fox hunting and catched a Fox after 35 minutes chase; returnd to Dinner & found the Attorney, his Lady & daughter there.

10. Rid to the Buck House & returnd to Dinner; after which went a dragging for sturgeon.

11. Dined at the Globe with Mr. Davis.

12. Went to New Kent Court with Colo. Bassett.

13. Went after sturgeon & a gunning.

14. Went to my Plantation in King William by water and dragd for Sturgeon & catchd one.

15. Rid to see Colo. Bassetts meadows at Roots's.

16. Fishing for Sturgeon from Breakfast to Dinner but catchd none.

17. Rid to Buck House & returnd to Dinner.

18. Did the same & got my Chariot & Horses over to Claibornes.

19. Went a shooting & hair huntg. with the Hounds who started a Fox which we catchd.

20. Set of from Colo. Bassetts for Nomony, crossed over to Claibornes; from thence by Frazer's Ferry to Hobs hole dining at Webbs Ordinary.

21. Reachd my Brothr. John's who & his wife were up the Country. Crossed over to Mr. Booths.

22. Went to Church (Nomony) & returnd to Mr Booths to Dinner, who was also from home in Gloucester. Mr. Smith, the Parson, dind with us.

23. At Mr Booth's all day with Revd. Mr. Smith. My Carpenter & House People went to work at my Mill repairing the Dams, hightening of them & opening the Race.

24. Came up to Pope's Creek & staid there all day.

25. Got up to my Brother Sams to Dinner, found Mrs. Washington &c. there.

26. Remaind at my Brother Sams where my Brother Jno. came, as also Mr. Lawr. Washington &c to Dinner.

27. Dined at Mr. L. Washingtons with the Compy. at my Bro.

28. Went to Boyd's hole & returnd to my Brothers to Dinr. where we found Colo. Lewis & my Br. Charles.

29. Went to St. Pauls church & Dined at my Brothers. The bitch Chanter brought five Dog puppies & 3 Bitch ditto which were named as follows: viz—Forrester,

Sancho, Ringwood, Drunkard, and Sautwell—and Chanter, Singer & Busy.

30. Went fishing & dined under Mr. L. Washington's store.
31. Returnd home crossing at Hooes Ferry—through Port
Tobacco.

The trips to Williamsburg represent Washington's
principal absences from Mount Vernon during the fifteen years next after his marriage. Occasionally he took
the family to the Bath Warm Springs, but on only two
other occasions did he go farther from his beloved home.
In 1770 he went to the Ohio and in 1773 to New York.

The Warm Spring trips were made partly in hopes of
benefiting Patsy Custis, and partly to counteract the
malaria imbibed at Mount Vernon, against which the
"Bark" seems not to have been wholly effective.
August was the month selected for the sojourn at the
Springs. Of his earliest experience there he said:
"Lodgings can be had on no terms but building for
them. . . . Had we not succeeded in getting a
tent and a marquee from Winchester we should have
been in a most miserable station here." Lloyd
Dulaney's inquiry about the rent of his house there in
1771 would suggest that he built at once, though his
diary clearly establishes the building of a new house,
kitchen, and stable there in 1784. The journey to the
Ohio in the autumn of 1770 was made to see the bounty
lands which he and his companions in arms, during the
campaigns against the French and their Indian allies,
had received from the Government for their military
services. He was accompanied by his friend, neighbor,
and fellow campaigner, "Dr. Craik, his servant, two of
mine, with a led horse and baggage." They departed

October 5th and on December 1st he "Reachd home, being absent from it nine weeks and one day," longer than he was away from Mount Vernon at any other time between 1759 and 1775.

The occasion of his trip to New York City in May and June, 1773, was to place Jack Custis in King's College. He was absent twenty-nine days, only four of which were spent in New York. The journey northward consumed sixteen days, the return nine days. In going and in returning he crossed the Potomac at the ferry above Mount Vernon, landing on Piscataway, and making his first stop with Mr. Calvert of Mount Airy. The points touched during the sixteen days' outward journey were Annapolis, Rockhall, Chestertown, "Georgetown on Sassafras," Newcastle, Wilmington, Chester, Philadelphia, Burlington, Trenton, Princeton, Bound Brook, "Lord Sterling's at Baskin's Ridge," and "Elisabeth town." Southward he stopped at New Ark, Amboy, Brunswick, Princeton, Bristol, Philadelphia, "the Sorrel House, 13 miles from it," "the Ship Tavern, 34 off," the Sign of the Bull, "13 miles from ye Ship," Lancaster, York Town, "the Sign of the Buck, 14 miles from York," Suttons, Slades, "Baltimore Town," the Widow Ramsay's, and Mount Airy, and he "reached home to dinner about 2 o'clock."

The earliest portrait of Washington was painted at this time at Mount Vernon. He wrote Dr. Boucher, in May, 1772: "Inclination having yielded to Importunity, I am now contrary to all expectation under the hands of Mr. Peale; but in so grave—so sullen a mood—and now and then under the influence of Morpheus, when some critical strokes are making, that I fancy the skill of this

Gentleman's Pencil, will be put to it, in describing to the World what manner of man I am."

The artist was Charles Willson Peale and the portrait was the three-quarter length picture in the uniform of a Virginia colonel. On "May 19. Found Mr. Peale and J. P. Custis.— 20. I sat to have my picture drawn.— 21. I set again to take the drapery.— 22. Set for Mr. Peale to finish my face." The artist found subjects also in Mrs. Washington, Martha and Jack Custis. These three productions, however, were in miniature. The cost of the four paintings was £57.4.0.

So passed the life at Mount Vernon, domestic and social, private and public, during the years which were for Washington among the happiest, if not quite the happiest, he ever enjoyed. The colony was at peace and was blessed with the serenity of a period practically without history. What Washington wrote to a relative in England was typical of this whole period: "I do not know that I can muster up one tittle of news to communicate. In short, the occurances of this part of the world are at present scarce worth reciting; for, we live in a state of peaceful tranquility ourselves, so we are at very little trouble to inquire the operations against the Cherokees, who are the only people that disturb the repose of this great continent, and who, I believe, would gladly accomodate differences upon almost any terms."

Not yet apparent was the significance of the increasing visits of the fathers of the colony to Mount Vernon and their earnest discussion with its first citizen; nor was it obvious as yet what would issue from the mass of correspondence rolling out of Mount Vernon library to every corner of the clustering colonies.

CHAPTER X

THE last two years before the Revolution brought many changes to Mount Vernon. They affected the house itself, the family circle, and the neighborhood, and the issues of which, in discussion and in correspondence, it was the storm centre were the most significant in character and effect in the history of our country.

The first grief that shadowed the house in more than twenty years came with the death of Martha Parke Custis, Mrs. Washington's daughter, the "Patsy" and "little patt" of their letters. She had been an invalid all her brief life, which endeared her the more to her devoted stepfather. On the night of June 19, 1773, he wrote briefly in his diary: "About five o'clock poor Patey Custis died suddenly," and in a letter to his wife's brother-in-law, Colonel Bassett: "It is an easier matter to conceive than to describe the distress of this Family; especially that of the unhappy Parent of our Dear Patsy

Custis, when I inform you that the Sweet Innocent Girl Entered into a more happy & peaceful abode than any she has met with in the afflicted Path she hitherto has trod." He begs that Mrs. Washington's mother come to make her home at Mount Vernon and concludes: "I do not purpose to add more at present, the end of my writing being to inform you of this unhappy change." He was about to start on a journey into the West with the Governor, Lord Dunmore, but he gave this up and remained with the bereaved mother, his own "dear Patsy," as he was wont to call her. Martha Custis left her entire and very considerable fortune to her step-father.

This year, too, Mount Vernon lost its long-time neighbors and friends, the Fairfax family, and thereafter the diary is silent of fox-hunting and dining and visiting across the creek at the merry old mansion. George William Fairfax fell heir to the ancestral estates in England, placed Belvoir in the care of Colonel Washington, who knew it and loved it better than any other man after its proprietor, and departed America never to return. Washington and his wife were with Colonel Fairfax and his family during their last hours at Belvoir, saw them embark, and from the noble height waved sad adieux as the ship sailed away to southward around the sharp turn in the Potomac.

Though Colonel Fairfax never returned to America, he and Washington kept up an intimate correspondence for the rest of his life. In 1774 most of the chattels at Belvoir were disposed of at public sale, and Washington bought at the prices below and brought to Mount Vernon the following items:

1 mahogany shaving desk 4 £, 1 settee bed and furniture 13 £, 4 mahogany chairs 4 £, 1 chamber carpet 1 £ 1s, 1 oval glass with gilt frame in the "green room" 4 £ 5s, 1 mahogany chest and drawers in Mrs. Fairfax's chamber 12 £ 10s, 1 mahogany sideboard 12 £ 5s, 1 mahogany cistern and stand 4 £, 1 mahogany voider, a dish tray and knife tray 1 £ 10s; 1 Japan bread tray 7s, 12 chairs and 3 window curtains from dining room 31 £, 1 looking glass and gilt frame 13 £ 5s, 2 candle sticks and a bust of Shakespeare 1 £ 6s, 3 floor carpets in gentlemen's room 3 £ 5s, 1 large carpet 11 £, 1 mahogany wash desk, &c., 1 £ 2s 6d; 1 mahogany close stool 1 £ 10s, 2 matresses 4 £ 10s, 1 pair andirons, tongs, fender and shovel, 3 £ 10s; 1 pair andirons, tongs, fender and shovel, 3 £ 17s 6d; 1 pair andirons, tongs, fender and shovel, 1 £ 17s 6d; 1 pair dog irons in great kitchen 3 £, 1 hot rache 4 £, 1 roasting fork 2s 6d, 1 plate basket 3s, 1 mahogany spider make tea table 1 £ 11s, 1 screen 10s, 1 carpet 2 £ 15s, 1 pair bellows and brush 11s, 2 window curtains 2 £, 1 large marble mortar 1 £ 1s, 1 hot rache in cellar 1 £ 7s 6d, 2 mahogany card tables 4 £, 1 bed, pair of blankets, 19 coverlets, pillows, bolsters and 1 mahogany table, 11 £; bottles and pickle pots 14s, 1 dozen mountain wine 1 £ 4s, 4 chariot glasses frames 12s 6d, 12 pewter water plates 1 £.

Colonel Fairfax presented Colonel and Mrs. Washington with the entire suite of furniture in "the Blue, or Dressing Room."

The Fairfaxes were moderate loyalists. Not only was it not on account of the presaging troubles with the mother country that Colonel Fairfax returned to England, but throughout the war he extended liberal assistance to Americans in England, to which Washington testified when the confiscation of his American property was threatened:

"I hope, I trust, that no act of Legislation in the State of Virginia has affected, or can affect, the property of this gentleman, otherwise than in common with that of every good and well disposed citizen of America. It is a well known fact that his departure for England was not only antecedant to the present rupture with Great Britian, but before there was the most distant prospect of a serious dispute with that country, and if it is necessary to adduce proof of his attachment to the interests of America since his residence there, and of the aid he has given to many of our distressed countrymen in that kingdom, abundant instances may be produced, not only by the Gentlemen alluded to in his letter of December 5, 1779, but by others that are known to me, and on whom justice to Col. Fairfax will make it necessary to call, if occasion should require the facts be ascertained."

John Parke Custis had now grown into young manhood, and he, too, was soon lost to Mount Vernon, but under consoling circumstances. He had spent the last few years away from home at college or under private tutors, with results that often tried and vexed his stepfather, who once said: "I can govern men, but I cannot govern boys." He supposed Jack was finally safely anchored when he placed him with the Rev. Mr. Boucher in Annapolis. There were frequent visits home from there, but the way lay past the door of Mount Airy, the seat of the Calverts of Maryland, and within was an irresistible temptation in the person of Miss Eleanor.

When the young people's intentions became obvious the politest letters passed between Mount Vernon and Mount Airy. Washington wrote Benedict Calvert, the young lady's father:

"My son-in-law and ward, Mr. Custis, has, as I have been informed, paid his addresses to your second daughter, and, having made some progress in her affections, has solicited her in marriage. How far a union of this sort may be agreeable to you, you best can tell; but I should think myself wanting in candor, were I not to confess, that Miss Nellie's amiable qualities are acknowledged on all hands, and that an alliance with your family will be pleasing to his. . . . It may be expected of me, perhaps, to say something of property; but, to descend to particulars, at this time, must seem rather premature. In general, therefore, I shall inform you, that Mr. Custis's estate consists of about fifteen thousand acres of land, a good part of it adjoining the city of Williamsburg, and none of it forty miles from that place; several lots in the said city; between two and three hundred negroes; and about eight or ten thousand pounds upon bond, and in the hands of his merchants. This estate he now holds independent of his mother's dower; which will be an addition to it at her death; and, upon the whole, it is such an estate as you will readily acknowledge ought to entitle him to a handsome portion with a wife. But as I should never require a child of my own to make a sacrifice of himself to interest so neither do I think it incumbent on me to recommend it as a guardian. At all times when you, Mrs. Calvert, or the young ladies, can make it convenient to favor us with a visit, we should be happy in seeing you at this place."

To which Mr. Calvert replied with the grace which became one of the family of the Lords Baltimore:

"I Received the favour of yours of the 3d Instant by Mr Custis which I feel myself highly honoured by, and am truly happy in your Approbation of that young Gentlemans future Union with my Second Daughter. I should be dead to Parental feelings, were I untouched with the polite manner in which you are pleased to compliment Nelly's Qualifications; Being her father, it would illy become me to sound her praise, perhaps I might be deemed partial —I shall therefore only say, That it has ever been the Endeavor of her Mother and me, to bring her up in such a manner, as to ensure the happiness of her future Husband, in which, I think, we have not been unsuccessful— if we have, we shall be greatly disappointed. . . . Mr. Custis I must acknowledge, is, as a match for my Daughter, much superior to the sanguine hopes which a parents fondness may have at any time encouraged me to indulge. . . . I can only add, on this subject, that, from the largeness of my family (having ten Children) no very great fortune can be expected: What that may be depends upon the Issue of my present depending Claim. Of this, Sir, however be assured, nothing in my power shall be left undone to promote so pleasing a Union— Nelly's portion, as far as my personal Estate will go, shall, at least, be equal to any of my other Children, nor will you, Sir, I am sure, desire more—I shall at all times, when convenient, be happy in bringing my family to wait on Mrs Washington, and equally glad to see her & Miss Custis with you at Mount Airy, where I hope it will suit you to call (next week early) in your way to Annapolis, and I will have the pleasure of attending you thither.

"I am Dear Sir Your most obed^t Humble Servt

"BENED^T CALVERT

"I expect the pleasure of the Governors & M^r. Haywoods Company a Saturday Evening, they stay with me till Monday Morning, when they set off for M^r. Bouchers where they propose to dine, and then go for Annapolis, I shall attend them there & return home in the Evening, without it will sute you to come here on Sunday and go up with them

"B C"

At the end of January, in 1774, the chariot was ferried across to Warburton, and Colonel Washington followed the next day in the great barge and rolled in state to the Calvert seat. Mrs. Washington still felt the loss of her daughter too keenly to enter into the bridal gayety. The fashion of the two colonies were there, and on February 3d the nuptials were celebrated amid much festivity. Jack was not wholly lost to Mount Vernon, however, for he and his wife made their home at Abingdon, a plantation on the Virginia side of the Potomac about four miles above Alexandria and formerly the home of their friend Robert Alexander. A large portion of their time and their children's was spent at Mount Vernon only a dozen miles away. It is, indeed, one of the traditions that "if any horse of the stables were started from Abingdon, and left to his own free will, it would be found in due time at the entrance of Mount Vernon."

The passage of the Stamp Act imposing duties on goods imported into the colony, though at first considered as a domestic difficulty which would yield to argument, was nevertheless resisted at once by the colonists. Washington was among the first by persuasion and example to oppose the injustice of the measure.

The non-importation Resolves were the weapon with which the colonists hoped to change England's attitude. They were the basis of a continual stream of letters from Mount Vernon advancing at first the formation of a local non-importation association, after the pattern of that established at Philadelphia, and later the more aggressive attitude which culminated in the conventions of Fairfax County, Williamsburg, Richmond, and the two Congresses at Philadelphia.

How Washington's principles bore upon the life of his own household is seen in his instructions to his London correspondents.   In sending one of his orders to Robert Cary & Company for domestic goods in 1769, he wrote:

"If there are any articles contained in either of the respective invoices (paper only excepted) which are taxed by act of Parliament for the purpose of raising a revenue in America, it is my express desire and request, that they may not be sent, as I have very heartily entered into an association (copies of which I make no doubt you have seen, otherwise I should have enclosed one) not to import any article which now is, or hereafter shall be taxed for this purpose until the said act or acts are repealed.   I am therefore particular in mentioning this matter as I am fully determined to adhere religiously to it, and may perhaps have wrote for some things unwittingly which may be under these circumstances."

This intention to import nothing for his home upon which Parliament had imposed a tax is repeated in another order on London in 1770:

"You will perceive, in looking over the several in-voices, that some of the goods there required, are upon condition, that the act of Parliament imposing a duty on tea, paper, &c. for the purpose of raising a revenue in America, is totally repealed; and I beg the favor of you to be governed strictly thereby, as it will not be in my power to receive any articles contrary to our non-importation agreement, which I have subscribed, and shall religiously adhere to, and should, if it were, as I could wish it to be, ten times as strict."

Washington and his neighbor, George Mason, were the leaders in the more aggressive attitude of the outraged colonists. In 1774 there were continual trips between Mount Vernon and Gunston Hall for conferences, and there eventuated the famous Resolves, written by Mason, and presented at a convention of the inhabitants of Fairfax County in July, at which Washington presided. In this meeting was the germ of the Second Continental Congress and in the Resolves was the inspiration of the Declaration of Independence.

Washington recorded this occasion with a simplicity which is the despair of the student; but in the light of what was accomplished and its effect on the destiny of a people, the few words are epic:

"July 17. Col. Mason came in the afternoon, and staid all night.
18. Went up to Alexandria to a meeting of the County. Returned in the evening."

After the Fairfax convention he was at Mount Vernon only long enough to pack up and hurry to the convention at Williamsburg, where the astonishing conduct of General Gage at Boston was discussed. The nominally

silent delegate from Fairfax showed the warmth of his
ardor when need be, as now, when, in "the most
eloquent speech that ever was made," he declared with
fire and force: "I will raise one thousand men, subsist
them at my own expense, and march myself at their
head for the relief of Boston."

Hurrying home he discovered the house full of company, but he found time for the Fairfax sale, letters to
England and elsewhere, the arrangement of domestic
affairs, and hurried off on the last day of the month for
the first Congress at Philadelphia. The day before his
departure Mount Vernon was the scene of another
significant conference with George Mason, Patrick
Henry, and Edmund Pendleton. They "came in the
evening and stay'd all night." Next day, August 31st,
"All the above gentlemen dined here; after which with
Colo. Pendleton and Mr. Henry, I set out on my journey
to Philadelphia." Pendleton said that before they set
out Martha Washington "talked like a Spartan mother
to her son on going to battle. 'I hope you will all stand
firm—I know George will,' she said."

When Washington returned home it was to pick up
again the threads of the life he loved so well. He began
at this time to make a reality of plans for the enlarge-
ment and perfection of his house and grounds, which
had long been maturing in his mind.

The house stood in 1773 exactly as he found it when
he took up his home there with his brother Lawrence,
save for the repairs he made in anticipation of his
marriage. The intervening fourteen years of domestic
and social life brought out the limitations of the villa.
It began to call again for repairs after so many years of

hard use. Washington desired a more ambitious and commodious residence, and as early as 1773 planned the house as it appears to-day. This included the extension of the length of the house by the additions at each end measuring the full width of the original house, thirty-two feet by twenty-two feet, which would extend the house by forty-four feet in length.

The new building operations were under way in the fall of 1773, as indicated by a quaint letter from a joiner in Washington's employ:

"Sir /

"I am apprehensive that in the Bill of Scantling that I sent you it was order^d so as to have the Sleepers of Both the additions to Ly Length ways with the house if so the will not be Right by that means the floor will be aCross and the Gelling plank the Length of the addition will not answer the intended purpose of haveing no heading Joints in the Lower floors, the S[l]eepers Need not be More then 16 feet Long to Join on a Summer in the Middle that must be Layd Length ways of House, the Sleepers Must be the same Breadth & thickness as them Mention^d in the Bill & the Two Summers 10 by 14 and 22 foot Long

"I am Sir Y^r Most Hum^{le} Servt
"Going Lanphier
"New Church Octr 16: 1773

"N B I prepos^d from the beginning to Lay the flooring & seeling Jousts Length way of the House it will be a Great Means to Strengthen the additions . . . . G L"

Washington no sooner began the cherished plans than
the war drew him away. He left Lund Washington
in charge of Mount Vernon, and the letters that passed
back and forth tell somewhat of the progress and duration of the work. At least one of the new additions was
completed within two years, for Washington wrote
home from Camp at Cambridge, August 20, 1775: "I
wish you would quicken Lanphier and Sears about the
Dining Room Chimney Piece (to be executed as mentioned in one of my last letters) as I would wish that end
of the House compleatly finished before I return."

Lund Washington referred to the "new room" in his
letters to his chief in 1775, as when, on October 15th, he
wrote: "As to pulling down the plastering in the new
room, it will not make a days odds in his doing the room.
Mrs. Washington seems desireous that whatever is to be
done to it, may be at once that she may get into it this
winter"; and again on December 10th: "Sears has
now painted the dining room twice over and the new
room once."

The further progress of Washington's extensive plans
for his dwelling and for the outbuildings, the gardens
and their walls, will appear later. At this time in-
terruptions checked the work. Mount Vernon seemed
destined to see its master's carefully planned efforts in
its behalf carried on in his absence now as when he first
put it in order to receive his wife.

During the winter of 1774–1775 he was frequently
from home. The house was the scene of continual conferences of the leaders of thought and action in the
neighborhood and in the colony at large. George
Mason was there; William Grayson, later first Senator

for Virginia but now arming the Independent Militia of
Prince William with funds he was promised on these
visits; Edmund Pendleton and Daniel of Saint Thomas
Jenifer, the latter now as Major Jenifer, neighbor,
coming to be directed in militia organization, but later
to live in history as Signer of the Declaration of Independence for Maryland; Charles Lee, British and un-
balanced, accompanied by his hounds, which he insisted on feeding in the dining-room; Horatio Gates,
Major now but Adjutant General in June next; old
companions in the French War, who, scenting powder,
found their way to their former chief's seat "in search
of courage and sympathy"; delegations from the various
counties who came to offer Washington the command
of their Independent Militia "should they be obliged to
have recourse to arms to defend their King and country"; and others in numbers, patriots for the most part,
who recognized in the master of Mount Vernon their
hope in the impending struggle.

Washington found time for his visitors and for endless
letters, and for the obligations placed upon him by the
neighborhood and the colony. He was still a member
of the House of Burgesses. As such he attended the
Virginia convention "in the old church in the town of
Richmond," in March (1775) and brought home his appointment to represent Virginia in the Second Continental Congress and the thrilling story of Mr. Henry's per-
oration: "I know not what course others may take, but
as for me, give me liberty or give me death!"

Less dramatically but not less fervently he wrote his
brother, John Augustine, his own "full intention to de-
vote my life and fortune in the cause we are engaged in."

He had scarcely returned to Mount Vernon when word followed him from the low country that the Royal Governor had confiscated the powder stored in Williamsburg, and he rode instantly to Fredericksburg to calm the six hundred men who had rushed to arms. Riders came to his door with messages from the militia of various counties offering to serve under his command. The pulse of the people was indeed throbbing.

Toward the end of April his chariot rolled away again to Philadelphia. There was not probably either in his heart or Mrs. Washington's a full understanding of what their good-byes meant. He left to be absent a few weeks, at most, as Virginia's delegate in the Congress. He remained under pressure of a unanimous Assembly to accept the command of the independent army of the colonies.

At this moment of such significance and obligation his thoughts flew at once to Mount Vernon. He wrote his "dear Patsey":

"I am now set down to write you on a subject, which fills me with inexpressible concern, and this concern is greatly aggravated and increased, when I reflect upon the uneasiness I know it will give you. It has been determined in Congress, that the whole army raised for the defense of the American cause shall be put under my care, and that it is necessary for me to proceed immediately to Boston to take upon me the command of it. . . . I shall feel no pain from the toil or the danger of the campaign; my unhappiness will flow from the uneasiness I know you will feel from being left alone. I therefore beg, you will summon your whole fortitude, and pass your time as agreeably as possible. Nothing will give me so much sincere satisfaction as to hear this, and to hear it from your own pen."

To Jack Custis he wrote:

"My great concern upon this occasion is, the thought of leaving your mother under the uneasiness which I fear this affair will throw her into; I therefore hope, expect, and indeed have no doubt, of your using every means in your power to keep up her spirits, by doing everything in your power to promote her quiet. . . . At any time, I hope it is unnecessary for me to say, that I am always pleased with yours and Nelly's abidence at Mount Vernon; much less upon this occasion, when I think it absolutely necessary for the peace and satisfaction of your mother; a consideration which I have no doubt will have due weight with you, and require no argument to enforce."

To his brother John Augustine:

"I am now to bid adieu to you, and to every kind of domestic ease, for a while. I am embarked on a wide ocean, boundless in its prospect, and in which, perhaps, no safe harbor is to be found. I have been called upon by the unanimous voice of the Colonies to take the command of the Continental army; an honor I have neither sought after, nor desired, as I am thoroughly convinced, that it requires greater abilities and much more experience, than I am master of, to conduct a business so extensive in its nature, and arduous in its execution. But the partiality of the Congress, joined to a political motive, really left me without a choice; and I am now commissioned a General and Commander-in-chief of all the forces now raised, or to be raised, for the defense of the United Colonies. That I may discharge the trust to the satisfaction of my employers, is my first wish; that I shall aim to do it, there remains as little doubt of. How far I shall succeed, is another point; but this I am sure of, that, in the worst event, I shall have the consolation of knowing, if I act to the best of my judgement, that the blame ought to lodge upon the appointers, not the appointed, as it was by no means a thing of my seeking, or proceeding from any hint of my friends. . . . I shall hope that my friends will visit and endeavor to keep up the spirits of my wife, as much as they can, as my departure will, I know, be a cutting stroke upon her; and on this account alone I have many very disagreeable sensations. I hope you and my sister, (although the distance is great) will find as much leisure this summer as to spend a little time at Mount Vernon."

Washington did not see Mount Vernon again for six years.

CHAPTER XI

MOUNT VERNON was indeed desolate to
Martha Washington as she read the message
of dreaded triumph which placed the destinies
of the country in her husband's hands. The sacrifice
was hers. In less than two years she had seen her family
completely disintegrate: her daughter lost by death; her
son by marriage; her husband by the call to the military
service of his country. A sympathetic sense of this
prompted Washington to write those first letters, after
receiving his commission, to her relatives and his, begging them to go to Mount Vernon and comfort his
lonely wife.

Jack Custis and his wife came down frequently from
Abingdon, as the years rolled by, bringing the growing
family of babies to their affectionate grandmother:
Elisabeth Parke the first; then Martha Parke, named
for Mrs. Washington; then Eleanor Parke, named for

her mother and hurried from her frail arms to Mount
Vernon to be nursed by sturdy Mrs. Anderson, wife of
the English steward; and finally the first boy, named
for the only father he ever knew, George Washington
Parke. Mrs. Washington's brothers and sisters, the
Dandridges and Bassetts, journeyed up from New
Kent, and friends from Alexandria and the neighboring
estates on both sides of the Potomac came to break Mrs.
Washington's loneliness. The house was "seldom with-
out company" while she was there and "our stables are
always full of horses," read the letters from home to the
General.

Mount Vernon was in charge of Lund Washington,
as manager for the General, with whom no doubt a
connection could be traced far out on some leafy branch
of the ancestral tree. But it is said that neither of them
knew what it was. Lund's lieutenant was Bishop, who
only once, since the memorable vigil outside Mr. Chamberlayne's door, had strayed from his chief. Too old
for the active service of the days of Braddock, "he was
left at home," wrote one who knew him well, "in charge
of the manufacturing establishments of the household,
wherein the veteran would flourish his cane, expecting
as perfect obedience as though he had been commanding
officer on parade. A comfortable house had been built
for him; he had married; and, looking no more toward
his native land, he was contented to pass the remainder
of his days on the domain of his patron, where he rested
from labor, in the enjoyment of every possible ease and
indulgence."

It may or may not be significant, but it is difficult
to discover the traces of cordial intercourse between the

Washingtons and the Custises. From the time of Washington's marriage his mother never came to Mount Vernon. His sister and brothers seem rarely to have appeared there. It is indeed suspected that on their wedding, Washington married into the Widow Custis' family, rather than that she married into his. When her grandson wrote his reminiscences of life at Mount Vernon he mentioned but one of the General's relatives, a young nephew whose first name appeared casually in a quoted letter. In the next generation, however, some of the children of the General's brothers and sister appeared somewhat more at home at their uncle's house than their parents before them.

When Washington accepted the command of the army he expressed no doubt that he would return safe to Mount Vernon and his wife in the fall. Instead of which he was detained in Massachusetts. Mrs. Washington, thereupon, was determined to go north and spend the winter in camp with him. For seven years this was her usual custom. When the stress of a summer campaign eased and the army settled in winter quarters, the General would send an aide-de-camp to Mount Vernon to be her personal escort to Cambridge, Morristown, Valley Forge, Middlebrook, New Winsor, or wherever the army happened to be. Her chariot was occasionally accompanied by a military escort, by the General's order if the road lay dangerously near the enemy's line, oftener as a spontaneous compliment of the citizens of the districts through which she passed.

Of the eight years and eight months that Washington was absent during the war Mrs. Washington spent nearly half the time with him. At such times Mount

Vernon was deserted indeed. The house was quiet, the woods no longer echoed to the hounds and horn, and the well-travelled roadways, deserted by the smart-hoofed mounts and the broad-tired chariots of the customary stream of visitors, felt the green creeping up from ditches to wheel-rut. His mother resented his military activities now as formerly and said she wished "George would come home and attend to his plantation."

However, even in the absence of both the master and mistress the doors of Mount Vernon were not entirely closed. The General wrote Lund Washington from Cambridge, shortly after Mrs. Washington joined him at headquarters: "Let the hospitality of the house, with respect to the poor, be kept up. Let no one go away hungry. If any of this kind of people should be in want of corn, supply their necessities, provided it does not encourage them in idleness; and I have no objection to your giving my money in charity, to the amount of forty or fifty pounds a year, when you think it well bestowed."

The progress of the war was followed with passionate but somewhat starved eagerness at Mount Vernon. The newspapers were few and without modern facilities for quick, precise, or ample news. There was no postal system to speak of. At intervals, usually of a week, express pony riders carried the mails north and south between the larger towns. England did nothing for the colonies in this respect and they did practically nothing for themselves. The mails were in the hands of private carriers, and important letters or consignments of money were not considered safe in their hands. If the matter was urgent and confidential a private bearer was despatched with the letter. Gentlemen about to undertake a journey allowed the fact to become known among their particular friends in the neighborhood and often started away with numerous packets of letters, large sums of money, and with negotiable papers of considerable value. Nevertheless it was upon the unreliable post-rider and the occasional accommodating traveller that Mount Vernon depended for communication with the General. Lund was faithful to the order that Washington ever put upon his managers in his absence, to write regularly and in full once a week about the condition of his estate. Many of his letters are preserved, and they afford an acquaintance with the life there to be found at no other source.

Washington had been gone but a few months when the presence of war in the land became evident at Mount Vernon. One of Governor Dunmore's first strokes was to threaten a declaration of freedom for all indentured servants in the colonies. Lund Washington wrote that such an order would wreck their working forces. But this fear dwindled presently before the larger alarm which spread along tidewater Potomac, as news came that English ships were on their way up the river to lay waste the towns and country, capture Mrs. Washington, and burn Mount Vernon.

Lund wrote the General in a tone obviously designed to allay his fears: "She does not believe herself in danger, nor do I," he said; "without they attempt to take her in the dead of night, they would fail, for ten minutes notice would be sufficient for her to get out of the way." A few days later he wrote: "Mrs. Washing-

ton was under no apprehension of Lord Dunmore doing
her an injury, until your mention of it in several of your
letters." Nevertheless, she postponed a trip down
country in order to pack the General's papers, the silver,
and other valuables, and hold herself and them in readiness for instant departure inland.

Dunmore's expedition came up as far as the mouth of
Occoquon Creek, into which flows the Bull Run of two
great battles nearly a century later. Here he en-
countered the Prince William Militia and a severe
storm, a combination which he found too forbidding for
his further progress; not, however, before he had thrown
the countryside into a panic. A few days later George
Mason wrote Washington: "Dunmore has come and
gone, and left us untouched except by some alarms.
I sent my family many miles back into the country, and
advised Mrs. Washington to do likewise as a prudential
movement. At first she said, 'No, I will not desert
my post,' but finally she did so with reluctance, rode
only a few miles, and—plucky little woman as she is,
stayed away only one night."

The dwellers along tidewater became active in considering measures to thwart the dreaded Dunmore; more
active in considering than in putting them into effect.
It was proposed to protect Mount Vernon and the upper
river by batteries on Lower Cedar Point where the
channel is narrowest, or at Maryland Point, or farther up
even on the commanding bluffs of Indian Head. Hob-
son's Santiago expedient was anticipated, Lund Washington writing his chief, October 29, 1775: "As I remembered hearing Captain Boucher say he would
undertake with three ships to stop the channel so that

no ship of force could get up the River, I proposed that he should be immediately sent to and consulted upon it." But in the end nothing was done.

The following January there were renewed rumors of the approach of British vessels to destroy Mount Vernon, and the neighborhood was in another panic. This time Lund did not conceal his apprehensions, perhaps because Mrs. Washington was with the General, and he did not have to dissemble to spare his chief's fears for his wife.

"Alexandria is much alarmed, and indeed the whole neighborhood," he wrote. "The women and children are leaving the town and stowing themselves in every hut they can find, out of the reach of the enemy's cannon. Every wagon, cart, and pack-horse, they can get, is employed. The militia are all up, but not in arms, for indeed they have none, or at least very few. I could wish, if we were to have our neighborhood invaded, that they would send a tender or two among us, that we might see how the people would behave on the occasion. Thay say they are determined to fight. I am about packing up your China and glass in barrels, and other things into chests, trunks, and bundles, and I shall be able at the shortest notice to remove them out of the way. I fear the destruction will be great, although the best care has been taken. Everybody I see tells me, that if the people could have notice they would immediately come and defend your property, so long as they have life, from Loudoun, Prince William, Fauquier, and this county."

But this time the ships did not even enter the Potomac. After cruising about the Chesapeake they finally felt the sting of the colonists' gunfire, and sped away, and Dunmore did not appear again to disturb the planters of the Potomac.

For the rest of the war Mount Vernon was unthreatened until its very last year. Early in 1781 British Tarleton with his band of red-coat raiders swung up from the southwest like a whirlwind. Word came that Jefferson's Monticello was their first objective and Washington's home would be the next. Tarleton reached Charlottesville, but his easterly course was aimed no higher than Fredericksburg.

When the fright about the river raid was first on at the beginning of the war, Lund wrote bravely: "I think fifty men well armd might prevent two hundred from burning Mount Vernon, situated as it is; no way to get up to it but up a steep hill, and if I remember right General Gates told me it could not be done by the shipping. I wish I had the muskets I would endeavor to find the men, black or white, that would at least make them pay dear for the attempt."

Apparently he never got the muskets, for shortly after the Tarleton scare British ships appeared in the river and actually anchored off Mount Vernon. Lund obviously was not without spirit; but without arms and the men, discretion seemed to him the better part of valor. What he did, and his chief's reflection on it, appear in the General's celebrated rebuke to the man for whom, however, he never lost admiration or affection:

"I am sorry to hear of your loss. I am a little sorry to hear of my own; but that which gives me most concern is, that you should go on board the enemy's vessels, and furnish them with refreshments. It would have been a less painful circumstance to me to have heard, that in consequence of your non-compliance with their request, they had burnt my House and laid the Plantation in ruins. You ought to have considered yourself as my representative, and should have reflected on the bad example of communicating with the enemy, and making a voluntary offer of refreshments to them with a view to prevent a conflagration. It was not in your power, I acknowledge, to prevent them from sending a flag on shore, and you did right to meet it; but you should, in the same instant that the business of it was unfolded, have declared explicitly, that it was improper for you to yeild to the request; after which, if they had proceeded to help themselves by force, you could have but submitted; and, (being unprovided for defense,) this was to be preferred to a feeble opposition, which only serves as a pretext to burn and destroy."

None of the military "alarums and excursions," however, disturbed the work on the place. The improvements on the house went forward. Before the end of 1775 Lanphier and Sears and "the stucco man" completed "the new room," the chimney piece, and the dining-room ceiling, which was "a handsomer one than any of Col. Lewis's [at Kenmore House, Fredericksburg] although not half the work on it." Lund had many other operations on the way at this time, among them the building or rebuilding of the storehouse, the washhouse, the garden walls, and their little octagon houses for school and seeds and tools. He was, moreover, eager to

complete the other addition to the mansion, but the fear
of new raids filled him with apprehension.

"I think if you could be of opinion that your buildings
would not be destroyed this summer," he wrote his
chief in February, 1776, "it would be best to have the
other addition to the end of your house raised   .   .   .
but this cannot be done without a master workman, unless you choose to once more try Lanphier." Washington evidently was forced to put up with this incorri-
gible, for in the spring of 1778 Lund still had him on hand
and wrote: "Of all the worthless men living Lanphier
is the greatest, no act or temptation of mine can prevail
on him to came to work notwithstanding his repeated
promises to do so. I wanted so much to get the windows
finished in the Pediment that I might have the garrett
passage plastered and cleared out before Mrs. Washington's return. Besides this the scaffolding in the front of
the house cannot be taken away before it is finished.
This prevents me from putting up the steps to the great
front door."

At this time, 1778, instead of after the war as generally stated, the mansion was raised to the extended proportions in which it has ever since been so familiar, and
the curved and colonnaded covered ways now rose to
connect the big house with the nearest of the many little
houses. To this time, too, may doubtless be attributed
the lofty portico extending the length of the river side of
the mansion, for so shortly after his return after the war
as to have made it impracticable for him to have built it
at that time, Washington ordered new stone flagging and
dug up the old pavement and laid the new.

The traditions which cluster about the old house include among the improvements made early in the war, the removal of the partition in the main passage or hall, thus making one extended hall from front to front, and the installation of the panelling of the new big hall as it has since remained.

Lund included in his letters all the personal news of the neighborhood and the estate, making them a gazette of life at home on the big river. After the receipt of one of these letters it was Washington's sad duty to be obliged to write Colonel Fairfax in England of the complete destruction of his house, Belvoir, by fire early in 1783. "But mine (which is enlarged since you saw it)," he hastened to add, "is most sincerely at your service till you can rebuild it." Belvoir was never rebuilt. Of it there remains neither authentic plan nor painting. Its site is an overgrown thicket where the lines of the foundation are scarcely to be traced. This beautiful and historic spot, which bound up some of the most agreeable and cherished experiences of Washington's life, was threatened with uses a few years ago which would have been at once a blight upon it and Mount Vernon. Friends of Washington's home and neighborhood, however, led by the Mount Vernon Ladies' Association, preserved it by securing the transfer of the threatened lands to the United States Army, which has dedicated it to the training of soldiers and officers.

It has been said that when Washington rode away in the spring of 1775, to attend the Second Continental Congress at Philadelphia, he did not return to Mount Vernon again for six years. In fact, during the whole course of the war, and for two years after Cornwallis sur-

rendered to him at Yorktown in 1781, he was in Virginia
only once. In passing south to Yorktown and in returning north again he stopped briefly at his home.
During his absence of eight years and eight months
he was at Mount Vernon only ten days.

The whole plantation was thrown into a commotion
in the early morning of Sunday, the 9th of September,
1781, by the announcement of the arrival of the General,
and old Bishop's younger rival, Billy Lee, his groom of
hunting days and personal attendant throughout the
war. They had pressed on ahead of the army which
was making a forced march south to join LaFayette at
Williamsburg.

Next to the greeting of his "dear Patsey," his return was
distinguished for him by his first sight of his now completed mansion, and by his first acquaintance with Mrs.
Washington's four grandchildren, the three daughters
and baby boy of Jack and Nelly Calvert Custis, all born
during his absence in the field.

On Monday General Count de Rochambeau came,
followed by General Marquis de Chastellux. After resting another full day Washington, accompanied by his
two French guests, their servants, and Jack Custis, set
off on Wednesday morning for the south.

On this trip there was no dallying at country houses.
The errand was stern and significant, and Washington
pressed across country in record time. He reached the
capital Friday afternoon and was welcomed by La-
Fayette and the French soldiers with military honors
which became his exalted command. One month and
five days later the fighting ceased.

This happy event was clouded by the news brought

Washington from Eltham, Colonel Bassett's place in New Kent, where Jack Custis lay at the point of death. Couriers had already speeded to Mount Vernon to summon the dying man's wife and mother. Doctor Craik hurried from Yorktown to give his friend what assistance he could. The General and his wife together watched the ebb of the young life of him who had been as son to both of them. By his death Mrs. Washington was now childless, but the General filled the gap in both their lives and gave promise of continued youthfulness at Mount Vernon by adopting the two youngest children, Eleanor Parke Custis and George Washington Parke Custis, as their own.

Six days later Washington was at Mount Vernon, where he remained a week, and departed to the north for another absence of two years, holding the army in that preparedness which would insure a desirable treaty of peace; then disbanding it and concluding his own relation to the military service. He resigned his commission at Annapolis on December 23, 1783; took affectionate leave of his companions in arms; and once more a private citizen, with Mrs. Washington by his side, and accompanied by Colonels David Humphreys, William Smith, and Benjamin Walker, he rode forward over the familiar Maryland roads toward his beloved Mount Vernon.

CHAPTER XII

Washington's Delight to Be at Mount Vernon Again—Letters
—Journeys to Fredericksburg, Philadelphia, and the Ohio
Country—Putting a Finish on Grounds and Buildings—The
Bowling Green and the Serpentine Drive—Trees—The Deer
Park—Gardens—Walls—Barns—Fences—A Toper's Con-
tract—The General's Warhorse, Nelson—Mrs. Washington's
Grandchildren—His Nephews and Nieces—First Wedding
in the Mansion—Dreaming of a Deed from the General—
Shiftless Harriott.

THE General and Mrs. Washington reached
home Christmas Eve. His "people" from
the various farms gathered at the gate and
along the drive to give them welcome. Among them
was Bishop, easily forgiven for any envy he felt of
young Billy Lee. They lighted the night with bonfires
and made it noisy with fiddling and dancing in the
quarters. At the great door of the mansion the home-
comers were greeted by a troop of relatives, and next
day the neighbors drove in from all directions to add
their welcome.

The unconscious historian of this occasion was a little
girl, one of the Lewis children of Fredericksburg, who
wrote a friend: "I must tell you what a charming day
I spent at Mt. Vernon with Mama and Sally. The
General and Madame came home on Christmas Eve,
and such a racket as the servants made! They were
glad of their coming. Three handsome young officers
came with them. All Christmas afternoon people

came to pay their respects and duty. Among these were stately dames and gay young women. The General seemed very happy and Mrs. Washington was up before daybreak making everything as agreeable as possible for everybody."

Washington's early letters after reaching Mount Vernon breathe the relief and joy he felt to have closed his "transactions with the public" and arrived at "the goal of domestic enjoyment."

It was perhaps natural that he should write with least reserve and most sentiment to his dear LaFayette:

"At length, my dear Marquis, I am become a private citizen on the banks of the Potomac; and under the shadow of my own vine and fig-tree, free from the bustle of a camp, and the busy scenes of public life, I am solacing myself with those tranquil enjoyments, of which the soldier, who is ever in pursuit of fame, the statesman, whose watchful days and sleepless nights are spent in devising schemes to promote the welfare of his own, perhaps the ruin of other countries, as if this globe were insufficient for us all, and the courtier, who is always watching the countenence of his prince, in hopes of catching a gracious smile, can have very little conception. I have not only retired from all public employments, but I am retiring within myself, and shall be able to view the solitary walk, and tread the paths of private life, with heartfelt satisfaction. Envious of none, I am determined to be pleased with all; and this, my dear friend, being the order of my march, I will move gently down the stream of life, until I sleep with my fathers."

In a somewhat similar sentimental vein he wrote the Marchioness de LaFayette, in reply to her felicitations:

"From the clangor of arms and the bustle of a camp, freed from the cares of public employment and the responsibility of office, I am now enjoying domestic ease under the shadow of my own vine and fig-tree; and in a small villa, with the implements of husbandry and lambkins around me, I expect to glide gently down the stream of life, till I am entombed in the dreary mansion of my fathers."

But to his fellow-campaigner, General Knox, he expressed his situation seven weeks after his return in more literal terms:

"I am just beginning to experience that ease and freedom from public cares, which, however desireable, takes some time to realize; for, strange as it may seem, it is nevertheless true, that it was not till lately I could get the better of my usual custom of ruminating, as soon as I waked in the morning, on the business of the ensuing day; and of my surprise at finding, after revolving many things in my mind, that I was no longer a public man, nor had anything to do with public transactions.

"I feel now, however, as I conceive a wearied traveller must do, who, after treading many a painful step with a heavy burthen on his shoulders, is eased of the latter, having reached the haven to which all the former were directed; and from his house-top is looking back, and tracing with an eager eye the meanders by which he escaped the quicksands and mires which lay in his way; and into which none but the all-powerful Guide and

Dispenser of human events could have prevented his falling."

Relief was the keynote of all he expressed, relief and a desire to remain undisturbed in the tranquillity of his home. "I feel myself relieved of a load of public care," he wrote Governor Clinton. "I hope to spend the remainder of my days cultivating the affections of good men, and in the practice of the domestic virtues." It was now his devoutly expressed wish "to glide silently and unnoticed through the remainder of life."

The ice and snow of a particularly rigid winter locked the family in the house during the first weeks of the General's return. During this time he laid out a scheme of work for his military secretaries, for improvements on the grounds and gardens and farms, and for the recovery of his extensive private interests from the confusion into which they had run during his long absence.

He settled down eventually to the routine of his life before the war, but not until he had made some trips during the first months after his return home. In February he braved roads and weather to pay his duty to his mother in Fredericksburg. In May he attended the meeting of the Society of the Cincinnati at Philadelphia. At the end of the summer he made his hasty journey to view his lands on the Kanawha and the Ohio. He was accompanied only by his nephew Bushrod Washington, Doctor Craik and his son William, and three servants. They travelled on horseback and covered the entire distance of six hundred and eighty miles in thirty-four days between September 1st and October 4th.

Save for three absences in Richmond he was not many miles from Mount Vernon until public service again made him an exile five years later. It is a notable fact that Washington rarely went far from his home except when called by duty or business. His interest and purpose attached to his house and lands and he left them only at the sacrifice of personal preferences.

It is not easy to see what Lund Washington left him to do by way of making those improvements to his house which have so often been attributed to the first years after the war. But the severe winter called out his ingenuity to make his house warmer, so it may have been at this time that he lathed and plastered the lower side of the floor planks between the joists in the cellar. The original laths and plaster have long since disappeared, but the unmistakable evidences of them remain. It was then not an uncommon method of keeping the floors free from draughts, for those were not days of tongue and groove lumber. He now prepared a dry well for ice in the cellar under the banquet hall, and possibly the cupola may be attributed to the work done at this time.

It is known that, in the spring of 1786, he renewed the paving of the great piazza on the river front. No portion of the house received more general or more severe usage than this out-of-door shelter with its magnificent views of the Potomac. Not only was it in constant service by the members of the household, but the great gatherings of visitors were received and entertained there, for which thirty windsor chairs were provided, and, when winter weather prevented the General from taking his usual exercise on foot or horseback, he paced

the portico for an hour before retiring to rest. Its
floor is, by Washington's own record, one hundred and
twenty-four feet and ten and a half inches above the
river level. Evidently the first pavement placed there
by Lund Washington did not stand well, for says the
diary (1786): "May 22, Began to take up the pavement
of the piazza," and "May 23, Began to lay the flags of
my piazza." Washington attributed the need of new
flags to the effect of frost on the old, but the new ones
have remained there to the present time.

In so far as concerned his house and grounds he had
passed the days of assembly, and now entered on a
period of decoration, polish, and finish. This appeared
especially in his attention to his west lawn, its encircling
drive, and the trees which border it; the two walled gardens, that to the south for vegetables and that to the
north for flowers and flowering shrubs in greenhouse
and box-patterned beds; the deer-park, the ha-ha walls,
and the miles of fences on the various farms. As in all
improvements of whatever character at Mount Vernon,
Washington made his own plans and drawings.

The great enclosed lawn on the west side of the mansion includes a level stretch of nearly two acres about
which he laid out a carriage drive, called his Serpentine
Road, and which in its courses passed the great door of
the mansion, the doors of four of the small or "office"
buildings, and the entrance to each garden, and described somewhat the outline of the shield of the United
States. The trees on either side of the Serpentine, as it
stretched away from the big house, terminated, by
Washington's own description, "with two mounds of
earth, one on each side, on which grow weeping willows,

leaving an open and full view of the distant woods.
The mounds are sixty yards apart."

In 1785 and 1786 his diary is a running guide to his
activities in the adornment of his grounds.   On January 19th he was "employd until dinner time in laying
out my Serpentine Road & Shrubberies adjoining."
In February he "Removed two pretty large & full-grown
lilacs to the N⁰ Garden gate—one on each side taking
up as much dirt with the roots as cᵈ be well obtained";
he "also removed from the woods and the old fields,
several young trees of sassafras, Dogwood & Redbud,
to the Shrubbery on the N⁰ side the grass plot"; and he
"planted all the Mulberry trees, Maple trees & Black
gums in my Serpentine walks—and the Poplars on the
right walk."   In the long list of trees that he planted
and grafted, earlier and later, at Mount Vernon, are
found: the Whitethorn, Hemlock, Mediterranean Pine,
Holly, Tulip, Sweet Gum, Oak, Balsam, Mulberry,
Aspen, Ash, Locust, Fringetree, Willow, Magnum
Bonum Plum, French Walnut, Mississippi Nut, Crab
Scions, Butter Pear, Spanish Pear "from Collo. Mason,"
Black Pear of Worcester, Bergamy Pear, Early June
Pear, Newton Pippin, Gloucester White Apple, Cullock
Heart Cherry, Early May Cherry, Large Duke Cherry,
Black May Cherry, May Duke Cherry, Carnation
Cherry, English Mulberry, Quince, Peach, and others.

He hunted the woods for miles to bring home a rare
or perfect specimen for his lawns.   He brought acorns
and buckeyes back from the Monongahela.   He sought
the coöperation of friends on both sides of the Atlantic
to help embellish his estate.   "Whenever you conceive
the season is proper," he wrote Governor Clinton of

New York, "and opportunity offers, I shall hope to receive the balsam trees, or any others, which you may think curious and exotics with us, as I am endeavoring to improve the grounds about my house in this way. If perchance the sloop *Pilgrim* is not yet sailed from your port, you would add to the favor you mean to confer on me, by causing a number of grape vines, sent to me by an uncle of the Chevalier de la Luzerne, brought over by Captain Williams, and deposited by him in the garden of Mr. Beekman near the City of New York, to be forwarded by that vessel. They consist of a variety of the most valuable eating grapes in France. A list of the kinds, and the distinctions of them, no doubt accompanied them. I pray you to take some of each sort for your own use, and offer some to Mr. Beekman."

The especial pride of his kitchen garden were the fig-trees which were trained on the warm side of the north wall. Amariah Frost, who wrote his account of a visit to Mount Vernon in Washington's lifetime, found the gardens "very elegant," and abounding in many curiosities, among which he enumerated "Fig-trees, raisins, limes, oranges, etc., large English mulberries, artichokes, etc." The "raisin" is more familiar to-day as the currant bush.

The unmanageable undergrowth on the faces of the bluff between the mansion and the river gave offense to Washington's sense of order and economy. To be rid of the thicket, without the trouble of keeping it down by labor, and at the same time add a new grace to his estate, he enclosed about one hundred acres with a wooden paling in 1785, and stocked the enclosure with

deer to beat it down to a park. It may be that his old
friend, Colonel Fairfax, suggested this characteristic
feature of a country estate, for in writing to him to
thank him for offering to secure him "a buck and doe
of the best English deer," Washington said: "but if
you have not already been at this trouble, I would, my
good sir, now wish to relieve you from it, as Mr. Ogle
of Maryland has been so obliging as to present me six
fawns from his park of English deer at Bellair. With
these, and tolerable care, I shall soon have a full stock
for my small paddock."

The brick walls about the two gardens, built during
the war, were not merely utilitarian; they were part of
the grand plan which united with architectural formality and proportion the big house, the little houses, the
gardens, and the bowling green. But as the place took
on finish it became exacting. It demanded that the
barns and open stable court be screened from the lawns
on the east side of the mansion, and Washington met
the demand with the stepped wall which descends the
hill with a grace that makes it almost imperceptible.
Those were days before lawn-mowers when the cattle
did the useful office of keeping the grass down. Un-
sightly pasture fences were no longer to be tolerated,
so he built the English ha-ha walls across the north
and south river lawns and beyond the west end of the
bowling green. These walls, in effect brick terraces,
were invisible from the house, but held the cattle at a
distance while admitting them to the landscape.

Mount Vernon was in reality completed in all its
adornments within a few years after the war. This
accomplished, Washington continually repaired, but

he did not materially alter the house or the fundamental plan of the grounds and small buildings. Changes in the outlying farms, however, were constantly under way. There was always a force of woodmen to cut and hew timber, and of carpenters and joiners to work the lumber up into farm buildings. Washington's pride as a farmer centred at this time on his new barn. It stood in the centre of Union Farm about halfway between the mansion and the mill, and measured one hundred feet long by more than one hundred feet deep. The plan was furnished by the celebrated English farmer, Arthur Young, but Washington modified it for his own emergencies.

Even at so early a period of the settlement of the country the astute Washington realized the necessity of economy in the use of timber. His thousands of acres were subdivided by miles of fences. The split-rail fence was commonly in use. He had begun several years before to replace these fences with hedges. "At least fifteen years," he said in 1795, "have I been urging my managers to substitute live fences in lieu of dead ones—which, if continued upon the extensive scale my farms require, must exhaust all my timber;—and to this moment I have not one that is complete:—nor never shall, unless they are attended to in the manner before mentioned; and if plants die, to replace them the next season; and so on, until the hedge is close, compact, and sufficient to answer the purpose for which it is designed."

Whatever other interests may have made their demands, wherever else he may have been called, neither now nor later did Washington cease to be the planter of, if not at, Mount Vernon. While away he kept in touch with his manager through the exchange of weekly reports and letters, and he dictated astonishingly minute details of policy and procedure. In exercising this genius for detail he did not always escape humorous results, as in the contract with a gardener; wherein, in consideration of his attending faithfully to his work and keeping himself from being "disguised with liquor," Washington agrees to allow him, among other emoluments, "four dollars at Christmas, with which he may be drunk four days and four nights; two dollars at Easter to effect the same purpose; two dollars at Whitsuntide to be drunk for two days; a dram in the morning and a drink of grog at dinner at noon."

So when he came back after the war, he complained a little that the farms were shabby and that farming was impoverishing him, but he resumed his old routine, nevertheless, easily and naturally. He was again in the saddle daily, riding his circuit from farm to farm, to reappear at the great front door at fifteen minutes before the dinner hour punctually as the needle on the sundial, with which he now invariably compared his watch.

Somewhere along the way, however, he compromised with time to allow himself a few extra minutes, for it is said that he now added one final unfailing stop to his daily rounds. It was at the pasture where a tall, aging chestnut, with white face and legs, came at his call to receive the caresses of his master's hand. This was his battle-horse, Nelson, his companion in the war, and "remarkable as the first nicked horse seen in America." He bore Washington on his back when Cornwallis surrendered to him at Yorktown. Then he was mustered out of service and a saddle was never put on his back again.

Nothing else in life seemed to delight Washington as Mount Vernon and its belongings, its development and upkeep. "Agriculture has ever been among the most favored of my amusements," he wrote Arthur Young, "though I have never possessed much skill in the art, and nine years total inattention to it has added nothing to a knowledge, which is best understood from practice; but with the means you have been so obliging as to furnish me, I shall return to it, though rather late in the day, with more alacrity than ever."

When Washington resumed life at Mount Vernon the household was curiously similar to that when he began his married life there twenty-four years before. Then there were himself and Mrs. Washington and her two children, John and Martha, respectively four and two years old. Now there were still himself and Mrs. Washington, and again a little girl and a little boy, but though adopted by Washington, they were her grandchildren this time, Eleanor Parke Custis and George Washington Parke Custis, respectively four and two years old.

Washington's marriage was childless, but his paternal affections spent themselves without reserve first on Mrs. Washington's children and then on her grandchildren. They found themselves as much at home at Mount Vernon as if it were their own father's house. Of the evidences of his petting of the children none perhaps is more charming than his thought of tiny Nellie and Washington when, in the confusion of settling the public business in Philadelphia, he took time to shop for toys

for them, in anticipation of that Christmas Eve return
from the war.   The items are recorded in his note-book
with his customary precision:

By Sundries bo^t. in Phil^a.

A Locket . . . . _ 5	5	
3 Small Pock^t. Books . . . . ¯ 1	10	
3 Sashes 1	5	0
Dress Cap 2	8	
Hatt 3	10	
Handkerchief 1		
Childrens Books	4	6
Whirligig	1	6
Fiddle	2	6
Quadrille Boxes 1	17	6

Washington had twenty-two nephews and nieces who
survived infancy.   His wife had almost as many.   They
were a humanly uneven group.   But their uncle was
generous and devoted to them according to their de-
serts.   He found commissions for several nephews in the
army.   It is said, though on what authority it does not
appear, that "he did not hesitate to give them posts of
danger, and their pay came out of his pocket."   Some
of the boys he sent to school at his own expense, and he
was glad to have the girls come to Mount Vernon and
meet the distinguished visitors with an eye to desirable
husbands for them.

When Lund Washington left Mount Vernon in 1785
and retired to his own estate, Hayfield, about four miles
back from the river, he was succeeded as manager by
George Augustine Washington, son of the General's
youngest brother, Charles.   While a member of his
uncle's family and in his house George met Frances

Bassett, Mrs. Washington's niece, and the second union of the Washington and Dandridge families followed in their marriage, on October 15, 1785. This appears to have been the first wedding ever solemnized at Mount Vernon. Before retiring that night the General noted in his diary with a quaint simplicity:

"The Reverend M^r. Grayson, and Doct^r Griffith; Lund Washington, his wife, & Miss Stuart came to Dinner—all of them remained the Evening except L. W. —After the Candles were lighted George Aug^e Washington and Frances Bassett were married by Mr Grayson."

Bushrod, son of John Augustine Washington, became his favorite nephew, even as his father was the General's favorite brother; and to him his uncle bequeathed Mount Vernon. There is something more to be told of him in its place in this story.

There is a tradition of another nephew, whose name is not given, who discovered his distinguished uncle's ownership of a plantation which the young man fancied. His desire for the place was so much on his mind that he one night dreamed his uncle had given it to him. The next time he was at Mount Vernon he called the General's attention to the piece of land which he had forgotten that he owned. The young man told of the dream. The General laughed outright and remarked: "You didn't dream Mount Vernon away from me, did you, sir?" The subject was then forgotten. The next morning as the young relative was leaving Washington placed a folded paper in his hand to be examined at his leisure. When he found the opportunity he discovered

MOUNT VERNON FROM THE POTOMAC RIVER

The wooded hillside in the foreground is the Deer Park.

THE GREAT WINDOW IN THE BANQUET HALL

it was a deed, made out after his uncle had retired for
the night, conveying to him the property they had
talked about, "for the consideration of natural affection."

As the boys and girls file by, none seizes the attention with more amusement than Harriott, the incorri-
gible daughter of much-married Samuel. She came to
her uncle's house in 1785, and made her home there for
seven years. Her uncle gives her portrait in a few
phrases, indicating at the same time what a trial she
must have been to one of his fine sense of order and
economy: "Harriott has sense enough but no disposition
to industry, nor to be careful of her cloathes. . . .
Direct her in their use and application of them, for without this they will be (I am told) dabbed about in every
hole and corner, and her best things always in use."
Then he adds with kindly justice: "But she is young
and, with good advice, may yet make a fine woman."
Surely there is apology for her in the inevitable neglect
of a father who could scarcely have found time with his
five wives to care properly for his five children.

These were, however, only the intimate details in the
domestic background after the war before which a new
and other phase of Washington's home life stood boldly
forth.

CHAPTER XIII

RELIEF that it was to have sheathed his sword and retired to the quiet of his home, Washington was no longer wholly free there and in the enjoyment of the privacy he desired. He now belonged to the country, for although there was no actual national entity, the pride and national aspirations of all the independent states in the confederation focussed on their recent military leader. Mount Vernon as the residence of such a figure typified the capital of the embryonic nation.

The first token of this new order invaded his household itself, the very privacy of his family. Henceforth, while he was there, the house was never without secretaries and clerks whose assistance was made necessary by the increasing volume of public and private correspondence and accounts. With added work he had less time, for a second evidence of the new order was the flow of visitors, no longer the casual neighbors riding in for dinner and a fox hunt, but dignitaries whose presence made demands, and amiable and often important strangers who came with the homage of curiosity.

In altering his house Washington made storage space for his letters and papers in recesses built on each side of his library. Eventually these became inadequate and he felt the necessity of building a separate house for this purpose. The bases of the archives of Mount Vernon were of course the copies of all his personal, business, and agricultural letters which he kept scrupulously in his own hand, his journals, and his account-books. To these were added, at the close of the war, the transcripts made by Colonel Richard Varick of the entire mass of his correspondence, public and private, from the beginning to the end of the Revolution. They filled thirty-seven volumes. After his death they passed by purchase into the archives of the national government. This mass was soon increased, in addition to his enormous personal correspondence, by the requests which came from all sources for his assistance and countenance; for he was asked "to write endorsements and recommendations, stand sponsor to books on every topic, subscribe money to all manner of undertakings and loan it to the needy."

The succeeding years brought to the Mount Vernon archives his vast correspondence on bounty lands in the West, on the development of waterways, on the organization of a stable national government, and on other public matters of which there was no end.

The first secretaries accompanied him home from the war. They were Colonels David Humphreys and William Smith. They remained long enough for

Colonel Smith to furnish an exploit which became one of the traditional stories of the estate.

Humphreys, it seems, was of a poetic turn and dreamed away his leisure hours in communion with the lovely views which at Mount Vernon stretch in all directions. Smith spent his recreation in more sociable walks. On one occasion he came upon the house of the petted old autocrat, Bishop, Washington's former body-servant, whose daughter was returning from the milking with a brimming pail. Smith made some kindly offer of assistance which the frightened girl took for the flirtatious license of a kind with that of the wantonly reputed British officers. She dropped the pail and ran into the house. The young colonel followed, muttering apologies and explanations, when he came face to face with her father. The ancient Bishop seems to have been a spoiled favorite who allowed himself all kinds of temper and temperament. He at once flew into a state of outraged wrath. The secretary's explanations did not make matters any better. "I know what you dashing young officers are," Bishop is said to have replied, folding his weeping daughter in his arms, feeling he was the hero of a sound dramatic situation and intending to do his full duty by it. "I am an old soldier and have seen some things in my day. I am sure his honor, after my services, will not permit my child to be insulted; and, as to the Madam, why the Madam as good as brought up my girl." And so he brought the curtain down on the first scene, or at least says the chronicle, "he retired into his house and closed the door."

Smith suspected Bishop to be as good as his threat

and sought out Billy Lee, a no less important figure at Mount Vernon than Bishop himself. Billy seemed to sense a part for himself in this little drama, and first fed the colonel on the ruthlessness of Bishop and then offered himself as ambassador to plead with him.

"Meantime," says the chronicler, who lived at Mount Vernon at the time and heard the story at first hand, "the old body-servant ransacked a large worm-eaten trunk, and brought forth a coat that had not seen the light for many long years (it was of the cut and fashion of the days of George II), then a vest, and lastly a hat, Cumberland cocked, with a huge ribbon cockade, that had seen service in the seven years' war. His shoes underwent a polish, and were covered by large silver buckles. All these accoutrements being carefully dusted and brushed, the veteran flourished his staff and took up his line of march for the mansion house.

"Billy met the old soldier in full march, and a parley ensued. Billy harangued with great force upon the impropriety of the veteran's conduct in not receiving the colonel's apology; 'for,' continued the ambassador, 'my friend Colonel Smith is both an officer and a gentleman; and then, old man, you have no business to have such a handsome daughter (a grim smile passing over the veteran's countenance at this compliment to the beauty of his child), for you know young fellows will be young fellows.' . . .

"The old body-servant, fully accoutred for his expedition, had cooled off a little during his march. A soldierly respect for an officer of Colonel Smith's rank and standing, and a fear that he might carry the matter a little too far, determined him to accept the colonel's assurance that there could be no harm where 'no harm was intended,' came to a right-about and retraced his steps to his home.

"The ambassador returned to the anxious colonel, and informed him that he had met the old fellow, *en grand costume*, and in full march for the mansion house, but that by a powerful display of eloquence he had brought him to a halt, and induced him to listen to reason, and drop the affair altogether. The ready guinea was quickly in the ambassador's pouch, while the gallant colonel, happy in his escape from what might have resulted in a very unpleasant affair, was careful to give the homestead of the old body-servant a good wide berth in all future rambles."

The first tutor for the children was Gideon Snow, who probably first used the quaint little octagon house in the garden wall as a schoolroom. His duties were so light that Washington decided to combine the offices of tutor and secretary, and he thus described the obligations and privileges attaching to the position: "To write letters agreably to what shall be dictated. Do all other writing which shall be entrusted to him. Keep Accts. —examine, arrange, and properly methodize my Papers, which are in great disorder.—Ride, at my expense, to such other States, if I should find it more convenient to send than to attend myself, to the execution thereof. And, ... to initiate two little children (a girl of six and a boy of 4 years of age, descendants of the deceased Mr. Custis, who live with me and are very promising) in the first rudiments of education." To which he shortly added that the secretary "will sit at my table, will live as I live, will mix with the company who resort to my house, and will be treated in every respect with civility and proper attention. He will have his washing done in the family, and may have his linen and stockings mended by the maids of it."

William Shaw came to fulfil those demands in July, 1785. He remained a year and seems to have had an easy time, for he hunted with the General, and went to the races, assemblies, and dances roundabout.

His successor was Tobias Lear, a native of Portsmouth, New Hampshire, and a Harvard graduate of 1783, who remained with Washington till the great man died. His second wife was Mrs. Washington's niece, the widow of George Augustine Washington. He lived at Wellington, an estate on the Virginia shore of the Potomac, about four miles north of Mount Vernon mansion, which Washington placed at his disposal, without charge, for his lifetime. After his chief's death Lear went into the consular service and died in Washington City, October 16, 1816.

During the Presidency Washington's secretaries often accompanied him from the seat of government to Mount Vernon, and he referred to them as "members of my family."

Though the hero was now merged in the planter, he found, as formerly, genuine satisfaction in the companionship of his friends. Nine years had made comparatively few changes in the neighborhood. The Fairfaxes were gone, to be sure, and Belvoir was no more, but a link with that treasured association remained in the person of Bryan Fairfax, younger half-brother of Colonel George William Fairfax. Later he was rector of Christ Church, Alexandria. His home, Mount Eagle, was and remains to-day on the heights across Great Hunting Creek from Alexandria. He was a picturesque figure, indeed, if he came to Mount Vernon dressed as he was when he went to England, "in a full suit of purple," which abroad was supposed to be "the custom of the clergy in Virginia."

The family now went to Christ Church much oftener than to Pohick. The latter church was practically abandoned. It suffered severely in the reaction against the established church, and all other things English, during the Revolution, and only at infrequent intervals were the doors open to itinerant preachers. Christ Church had been built about the same time as the second Pohick Church, and from the beginning Washington had owned a pew there. The family and their guests drove up when the roads and the weather encouraged a round trip drive of eighteen miles. But he never gave up his pew at Pohick, and went there occasionally when it was open.

Another link between Mount Vernon and Alexandria was forged as early as 1784, when the General and Mrs. Washington drove up to attend the first of the Birth Night Balls. These were the predecessors of the later holiday, Washington's Birthday, and succeeded to the colonial custom of celebrating the sovereign's birthday.

His exalted position now attracted a constant stream of visitors. Among them were his recent French and American companions in arms, and even English officers; leaders of political thought from all over the country; a variety of strangers, curious, speculative, petitioning; and distinguished foreigners from many European countries. It is to some of these foreigners, who afterward published the journals of their travels, that the story of Mount Vernon owes many valuable sketches of the life there at this time.

Among the first to come and write his impressions was John Hunter, merchant of London. He spent a day and a night there in 1785. In his diary is found:

"Wednesday 16th. of Nov'r.—When Colonel Fitzgerald introduced me to the General I was struck with his noble and venerable appearance. . . . The General is about six feet high, perfectly straight and well made; rather inclined to be lusty. His eyes are full and blue and seem to express an air of gravity. His nose inclines to the aquiline; his mouth small; his teeth are yet good and his cheeks indicate perfect health. His forehead is a noble one and he wears his hair turned back, without curls and quite in the officer's style, and tyed in a long queue behind. Altogether he makes a most noble, respectable appearance, and I really think him the first man in the world. After having had the management and care of the whole Continental army, he has now retired without receiving any pay for his trouble, and though solicited by the King of France and some of the first characters in the world to visit Europe, he has denied them all and knows how to prefer solid happiness in his retirement to all the luxuries and flattering speeches of European Courts. . . .

"People come to see him here from all parts of the world—hardly a day passes without; but the General seldom makes his appearance before dinner; employing the morning to write his letters and superintend his farm, and allotting the afternoon to company; but even then he generally retires for two hours between tea and supper to his study to write.

"He is one of the most regular men in the world. When no particular Company is at his house, he goes to bed always at nine and gets up with the sun. It's astonishing the packets of letters that daily come for him, from all parts of the world, which employ him most of the morning to answer, and his Secretary Mr. Shaw . . . to copy and arrange. The General has all the accounts of the war yet to settle. Shaw tells me he keeps as regular Books as any Merchant whatever, and a daily Journal of all his transactions. . . .

"When I was first introduced to him he was neatly dressed in a plain blue coat, white cassimer waistcoat, and black breeches and Boots, as he came from his farm. After having sat with us some time he retired and sent in his lady, a most agreeable woman about 50, and Major Washington his nephew, married about three weeks ago to a Miss Bessot. . . . After chatting with them for half an hour, the General came in again, with his hair neatly powdered, a clean shirt on, a new plain drab coat, white waistcoat and white silk stockings. At three, dinner was on table, and we were shewn by the General into another room, where everything was set off with a peculiar taste, and at the same time very neat and plain. The General sent the bottle about pretty freely after dinner, and gave success to the navigation of the Potomac for his toasts, which he has very much at heart. . . .

"After tea General Washington retired to his study and left us with the President, his lady and the rest of the Company. If he had not been anxious to hear the news of Congress from Mr. Lee, most probably he would not have returned to supper, but gone to bed at his usual hour, nine o'clock, for he seldom makes any ceremony. We had a very elegant supper about that time. The General with a few glasses of champagne got quite merry, and being with his intimate friends laughed and talked a good deal. Before strangers he is generally very reserved, and seldom says a word. . . . At 12 I had the honor of being lighted up to my bedroom by the General himself.

"Thursday 17th. November.—I rose early and took a walk about the General's grounds—which are really beautifully laid out. . . . Indeed his greatest pride now is, to be thought the first farmer in America. He is quite a Cincinnatus, and often works with his men himself—strips off his coat and labors like a common man. . . . It's astonishing with what niceness he directs everything in the building way, condescending even to measure the things himself, that all may be perfectly uniform. The style of his house is very elegant, something like the Prince de Condé's at Chantille, near Paris, only not quite so large. . . . The situation is a heavenly one, upon one of the finest rivers in the world. I suppose I saw thousands of ducks upon it, all within gun shot. There are also plenty of blackbirds and wild geese and turkies.

"After breakfast I went with Shaw to see his famous race-horse Magnolia—a most beautiful creature. . . . He also showed me an elegant State Carriage, with beautiful emblematical figures on it, made him a present by the State of Pennsylvania. I afterwards went into his stables, where among an amazing number of

horses, I saw old Nelson, now 22 years of age, that
carried the General almost always during the war:
Blueskin, another fine old horse next to him, now and
then had that honor. . . . They have heard the
roaring of many a cannon in their time. Blueskin was
not the favorite, on account of his not standing fire so
well as venerable old Nelson. . . .

"When the General takes his coach out he always
drives six horses; to his chariot he only puts four. . . .
I fancy he is worth 100,000 Pounds sterling and lives at
the rate of 3 or 4000 a year; . . . There is a fine
family picture in the Drawing room of the Marquis de
LaFayette, his lady and three children—another of the
General with his marching orders, when he was Colonel
Washington in the British Army against the French in
the last war; and two of Mrs. Washington's children:
her son was reckoned one of the handsomest men living, also a picture of Mrs. Washington when a young
woman."

Watson, formerly a merchant of Nantes, came one
bitter January evening, suffering with a severe cough,
which increased during the night; when his door opened
gently, the bed curtains were parted and there stood
"Washington himself with a bowl of hot tea in his
hand." J. B. Brissot de Warville appeared in the
course of his travels in North America and noted the
simplicity in the house, and declared that Washington's
"modesty is astonishing to a Frenchman; he speaks of
the American war, and of his victories, as of things in
which he had no direction."
Robert Edge Pine, "a pretty eminent Portrait & His-

torical-Painter," spent three March weeks at Mount
Vernon in 1785 to make studies of Washington for historical canvases. These were never painted, but he did
portraits of the General and the Custis children. It
was while Pine was at Mount Vernon that Washington
wrote:

"*In for a penny, in for a pound*, is an old adage. I
am so hackneyed to the touches of the painter's pencil,
that I am *now* altogether at their beck; and sit, 'like
Patience on a monument,' while they are delineating the
lines of my face. It is a proof, among many others, of
what habit and custom can accomplish. At first I was
as impatient at the request, and as restive under the
operation, as a colt is of the saddle. The next time I
submitted very reluctantly, but with less flouncing.
Now, no dray-horse moves more readily to his thill than
I to the painter's chair."

The imagination responds readily to the suggestion of
astonishment and confusion produced by the event
noted as of Sunday the 2d of October following:

"Went with Fanny Bassett, Burwell Bassett, Doct^r
Stuart, G. A. Washington, Mr Shaw & Nelly Custis to
Pohick Church; to hear a Mr Thompson preach, who
returned home with us to Dinner, where I found the
Rev. Mr Jones, formerly a Chaplin in one of the Pennsylvania Regiments.—After we were in Bed (about Eleven
oclock in the Evening) Mr Houdon, sent from Paris
by Doct^r Franklin and Mr Jefferson to take My Bust,
in behalf of the State of Virginia, with three young men
assistants, introduced by a Mr Perin a French Gentle-

man of Alexandria arrived here by water from the latter place."

During nearly three weeks spent at Mount Vernon, Houdon made a life mask and modelled a bust which has remained in the mansion ever since. With this life mask and measurements of the person of the General, and memoranda concerning his dress, he returned to Paris. There Gouverneur Morris posed for the figure and Houdon modelled the head from the mask and memory, and thus completed the exquisite statue in marble which stands in the rotunda of the Capitol at Richmond. The clay bust at Mount Vernon remains unique as the only bust of Washington made from life.

So the procession filed on. It included among others Charles Vallo, who contributed to the descriptive literature of the place; Chevalier de la Luzerne, who found nothing to recall "the important part he [Washington] has played except the great number of foreigners who come to see him"; two English visitors perpetuated in the significant entry in the diary, "Mrs. Macauley Graham and Mr. Graham"; the French Minister, the Comte de Moustier, and his sister the "Marquise de Brehan," and, though Washington did not appreciate Madame's penchant for fondling negro babies, he admired a miniature profile of him which she painted; Jno. Fitch with "a draft & model of a machine for promoting navigation, by means of steam," and Robert Fulton, then only twenty years of age; Noah Webster, on a copyright errand, not yet busy with his dictionary; Captain Littlepage, of Virginia, who had been "Aid de Camp to the Duke de Crillen—was at the Seiges of Fort

St. Phillip (on the Island of Minorca) and Gibralter; and is an extraordinary Character"; André Michaux, sent by the French Government to establish in America nurseries of plants to be naturalized in France; "a Gentleman calling himself the Count de Cheiza D'arteignan officer of the French Guards" presented himself for dinner and spent the night, "bringing no letters of introduction, nor any authentic testimonials for his being either; I was at a loss how to receive or treat him—"; Parson Weems, meditating the hatchet story for his life of Washington, which was to be more widely known and read than any other; and Jedediah Morse, author of the first American geography. "My house," wrote Washington at about this time, "may be compared to a well resorted tavern."

With uniform hospitality for all who came under his roof, there was, however, no one else who received a welcome equal to that of General the Marquis de LaFayette, "the French boy," as Mrs. Washington called him, who made two visits to Mount Vernon on his return to America in 1784. He came first in August for twelve days and returned in November for a week. Washington's attachment for LaFayette was one of the unique affections of his life. On the occasion of his second visit Washington travelled all the way to Richmond to meet him and accompany him to Mount Vernon. And when the precious seven days had passed he was so loath to give up his friend that he journeyed on with him to Annapolis. Washington returned home and dispatched thence these lines of farewell which are more nearly sentimental than any others of his which are preserved:

"In the moment of our separation, upon the road as I travelled, and every hour since, I have felt all that love, respect and attachment for you, with which length of years, close connection, and your merits have inspired me. I often asked myself, as our carriages separated, whether that was the last sight I ever should have of you? And though I wished to answer No, my fears answered Yes. I called to mind the days of my youth, and found they had long since fled to return no more; that I was now decending the hill I had been fifty two years in climbing, and that, though I was blessed with a good constitution, I was of a short lived family, and might soon expect to be entombed in the mansion of my fathers. These thoughts darkened the shades, and gave a gloom to the picture, and consequently, to my prospect of ever seeing you again."

His premonition was correct. They did not see each other again. LaFayette, however, came to Mount Vernon forty years later to pay homage at the tomb of his chief and friend.

Washington was also reminded of the enlarged sphere of his fame by the numerous and sometimes extraordinary gifts which now reached Mount Vernon. Most interesting of these were the Italian mantel, the French hunting hounds, and the Maltese and Spanish asses.

The mantel, which at once found an ideal position in the banquet room, opposite the large ornamental window, came in February, 1785, from Samuel Vaughan, of London. He was a stranger to Washington but had a passionate admiration for his character and achievements. The mantel is of "white and Sienite marbles."

THE CENTRAL HALL OR PASSAGE

On the wall to the left in the crystal case is the key of the Bastille. In the cases on the right wall are swords which belonged to General Washington. Suspended from the ceiling is the crystal and wrought-iron lantern presented by Admiral Vernon to Lawrence Washington

A Vista

Through the lofty portico on the river side of the Mansion, looking down the
Potomac. The right shore is Virginia, the left shore is Maryland

Its most striking feature, aside from its simplicity and symmetry, are the three panels, sculptured in high relief, celebrating agricultural life. It has never been removed from its original position and, with the white marble hearth, the grate, clock, vases, candlesticks, and flanking pedestals, it forms the one complete original group assembled in the mansion to-day exactly as in the lifetime of its owner.

The hounds were sent by LaFayette on his return to France after his visit to Mount Vernon. They were in favor until one day the family sat down to dinner to discover that Vulcan had stolen the ham about which the meal was to have been assembled. They were a natively fierce pack and Mrs. Washington is suspected of having used the stolen ham as an excuse to get rid of them. At any rate the French hounds soon followed the ham. Washington's adopted son says apropos of this that the General gave up hunting in 1785, but he did in fact hunt until 1788. Then for eight years his absence at the seat of government kept him away from Mount Vernon during the hunting season. When he returned in 1797 he was somewhat advanced in years for the vigorous sport he had followed until his fifty-sixth year.

There were few and only inferior mules in America at this time and Washington desired to improve the breed. This became known abroad, and in 1788 he received from LaFayette a jack called Knight of Malta and two Maltese she asses; also a jack called Royal Gift and two jennies from the King of Spain. "From these altogether," he said, "I hope to secure a race of extraordinary goodness, which will stock the country."

The presents did not all move in one direction by any means. In 1785 Washington was making an effort to get seeds in "Kentucke" for the French King's Gardens at Versailles, and three years later he was hunting a healthy family of opossums to send an English friend, Sir Edward Newenham.

Such were some of the conspicuous details at Mount Vernon of the early days of Washington's military fame. If it robbed the home of some of its privacy, there were compensations. It has been said Mount Vernon typified the capital of the embryonic nation. There now centred the ideas, the discussions, and the initiative which finally prevailed in giving birth to the nation.

CHAPTER XIV

Mount Vernon the Cradle of Constitutional Agitation—Union
of States First Effected at Mount Vernon Conference—Off
to the Constitutional Convention—Washington's Passion for
the Constitution—Virginia in a Turmoil—Ratification—
Dreading the Interruption of His Home Life—Elected First
President of the United States—The Formal Notification at
Mount Vernon—Breaking Home Ties—End of His Furlough
—Departure for the Inauguration.

IT HAS been said that Washington left Mount Vernon a distinguished Virginian and returned after
the war one of the most famous men in the world.
More significant is Henry Cabot Lodge's other remark
that Washington passed at a single step from being a
Virginian to being an American.

In the midst of his domestic, social, and agricultural
activities by the Potomac his mind dwelt continually
on the conditions which his military success had imposed on the disunited states. His vision revealed to
him the ruin ahead under the Articles of Confederation
and the opportunity and salvation which lay only in a
nation united with a firm, centralized government.

He realized the truth of the British taunt that if the
now independent states were left to themselves they
would soon dissolve. And so, while he wrote LaFayette
and Knox and others of his complete retirement, his intention to confine his activities to the cultivation of the
friendship of good men and to the practise of the domestic virtues, the enigma of his country's future was

never wholly out of his mind. To his perception he added a patriotism which embraced all the states, and at Mount Vernon was conceived and developed, urged, and in a measure consummated, the idea of union and of the means to national strength and life.

In the library were written the constant stream of letters which carried the constitutional idea into every other state. During hours and days of consultation and discussion with thoughtful leaders, in walks beneath the trees, seated about his hospitable board, or during long sessions under the canopy of his riverside piazza, he argued and persuaded for the firm union of the states.

The common enemy had drawn the colonies together during the war, but once peace was declared the units flew asunder. Jealousy displaced fraternal confidence. The states discredited each other's currency. They set up import taxes against each other. Under these menacing conditions the representatives of Maryland and Virginia met at Mount Vernon in March, 1785, to devise some means of securing uniform action between the two states on the problem of the commerce and fishing of the Chesapeake and the Potomac. It was then and there decided that the two states should adopt uniform laws on imports, currency, and commercial regulations; that a naval force should be maintained at the expense of both states and for the protection of both; that the commissioners should propose to their respective state governments the establishment of conjoint laws under the assent of Congress. Here appeared the first evidence of union. It was the union of only two states, Virginia and Maryland, but it was

union, and it submitted itself to the Congress of all the
states. Mount Vernon was the scene of this first step
toward national union.

The following January, 1786, Virginia joined Maryland in a proposal that every state should send delegates to a convention at Annapolis in September, to
regulate the commerce of all the states. From the
Annapolis convention emanated the call for the convention to be held in Philadelphia, in the spring of 1787, to
frame a constitution for the union of all the states.

Washington was unanimously elected to head Virginia's delegation. He pleaded his retirement, rheu-
matism, and other reasons for declining to serve. But
when there was question of his republicanism he
brushed all considerations aside, began an exhaustive
study of constitutional governments, of which he left
lengthy autograph evidence in his library, and on Wednesday, May 9, 1787, "crossed from Mount Vernon to
Mr. Digges a little after sunrise," and was one of the
first delegates to reach Philadelphia. He was made the
president of the Constitutional Convention, remained
in the city throughout the fatiguing summer, and
reached home September 22d, after an absence of four
months and fourteen days.

He at once dispatched riders from Mount Vernon
with copies of the Constitution to Thomas Nelson,
Benjamin Harrison, and Patrick Henry, former governors of Virginia, and to other prominent men, stating
his wish that it had been more perfect and his belief
that it was the best that could be obtained at the time,
and urging their support. A storm of discussion broke
over the state. Among those arrayed against the Con-

stitution were Patrick Henry, Benjamin Harrison, George Mason, Richard Henry Lee, and James Monroe. Among those in its defense were James Madison, John Marshall, Edmund Pendleton, and General Henry Lee ("Light Horse Harry").

Washington remained at home and somewhat in the background of the "passionate agitation." But he stood committed to the Constitution as drawn, with a door open for subsequent amendments, and gave it the full force of his support. A visitor to Mount Vernon shortly after his return from Philadelphia wrote Thomas Jefferson in November:

"I stayed two days with General Washington at Mount Vernon about six weeks ago. . . . I never saw him so keen for anything in my life as he is for the adoption of the new scheme of government. As the eyes of all America are turned towards this truly great and good man for the first President, I took the liberty of sounding him upon it. He appears to be earnestly against going into public life again; pleads in excuse for himself his love of retirement and his advanced age, but notwithstanding of these, I am fully of opinion that he may be induced to appear once more on the public stage of life."

He subscribed for a number of copies of the *Federalist*, in which Madison, Jay, and Hamilton defended the Constitution. One set he had bound and placed in his library. The others he sent broadcast on their propaganda. Another and more unique addition to Mount Vernon at this time was the good ship *Federalist*, a present to Washington from the merchants and shipowners of Baltimore. That city celebrated the adoption of the Constitution by Maryland with a procession in which a conspicuous feature was a full-rigged ship, named the *Federalist*, fifteen feet long, mounted on wheels and drawn by four horses. After the celebration it was launched in the Chesapeake and navigated down the bay by Captain Barney and up the Potomac to Mount Vernon wharf. It remained there an amusing curiosity for nearly two months, when it was torn from its moorings by a high wind and was sunk.

The bitter fight for the Constitution in Virginia was waged for nearly a year. During that time Washington was more active than ever with his correspondence. He saw an increasing number of people and spent himself in persuasion. It was his conviction that the alternative to the adoption of the Constitution was the total dissolution of the uniting states. Without his influence Virginia would not have ratified, and it is probable that without Virginia the great experiment would not have succeeded. Hence it was with relief and exultation that news came telling of Virginia's ratification on June 25th. Three days later the citizens of Alexandria prepared a public dinner as part of the celebration of the event, which the General, Colonel Humphreys, and George Augustine Washington attended from Mount Vernon. Returning home, he noted with neighborly pride, in a letter to Charles Cotesworth Pinckney: "Thus the citizens of Alexandria, when convened, constituted the first public company in America, which had the pleasure of pouring [a] libation to the prosperity of the ten States that had actually adopted the general government."

When Congress received the testimonials of ratification it appointed a day for the choice of electors of a
President, who, being chosen, unanimously elected
George Washington first President of the United States.
So little was this unexpected that from the time of the
General's return home from the Constitutional Convention requests poured in upon him to accept the office.
It was the fixed idea that Washington should be the
first executive of the new nation not only in every mind
in America at all times, but Europe likewise accepted
his choice as inevitable. In answer to LaFayette's
letter on this subject, the General wrote him:

"Knowing me as you do, I need only say, that it
has no enticing charms and no facinating allurements for
me. However, it might not be decent for me to say I
would refuse to accept, or even to speak much about an
appointment, which may never take place; for, in so
doing, one might possibly incur the application of the
moral resulting from that fable, in which the fox is
represented as inveighing against the sourness of the
grapes, because he could not reach them. All that it
will be necessary to add, my dear Marquis, in order
to show my decided predelictions is, that, (at my time
of life and under my circumstances,) the increasing
infirmaties of nature and the growing love of retirement
do not permit me to entertain a wish beyond that of
living and dying an honest man on my own farm."

Later, as the time drew near for the counting of the
electoral votes, there was some delay, and Washington
wrote Henry Knox:

"For myself the delay may be compared to a reprieve; for in confidence I tell you, (with the *world* it would obtain little credit,) that my movements to the chair of government will be accompanied by feelings not unlike those of a culprit, who is going to the place of his execution; so unwilling am I, in the evening of a life nearly consumed in public cares, to quit a peaceful abode for an ocean of difficulties, without that competency of political skill, abilities, and inclination, which are necessary to manage the helm."

Mrs. Washington shared their regret to tear away again from the peace and retirement of their riverside home. "I little thought when the war was finished that any circumstances could possibly happen which would call the general into public life again," she wrote a friend. "I had anticipated that from that moment we should be suffered to grow old together, in solitude and tranquility. . . . When I was much younger I should probably have enjoyed the innocent gayeties of life as much as most persons of my age; but I had long since placed all the prospects of my future worldly happiness in the still enjoyments of the fireside at Mount Vernon."

A notable scene was acted at Mount Vernon on the 14th of April, this year of 1789. Shortly after noon there arrived from New York the Secretary of Congress, Mr. Charles Thompson, who had been appointed to notify Washington of his election to the office of President. He was an old friend of the General's and had been Secretary of Congress for nearly fifteen years. He delivered the certificate of election and added a few words of personal address. Washington's reply is preserved. He said:

"I am so much affected by this fresh proof of my country's esteem and confidence that silence can best express my gratitude. While I realize the arduous nature of the task which is imposed upon me and feel my own inability to perform it, I wish that there may not be reason for regretting the choice; for indeed all I can promise is to accomplish that which can be done by an honest zeal. Upon considering how long time some of the Gentlemen of both Houses of Congress have been at New York, how anxiously desirous they must be to proceed to business, and how deeply the public mind appears to be impressed with the necessity of doing it speedily, I cannot find myself at liberty to delay my journey. I shall therefore be in readiness to set out the day after tomorrow; and shall be happy in the pleasure of your company; for you will permit me to say that it is a peculiar gratification to have received this communication from you."

In anticipation of an early departure he had paid a visit of farewell to his mother at Fredericksburg, when he then saw her for the last time, and in Alexandria borrowed five hundred pounds to discharge his personal debts and another one hundred pounds to defray his expenses to the seat of government at New York City. He set out on his journey Thursday morning, April 16th. "About ten o'clock," he wrote in his diary, "I bade adieu to Mount Vernon, to private life, and to domestic felicity, and with a mind oppressed with more

anxious and painful sensations than I have words to
express, set out for New York in company with M^r
Thomson and Col^o Humphreys, with the best disposition to render service to my country in obedience to its
calls, but with less hope of answering its expectations."

When he reached the West Lodge gates he found a
mounted escort of neighbors and friends from Alexandria, who accompanied him up to town. They said
their mutual farewells at a dinner in his honor, when,
suggestive of the number of units of the union, the
toasts were thirteen. "Farewell," said the mayor on
behalf of his fellow-townsmen: "Go and make a
grateful people happy—a people who will be doubly
grateful when they contemplate the recent sacrifice for
their interests." Washington's emotions could with
difficulty be concealed. "Unutterable sensations,"
said he, in closing his reply, "must then be left to more
expressive silence, while from an aching heart I bid you
all, my affectionate friends and kind neighbors, farewell."

CHAPTER XV

Mount Vernon During the Presidency—Visits Home—Arrival of the Key of the Bastille—Mode of Travel—The Hard Riding Aide and the General's Anger—Directions for Hospitality at Mount Vernon in His Absence—Managers of the Estate: George Augustine Washington, Anthony Whiting, Howell Lewis, William Pearce, and James Anderson—Keeping in Touch with His Estate When Absent—New Barns—Mrs. Washington Homesick in Philadelphia—The General's Love for His Home—Retires from Public Life—Returns to Mount Vernon.

THE six years' respite from official life at Mount Vernon after the war Washington called his "furlough." During the next eight years his home saw him only by glimpses.* He found opportunities during his two terms as President to journey fifteen times to Mount Vernon, an average of about twice a year. These visits were always made between the first of April and the first of November. Once only he remained later by three weeks. Winter was the period of the sittings of Congress, and the season when the roads were less passable and when the city offered the greater comfort, which accounts for his presence at the seat of government during the colder months.

His stays on the Potomac were generally brief. Five times he remained only from seven to twelve days. Once he remained a part of four months. The other visits covered four to eight weeks. To be exact, of the

*See Appendix B.

eight years of the Presidency he allowed himself in all
less than fifteen months at his home.

His first absence was his longest. He did not come
back to Mount Vernon until a year and a half after his
inauguration, September, 1790. On this trip he probably brought with him the main key of the Bastille and
the drawing of the fortress which LaFayette sent him
"as a missionary of Liberty to its patriarch." The key
hung in a glass cabinet on the south wall of the main hall
and it has not left Mount Vernon since. The Bust of
Necker, French Revolutionary Minister of Finance, also
came at this time, and for many years after occupied a
position in the library. Mrs. Washington and her
grandchildren, Nellie and George Washington Parke
Custis, did not accompany the General to the inauguration, but they soon followed, and spent the period of his
Presidency in New York with him. In the fall of 1790
Philadelphia succeeded New York as the seat of government, and thither Washington returned at the end
of November.

He was at home three periods in 1791: the first for
three days early in April, "visiting my Plantations every
day," on his way to make the grand tour of the South;
the second to rest for a fortnight on his way north in
June, and the third for three weeks in September and
October.

The next year he came twice: for nine days in May,
and in July for the longest vacation he spent at his home
while President, when he was so far disposed not to
accept a second term that he wrote Madison asking his
suggestions about a farewell address. A unique souve-
nir of this summer on the Potomac survives to-day

scratched in one of the panes of glass in the sleeping-room known as the Green Room. The frail but precious window pane is heavily reinforced with putty, for it bears the autograph of Eliza P. Custis, and the date of its etching, August 2, 1792.

After the ceremonies of his second inauguration, in 1793, the President rode away as soon as he could for a spring visit to Mount Vernon, but the outbreak of the war between France and England drew him back to Philadelphia after a rest of less than three weeks. The death of the manager of his estate made it necessary for him to return southward early in the summer. He remained nine days and was the guest of honor of his friends and neighbors at Alexandria at a Fourth of July celebration, when "mighty twelve pounders" thundered salutes and a company of one hundred and ten "sat down to an elegant dinner in Mr. Wise's long room." His real vacation came in September and October, loveliest time of the year in Fairfax. It was an unexpected and unwilling flight from Philadelphia, but the yellow fever had broken out in the city, and every one who could deserted it. Although Washington expressed a wish to remain in the north longer than the 10th of September, it is difficult to see how that could have been possible in view of an important engagement for the 18th of that month in Washington City. On that day he came up from Mount Vernon to "The Federal City," as he was accustomed to call it, and assisted at the laying of the cornerstone of the Capitol of the United States.

Having accepted a second term in the chair of government, Washington at this time began to think of re-

ducing his responsibilities as a planter by renting all his
land except the farm on which the mansion house stood.
It was the passing whim of a tired man. His farms
were the great plaything of his life. Nothing came of it
except an advertisement in a local paper and an elaborate letter to his English friend, Arthur Young, in which
is preserved a detailed account of the physical features of
his lands and their improvements and stock.

Twelve days in June and July were the sum of the next
year's time spent at Mount Vernon. In 1795 he came
for seven days in April, in July for seventeen, and on
September thirteen for a full month lacking only a day.
It was on the last visit that he found two old friends of
the Mount Vernon household married and at home in
Alexandria. They were his secretary, Tobias Lear, and
Frances Bassett Washington, widow of George Augustine Washington. Her husband and Lear's wife both
died in 1793. The young widow and the widower were
married in August, 1795, and in September the President
and Mrs. Washington drove up to Alexandria and dined
with them. This was the first time in over thirty years
that the master and mistress of Mount Vernon had
driven through its gates and missed the welcome of
ancient Bishop. He died in his cottage on the mansion
house farm, in his eightieth year, in January, 1795,
mourned by the master he had served as long as
strength permitted and by whose bounty he enjoyed a
green old age of ease and plenty.

Every morning saw the President on horseback, riding
over his farms. The house was never free of company
and usually the guests packed it. He often entertained
the foreign ministers, the members of his cabinet, and

other high governmental officials, ranking veterans of the army, and natives and foreigners of various distinctions. Time for work on his letters and papers was made possible only by his custom of rising hours before others of the household and closeting himself in the library.

During the final year of the Presidency Washington was at home for nearly two months, from June 20th to August 17th, and returned in September to take Mrs. Washington and the children back to Philadelphia for the winter. On the latter occasion he remained thirty-three days. Much of his time while at home this summer was spent in his library over his Farewell Address. He had by him Alexander Hamilton's extensive suggestions, and to him he wrote after some work on it: "All the columns, of a large gazette would scarcely, I believe, contain the present draught."

He left Mount Vernon for Philadelphia for the last period of his term in office at the end of October, 1796. He arrived at the seat of government on the last day of the month. In general the trip between Mount Vernon and Philadelphia, with fair roads and no delays, occupied four or five days. When his horses were fat or "out of exercise" he allowed for an extra day of rest on the route somewhere. If the trip were made without Mrs. Washington or her grandchildren he generally pushed forward with secretary and servants and five horses, or at most with the light coachee and outriders. But with his family he travelled with chariot and four or six horses, coachman and postilions, secretaries on horseback, a light baggage wagon, perhaps a two-horse phaeton, and from six to twelve servants. There were

often as many as sixteen horses in the train. The heavy
luggage was usually sent from Philadelphia to Mount
Vernon by vessel. Washington rode in the coach only a
fraction of the time, often mounting a horse and resting
himself with a ride by the side of Mrs. Washington's
chariot.

One of the rare scenes reported of these journeys confirms the belief that behind Washington's placid mask
he had a very human nature capable of being stirred to
high anger and, moreover, it glimpses his concern for his
horses.

"I never saw him angry but once in my life," said a
relative of the General's whom a writer in the *Demo-
cratic Review* for March, 1843, merely styles "Captain
L"; "and this was considered so remarkable . . .
we looked upon it as quite an anomaly in the General's
life. It happened while he was President and travelling
in his carriage, with a small retinue of outriders, from
Mount Vernon to Philadelphia. It was during the first
day of our journey, and we were passing through the
barrens of Maryland, where, at intervals of a few miles,
the solitude of the road was relieved at that time by a set
of low taverns or groggeries, at which we did not think
of stopping. But we had a thoughtless young man in
our train, who by favour had been admitted into the
family as a sort of gentleman attendant, and who
seemed much more inclined to patronize these places.
The General, at his request, had permitted him to ride a
favorite young mare which he had raised on his plantation, and of which he was exceedingly careful, the ani-
mal being almost as slight as a roebuck and very high
spirited. But the young fellow, notwithstanding the

intimations he had received at starting to deal gently
with her, appeared bent on testing her speed and other
qualities, and that too in a manner little likely to meet
with favour in a man of Washington's high sense of
propriety. He would leave the train, and riding up to
one of the liquoring establishments, there remain until
we were out of sight; when he would come up upon the
run, ride with us awhile, and gallop on forward to the
next. This he repeated three times, the last of which
brought the mettlesome creature to a foam and evidently much fretted her. At the first transgression
thus committed against the General's orders respecting
the mare, as well as against his known sense of propriety, he seemed surprised, looking as if he wondered at
the young man's temerity, and contented himself with
throwing after the young man a glance of displeasure.
At the second he appeared highly incensed although he
said nothing, and repressed his indignation, acting as if
he thought this must be the last offense, for the punish-
ment of which he chose a private occasion. But as the
offender rode up the third time, Washington hastily
threw open the carriage window, and asking the driver
to halt, sharply ordered the former alongside; when with
uplifted cane, and a tone and emphasis which startled
us all, and made the culprit shrink and tremble like a
leaf, he exclaimed, 'Look you, sir! Your conduct is in-
sufferable! Fall in behind there, sir; and as sure as you
leave us again, I will break every bone in your skin!'"

In the absence of the family Mount Vernon was fre-
quented by travellers eager to see the home of the re-
nowned Washington, and he maintained a generous hospitality for all who presented themselves. It was taken

advantage of, however, not merely by the guests but by
the servants, and the President felt obliged to write his
manager defining the treatment he wished the visitors to
receive:

"Speaking of Gentlemens Serv^{ts} it calls to my mind,
that in a letter from Mrs. Fanny Washington to Mrs.
Washington (her Aunt) she mentions, that since I left
Mount Vernon she has given out four doz^n and eight
bottles of wine.—Whether they are used, or not, she does
not say;—but I am led by it to observe, that it is not my
intention that it should be given to every one who may
incline to to make a convenience of the house, in traveling; or who may be induced to visit it from motives of
curiosity.—There are but three descriptions of people to
whom I think it ought to be given:—first, my *particular*
and intimate acquaintances, in case business should call
them there, such for instance as Doct^r Craik.—2dly
some of the *most* respectable foreigners who may, perchance, be in Alexandria or the federal city; and be
either brought down, or introduced by letter, from some
of my particular acquaintances as before mentioned;—
or, thirdly, to persons of some distinction (such as members of Congress &c^t) who may be traveling through the
Country from North to South, or from South to North;
—to the first of which, I should not fail to give letters,
where I conceive them entitled.—Unless some caution
of this sort governs, I should be run to an expence as improper, as it would be considerable. . . . I have no
objection to any sober, or orderly person's gratifying
their curiosity in viewing the buildings, Gardens &c^t
about Mount Vernon;—but it is only to such persons as

I have described, that I ought to be run to any expence
on account of these visits of curiosity, beyond common
civility and hospitality."

The above directions were sent his manager, William
Pearce.

During the first sixteen years of his married life,
which he spent at home, Washington managed the
estate himself with overseers on each of the farms.   At
the outbreak of the Revolution he engaged a distant relative, Lund Washington, as manager, and left the charge
of Mount Vernon in his hands for ten years.   At the end
of this term the General had then been at home two
years and recovered his grasp on the place.   His
nephew, George Augustine Washington, was at Mount
Vernon at this time, and to the affections of his uncle he
added his confidence to such a degree that when called
to the Presidency Washington placed the estate under
the management of this nephew.   The young man
seems not to have been without ability, but his health
failed him and in the winter of 1791-2 he was succeeded
by Anthony Whiting, a man who, it was reported to
Washington, "drank freely—kept bad company at my
house and in Alexandria—and was a very debauched
person."   His habits probably hastened the relief his
employer had of him for he died in July, 1793.   Washington's nephew, Betty's son, Howell Lewis, took
charge during the few months pending the arrival of
William Pearce, in December.   There may be a hint to
the curious in Washington's remark when he heard that
Howell's brother Lawrence was available at the time of
the former's engagement: "But after all is not Law-

rence Lewis on the point of matrimony? Report says
so, and if truly, it would be an effectual bar to a *permanent* establishment in my business, as I never again
will have two women in my house when I am there myself."

Pearce's stewardship covered three full years. He
was succeeded by James Anderson in the last year the
President was absent in Philadelphia. Both these men
gave their chief great satisfaction. Anderson was manager during the remaining years of Washington's life and
to him was addressed the last letter the great man wrote.

During the first five years of the General and Mrs.
Washington's absence at the seat of government the
mansion was under the personal control of Fanny Washington. Both her uncle and aunt were very fond of
her and Mrs. Washington was constantly sending her
presents. In forwarding a newly imported watch on
one occasion, her Aunt Martha closed the letter with
this remembrance of her little girl: "Kiss Marie I send
her two little handkerchiefs to wipe her nose. Adue."

Mount Vernon never lost the direct influence of its
master even during his long absences. He exacted a
weekly report from his manager by the post leaving
Alexandria each Thursday, and he, on his part, wrote
every week, usually devoting Sunday afternoon to the
preparation of the long letters which covered two or
three and even four large, closely written pages. Such
was the importance which he attached to these letters
that he first made a rough draft of them, then copied
them out in full in his own handwriting, and finally
preserved a letter-press copy. They directed the planting. cultivating, and harvesting of crops; building and

repairs; the engaging, discharge, discipline, and comfort
of his servants and slaves; all with the same intimate
acquaintance he might have shown in his library in a
talk with his manager after a morning ride of inspection
over his farms.

He referred to the hundreds of slaves by name, and
knew each of their children's; he knew exactly where
windows and doors were to be placed and their dimensions; what was boarded and what was free; what carpenters were available and best suited to the various
jobs; what money he owed and what money was owed
him; the condition of his growing crops, the potentiality
of each field, the stage of the foaled mares; and seemingly every other imaginable detail.

That an absent proprietor with no other concerns
should exhibit such a grasp would be remarkable; that it
was the concurrent if not the secondary interest at first
of a general conducting a great war and later of a president organizing an infant nation, excites a truly natural
wonder.

One of the new and important works put under way
during the early years of the Presidency was the circular or sixteen-sided barn, of his own invention, on Dogue
Run Farm. It was two stories high and sixty feet in
diameter, and was so arranged that when rain drove the
farm help out of the fields they could here under shelter,
in the second story, thresh out the grain on a ten-foot
floor of open slats which entirely surrounded the central
mows. Another feature of this barn, in which he took
so much pride, and which was the wonder of the
neighbors, was an inclined runway which admitted the
oxen or horses up to the circular treading floor.

When Pearce arrived in 1793 the President wrote him a characteristic letter giving a schedule of work for the carpenters. They were to begin at once the completion of the circular barn and the stables attached thereto for horses and cattle. After that "the work essentially necessary to be done," he wrote, was "building the house for Crow—Repairing my house in Alexandria for Mrs. Fanny Washington—which must be done before the first of May—Inclosing the lot on which it stands for a Garden or Yard.—Repairing the Millers house.—Removing the larger kind of Negro quarters (the smaller ones or cabbins, I presume the people with a little assistance of Carts can do themselves) to the ground marked out for them opposite to Crow's New house.—Repairing at a proper time those he will remove from.—Lending aid in drawing the houses at River farm into some uniform shape, in a convenient placc. Rcpairing the Barn and Stables at Muddyhole.—Compleating the Dormant Windows in the back of the Stable at Mansion house and putting two in the front of it agreeably to directions already given to Thomas Green—after which, and perhaps doing some other things which do not occur to me at this moment, my intention is to build a large Barn, and sheds for Stables upon the plan of that at Dogue Run (if, on trial it should be found to answer to the expectation wch is formed of it) at River Farm."

In another letter he enclosed a schedule of the bricks needed for the barn on the River Farm. They were 139,980 in number. In view of these extensive improvements something had to be neglected, and it appears to have been the palings of the deer park. When

Pearce forwarded the gardener's complaint of the injury the roving animals did the shrubbery, the General did not consider new palings, rather he was "at a loss . . . whether to give up the Shrubbery or the Deer!" The only new feature of the mansion at this time seems to have been the "Venetian blinds . . . painted green, for all the windows on the West side of the House."

Whenever away from Mount Vernon not only a portion of his mind but all his heart seems to have been there. He had better control of his emotions in this respect, however, than Mrs. Washington; with greater need. She was downright homesick. When the war ended they had hoped to pass the remainder of their days at their river home in peace and tranquillity. The renewed absences during the Presidency fretted Mrs. Washington, she longed for home and said so. She found official life dull and went about little. "Indeed I think I am more like a State prisoner than anything else," she said; "there is certain bounds set for me which I must not depart from—and as I cannot doe as I like, I am obstinate and stay at home a great deal."

Her husband's love for Mount Vernon was even more passionate. It breathes forth in letter after letter in spite of his excellent self-control. It was his "goal of domestic enjoyment"; his "vine and fig-tree" over and over again; and he dwelt caressingly on its "tranquil scenes" whether absent or among them. It was his pride to be thought the first farmer in America. He declared no estate to be so pleasantly situated as his. "I can truly say," he exclaimed, "I had rather be at Mount Vernon with a friend or two about me, than to be

attended at the seat of government by the officers of
state and the representatives of every power in Europe."
As the time approached to relinquish office and return
to his plantation, he looked forward to this last journey
with the eagerness of a freed schoolboy, declaring, "No
consideration under heaven, that I can foresee, shall
again withdraw me from the walks of private life."

John Adams was inaugurated March 4, 1797. Washington thus once more became a private citizen. Mr.
Adams, writing his wife, said: "A solemn scene it was
indeed, and it was made more affecting to me by the
presence of the General, whose countenence was as se-
rene and unclouded as the day. He seemed to me to
enjoy a triumph over me. Methought I heard him say,
'Ay! I am fairly out and you fairly in! See which of
us will be the happiest!'"

The citizens of Philadelphia gave Washington a farewell dinner under the great roof of Rickett's Circus.
As the extensive company marched in to the tables,
said a journal of the day, "*Washington's march* re-
sounded through the place, and a curtain drew up which
presented to view a transparent full length painting of
the late President, whom Fame is crowning with a
Wreath of Laurel, taking leave after delivering to her
his valedictory address, of the Genius of America, who
is represented by a Female Figure holding the Cap of
Liberty in her hand, with an Altar before her, inscribed
PUBLIC GRATITUDE. In the painting are introduced several emblematic devices of the honours he had
acquired by his public services, and a distant view of
Mount Vernon the seat of retirement."

On March 9th Washington left Philadelphia. A

Baltimore paper reported the party made up of "His Excellency . . . his lady and Miss Custis, the son of the Unfortunate LaFayette and his preceptor." But Washington in a postscript to a letter, written on the way, to Lear, indicated others: "On one side I am called upon to remember the Parrot, and on the other to remember the dog. For my own part I should not pine much if both were forgot."

Everywhere along the route the illustrious traveller was met by escorts of military, by processions, salutes, entertainments, and ovations from the assembled crowds. An escort of mounted troops from Alexandria finally accompanied him to the gates of Mount Vernon, where he arrived on Saturday, April 1, 1797.

CHAPTER XVI

Planter Once More—Repairing the Neglect of Years of Absence—
    Refurnishing the Mansion—Joking About Death—Renewed
    Social Gayety—A Letter to Mrs. Fairfax—George Wash-
    ington LaFayette—Distinguished Visitors—Bushrod Wash-
    ington and John Marshall Bring a Peddler's Pack—General
    Henry Lee and His Liberties—The Polish Gentleman's
    Visit—Washington's Own Account of How He Spent His
    Time.

WASHINGTON left the pageantry of public
life outside the gates of Mount Vernon. As
he turned in and they closed behind him, it
was with a profound relief and a tranquil delight that he
beheld, across the rolling green lands, centred through
the opening in the wall of woods, his tabernacle of
peace. Just one-half of all the years of his ownership of
Mount Vernon were given to the public service.

He had come home to stay. He sensed it and, though
a man's sixty-fifth year would be late for him to resume
the interests of youth, he began where he left off when
his country called him thence, nearly a quarter of a century before, to lead her armies.

He acknowledged that he felt himself a permanent
resident of Mount Vernon now for the first time in
twenty-five years. During that period he had been the
public's servant, an exile from his much-desired retirement, save for his brief "furlough" between the end of
his military service and his call to the Presidency, an
interval crowded with the penalties of fame and the

anxieties of the prophetic patriot who foresaw the necessity of a coherent union and worked unceasingly to
effect it.

The house and the lands and "his people" retained a
hold over him which he had never relinquished. In his
letters he defers a little to the current literary fashion
for sentimental melancholy—"To the wearied traveller,
who sees a resting-place, and is bending his body to
rest thereon, I now compare myself"—but for the most
part they teem with his interest in the renewed activity.

"For myself," he wrote Oliver Wolcott, "having
turned aside from the broad walks of political, into the
narrow paths of private life, I shall leave it with those,
whose duty it is to consider subjects of this sort, and,
(as every good citizen ought to do,) conform to whatever
the ruling powers shall decide. To make and sell a
little flour annually, to repair houses (going fast to
ruin), to build one for the security of my papers of a
public nature, and to amuse myself in agricultural and
rural pursuits, will constitute employment for the few
years I have to remain on this terrestrial globe. If, to
these, I could now and then meet the friends I esteem,
it would fill the measure and add zest to my enjoyments;
but, if ever this happens, it must be under my own vine
and fig-tree, as I do not think it probable that I shall
go beyond twenty miles from them."

"Rural employments. . . . will now take place
of toil,— responsibility—and the solicitudes of attending the walks of public life," he wrote another, and
Nellie Custis wrote Mrs. Wolcott of how much pleased
her "Grandpapa," as she called him, was "with being
once more *Farmer Washington.*"

Every aspect of the place now reminded him of his absence, for it had let down perceptibly at all points. He pushed repairs on his barns, overseers' houses, slave quarters and fences. This was all done with such thoroughness that "the expense was almost as great and the employment of attending to the workmen almost as much" as if he had "commenced an entire new establishment."

In spite of all the outlying work, however, his first and most cherished interest was to put his house in order. "I find myself in the situation nearly of a young beginner," he wrote McHenry, "for, although I have not houses to build (except one, which I must erect for the accomodation and security of my Military, Civil, and private Papers, which are voluminous and may be interesting), yet I have not one, or scarcely anything else about me that does not require considerable repairs. In a word, I am already surrounded by Joiners, Masons, Painters, &c., &c.; and such is my anxiety to get out of their hands, that I have scarcely a room to put a friend into, or to sit in myself, without the music of hammers, or the odoriferous smell of paint."

The exact nature of the work on the mansion he revealed in a letter to his faithful and much-appreciated Lear, who remained behind in Philadelphia to close the house the President had occupied, pack and ship such furnishings as were wanted at Mount Vernon, and sell the balance:

"The work *immediately* foreseen and which must be done without delay, is to refix the marble Chimney piece in the parlour, which is almost falling out, to fix

the new one (expected from Philadelphia) in the small
dining Room; to remove the one now there, into what
is called the School room,—to fix the grate which is
coming round in the large dining room;—and to give
some repairs to the steps; which (like most things else
I have looked into since I have been home) are sadly
out of repair."

That twelve busy months were exacted for this work
is learned from a letter written a year later to his old
neighbor, Sarah Fairfax, the widow of Colonel George
William Fairfax, a letter which confirms again the time
when he made the last former repairs to the mansion:

"Before the war, and even while it existed, although
I was eight years from home at one stretch, (except the
en passant visits made to it on my marches to and from
the seige of Yorktown,) I made considerable additions
to my dwelling-houses, and alterations in my offices and
gardens; but the delapidation occasioned by time, and
those neglects, which are coextensive with the absence
of proprieters, have occupied as much of my time within
the last twelve months in repairing them, as at any
former period in the same space; and it is matter of sore
regret, when I cast my eyes towards Belvoir, which I
often do, to reflect, the former inhabitants of it, with
whom we lived in such harmony and friendship, no
longer reside there, and that the ruins can only be
viewed as the memento of former pleasures."

The interior of the mansion took on a more elaborate
effect at this time by reason of the addition of much of
the fine furniture, silver, china, glass, and other fur-

nishings which the General and his wife had accumulated at the Presidential Mansion in Philadelphia, and of numerous curious and elegant presents admirers had sent Washington. Among them were the harpsichord which he imported from London for Nellie Custis, and over which she spent so many many hours of practice under the disciplinary eye of her grandmother; the small (twenty by thirty inches) Trumbull portrait of the General standing by the side of his horse; the shaving stand which was presented to him by the first French Minister to this country; and the oak box made from the tree which sheltered the great Sir William Wallace after the battle of Falkirk, and sent to Washington by the Earl of Buchan.

As the General had ridden home amid the applause of the crowds which saluted him on every hand, his thoughts seem to have been well fastened on the refurnishing of his house, for directions for the choice and packing of what he desired filled letters which he posted to Lear at each principal stop after they left Philadelphia. The large looking glasses, "the grate (from Mr. Morris's)," the "bedstead which Nellie Custis slept on," and "the trundle under it" were all to be packed carefully against tossing in the vessel's hold. He desires "*new* Carpeting as will cover the floor of my blue Parlour," Wilton if it is "not much dearer than Scotch Carpeting." . . . "a suitable border if to be had, should accompany the Carpeting" . . . "all the Carpeting belonging to me I would have sent;— and Mrs. Washington requests that you would add the Bellows and the Vessels (Iron & Tin) in which the ashes are carried out." . . . "Desire *Peter Por-*

cupine's Gazette to be sent to me (as a subscriber)."
. . . "Pray get me of those Thermometers that
tell the state of the Mercury within the 24 hours—
Doctor Priestly or Mr. Madison can tell where it is
to be had." . . . "Let me request the favour of
you to purchase for me half a dozen pair of the best
kind of White Silk stockings (not those with gores but)
to be large, and with small clocks (I think they are
called) I want the same number of raw silk, for boot
stockings; large and strong."

In connection with these attentions to refurnishing,
there are traditions that he kept certain curtain cornices and the painting of Vernon's fleet riding before
Carthagena, both of which were in the house when he
first came there to live, and have been there ever since,
accredited veterans of the chattels of the mansion.

Life appeared very full and very sweet, in spite
of minor occasional complaints. As Christmas approached the General made a draft of a letter to Mrs.
Powell for Martha, who seems not to have been willing
to compose her own letters in later life, and it reflected
their gay mood:

"I am now, by desire of the General to add a few
words on his behalf; which he desires may be expressed in the terms following, that is to say,—that
despairing of hearing what may be said of him, if he
should really go off in an apoplectic, or any other fit
(for he thinks that all fits that issue in death are worse
than a love fit, a fit of laughter, and many other kinds
that he could name)—he is glad to hear *beforehand*
what will be said of him on that occasion;—conceiving

that nothing extra: will happen between *this* and *then*
to make a change in his character for better, or for
worse.—And besides, as he has entered into an engagement with M^r. Morris, and several other Gentlemen,
not to quit the theatre of *this* world before the year
1800, it may be *relied upon* that no breach of contract
shall be laid to him on that account, unless dire necessity should bring it about, maugre all his exertions to the
contrary.—In that case, he shall hope they would do by
him as he would do by them—excuse it. At present
there seems no danger of his giving them the slip, as
neither his health nor spirits, were ever in greater flow,
notwithstanding, he adds, he is descending, and has
almost reached, the bottom of the hill;—or in other
words, the shades below."

Life in the mansion was never gayer than now.
Young Custis was away part of the time, to be sure,
pursuing his studies at college, but his sister Nellie
was now a beautiful young woman of nearly twenty
and enlivened the house with her girlish spirit, her
troops of friends, and not least with the piquancy of
an inevitable romance. Her elder sisters, Mrs. Law
and Mrs. Peter, with their husbands and children
drove down frequently from their homes in Georgetown and Washington; so did their mother, now Mrs.
Doctor Stuart, from her new home, Hope Park, westward, near Ravensworth. The Lewis boys, sons of
Betty Washington Lewis, were frequent visitors; as
were other nephews and nieces of both the General
and Mrs. Washington.

Mount Vernon was the rallying point as formerly for

the extended neighborhood, though there were changes enough since the days of hunts and dinners and dances at Belvoir and Gunston Hall, the sprightly racing seasons at Annapolis, and the frequent balls at Alexandria. In another letter which the General wrote for his wife to copy and send to their friend Mrs. Fairfax in England, he reviews the neighborhood changes:

"It is among my greatest regrets, now I am again fixed (I hope for life) at this place, at not having you as a neighbor and companion. This loss was not sensibly felt by me while I was a kind of perambulator, during eight or nine years of the war, and during other eight years which I resided at the seat of the general government, occupied in scenes more busy, tho' not more happy, than in the tranquil employment of rural life with which my days will close.

"The changes which have taken place in this country, since you left it (and it is pretty much the same in all other parts of this State) are, in one word, total. In Alexandria, I do not believe there lives at this day a single family with which you had the smallest acquaintance. In our neighborhood Colo. Mason, Colo. McCarty and wife, Mr. Chichestor, Mr. Lund Washington and all the Wageners, have left the stage of human life; and our visitors on the Maryland side are gone and going likewise. . . . With respect to my own family, it will not I presume, be new to you to hear that my son died in the fall of 1781. He left four fine children, three daughters and a son; the two eldest of the former are married, and have three children between them, all girls. . . . Both live in the federal city. The youngest daughter, Eleanor, is yet single, and lives with me, having done so from an infant; as has my grandson George Washington, now turned seventeen, except when at college; to three of which he has been—viz—Philadelphia, New Jersey and Annapolis, at the last of which he now is."

To Mrs. Knox she wrote:

"The General and I feel like children just released from school or from a hard taskmaster, and we believe that nothing can tempt us to leave the sacred roof tree again, except on private business or pleasure. We are so penurious with our enjoyment that we are loth to share it with any one but dear friends, yet almost every day some stranger claims a portion of it, and we cannot refuse. . . . Our furniture and other things sent us from Philadelphia arrived safely, our plate we brought with us in the carriage. . . . I am again fairly settled down to the pleasant duties of an old-fashioned Virginia house-keeper, steady as a clock, busy as a bee, and cheerful as a cricket."

When returning from Philadelphia the General brought home with him George Washington LaFayette, son of his dear Marquis, who was accompanied by his tutor, M. Frestel. The young man had been in America nearly two years, but so long as Washington held an official position reasons of state made it inexpedient to invite him into his own family, but when he was again a private citizen he at once welcomed the young man to his home with the tenderness of a father. A report of LaFayette's release from prison reached America in the autumn and his son sailed for France October 26th. It was not his last visit to American or to Mount Vernon.

Other distinguished *emigrés* who had not been received by the President in Philadelphia, but were later welcomed at his home on the Potomac, included the Duc d'Orleans, afterward Louis Philippe, and his brothers, Montpensier and Beaujolais.

During '97 and '98 came Volney, the freethinker, for a recommendation, and received the equivocal "C. Volney needs no recommendation from Geo. Washington"; Benjamin H. Latrobe, Amariah Frost, and Mr. Niemcewitz, "the companion of General Kosciaski," all of whom wrote valued descriptions of Mount Vernon and of Washington; young Charles Carroll of Carrollton, suspected of sentimental intentions in regard to Nellie Custis; and once, on the same day, "Mr Lawe Washington of Chotanck & Mr Lawe Washington of Belmont came to dinner."

The arrival one autumn day of Bushrod Washington and his friend John Marshall, later Chief Justice of the United States, afforded one of the most amusing traditions of the place. They came, as the story runs, on horseback, "attended by a black servant, who had charge of a large black portmanteau containing their clothes. As they passed through a wood on the skirts of the Mount Vernon grounds they were tempted to make a hasty toilet beneath its shade; being covered with dust from the state of the roads. Dismounting, they threw off their dusty garments, while the servant took down the portmanteau. As he opened it, out

flew cakes of windsor soap and fancy articles of all
kinds. The man by mistake had changed their portmanteau at the last stopping place for one which re-
sembled it, belonging to a Scotch pedlar. The con-
sternation of the negro, and their own dismantled state,
struck them so ludicrously as to produce loud and repeated bursts of laughter. Washington, who happened
to be out upon his grounds, was attracted by the noise,
and was so overcome by the strange plight of his friends,
and the whimsicality of the whole scene, that he is said
to have actually rolled on the grass with laughter."

More frequently than many others came General
Henry Lee who, of all of them, stood least in awe of the
majestic Washington. Tradition has floated down numerous anecdotes of his table talk at Mount Vernon.

On one occasion Lee quoted Gilbert Stuart, the portrait painter, as having said that the General had a
tremendous temper. Mrs. Washington colored and
said that "Mr. Stuart took a great deal on himself."
Lee then said that Stuart had added that the General
had his temper under wonderful control. After a
thoughtful pause the General himself smiled and remarked, "Mr. Stuart is right."

On another occasion General Lee expressed the wide-
spread amazement at the vast amount of work Washington did. "Sir," he replied, "I rise at four o'clock
and a great deal of my work is done while others sleep."

Lee's great impertinence was committed at table one
day when Washington remarked that he wanted new
carriage horses and asked Lee if he could get him a pair.
"I have a fine pair, General," answered Lee, "but you
cannot get them." "Why not?" asked his host. "Be-

cause," Lee replied, "you will never pay more than half price for anything; and I must have full price for my horses." At this Mrs. Washington laughed and was joined by her parrot, perched near her, doubtless the same one the General had the care of on his way home. Washington yielded to the situation and said with good humor: "Ah, Lee, you are a funny fellow, see that bird is laughing at you."

The General and Mrs. Washington defended themselves from the overrunning visitors, who would have left them no life of their own, by a well-understood formality which restricted certain time for their own. It was at the dinner hour after his ride over the farms that Washington's visitors saw him first. After dinner he spent an interval talking with them, "with a glass of Madeira by his side," and then withdrew to his library again where he made a hasty survey of the newspapers, of which he received a great many, and retired for the night at nine o'clock, if possible without appearing at supper.

Mrs. Washington's first appearance in the morning seems to have been "precisely at eleven," when she spent an hour with her guests, who were expected to be waiting her at that time. When the clock struck twelve she would bid them good-morning and ascend to her chamber, to reappear punctually on the stroke of one. At this time she was followed by a servant with a bowl of punch which was served. She presided at the supper table and spent the evening with her guests.

It was Kosciuszko's friend who left one of the most graphic sketches of life and conditions at Mount Vernon at this time which survives. He journeyed thither with

Mr. Law. When they arrived the General was absent on his morning tour of his estate, but "his lady appeared in a few minutes, welcomed us most agreeably, and hastened to serve punch. At two o'clock the General arrived on the back of a grey horse. He descended, shook hands, and gave a lash to his horse, which went alone to the stable. After a short conversation he retired in order to change his dress."

The visitor then inspected the house. In the hall he found "a kind of crystal lantern contains the true key of the Bastille" and underneath it hung "a picture representing the destruction of that formidable castle." The model of the Bastille carved from one of its stones stood on the piazza, "it is a pity that children have spoiled it a little." At this time, from the Polish gentleman's account, Washington's bedroom seems to have been on the ground floor; probably a temporary arrangement. The views from the portico excited his liveliest enthusiasm. "This gallery is the place where the General and his family spend their afternoons with their guests, enjoying fresh air and the beautiful scenery." . . .

He gives this glimpse of the spirit of youth which Nellie Custis brought into the picture: "About three o'clock a carriage drawn by two horses, accompanied by a young man on horseback, stopped before the door. A young lady of the most wonderful beauty, closely followed by an elderly attendant, descended. She was one of those celestial beings so rarely produced by nature, sometimes dreamt of by poets and painters, which one cannot see without a feeling of ecstacy. Her sweetness equals her beauty, and that is perfect. She has many accomplishments. She plays on the piano, she sings and designs better than the usual woman of America or even of Europe."

The deer-park palings had now rotted and the deer were scattered. But when a group of bucks came browsing in sight of the mansion, "the General proposed to me to go to see them nearer. We went. He walks very quickly. I could scarcely follow him." But the bucks observed their approach and disappeared in the woods.

How the time passed with Washington himself, he told, when he became the historian of one of his days, "which will serve for a year," in a letter to his friend James McHenry:

"You are at the source of information, and can find many things to relate; while I have nothing to say, that could either inform or amuse a Secretary at War in Philadelphia. I might tell him, that I begin my diurnal course with the sun; that, if my hirelings are not in their places at that time I send them messages expressive of my sorrow at their indisposition; that, having put these wheels in motion, I examine the state of things further; and the more they are probed, the deeper I find the wounds are which my buildings have sustained by an absence and neglect of eight years; by the time I have accomplished these matters, breakfast (a little after seven o'clock, about the time I presume you are taking leave of Mrs. McHenry), is ready; that, this being over, I mount my horse and ride round my farms, which employs me until it is time to dress for dinner, at which I rarely miss seeing strange faces, come as they say out of respect for me. Pray, would not the word curiosity answer as well? And how different this from having a few social friends at a cheerful board! The usual time of sitting at table, a walk, and tea, brings me within the dawn of candlelight; previous to which, if not prevented by company, I resolve, that, as soon as the glimmering taper supplies the place of the great luminary, I will retire to my writing-table and acknowledge the letters I have received; but when the lights are brought, I feel tired and disinclined to engage in this work, conceiving that the next night will do as well. The next comes, and with it the same causes for postponement, and effect, and so on.

"This will account for your letter remaining so long unacknowledged; and, having given you the history of a day, it will serve for a year, and I am persuaded you will not require a second edition of it. But it may strike you, that in this detail no mention is made of any portion of time alloted for reading. The remark would be just, for I have not looked into a book since I came home nor shall I be able to do it until I have discharged my workmen, probably not before the nights grow longer, when possibly I may be looking in Doomsday-Book."

CHAPTER XVII

The Year 1799—Washington's Fortieth Wedding Anniversary
—Two Birthday Celebrations—Wedding of Nellie Custis
and Lawrence Lewis—A Gay Summer—First Dinner Alone
with Mrs. Washington in Twenty Years—Bankruptcy by
Hospitality—Mount Vernon Washington's Consuming In-
terest—A Luxury—The Rickety Stairway at the Polls—A
Birth in the Mansion—Washington Survives His Sister and
All His Brothers—Last Dinner Parties at Mount Eagle and
Mount Vernon—Caught in a Storm—Last Illness—Death
—Funeral.

THE year of 1799 was one of singular range and variety at Mount Vernon. It found the estate in its highest stage of development. The mansion was in perfect condition and was adorned with the taste and the trophies of Washington's matured career. From without the admiration and applause of the world centred here on its illustrious master.

As month after month slipped by the round of gayety, the number of visitors, and the events of significance were, perhaps, more numerous than in any other year of its long life. It saw the culmination of a romance in marriage, the fruition of that union in birth and, in its last month, transpired the final scene in the immortal career of which Mount Vernon was the principal setting.

The sixth day of the first month brought the fortieth anniversary of the General's marriage to Martha Custis. If it was not celebrated, the day did not pass unnoticed by them, for Washington was not without sentiment. On a gold chain about his neck, for many years, until the end of his life and beyond, he wore a miniature portrait of his wife.

In February he was the guest of the citizens of Alexandria for their customary celebration of his birthday. "Many Manœuvres were performed by the Uniform Corps—and an elegant Ball & supper at Night." This was the entry in the diary for the 11th of the month. Washington was born February 11th, old style. The new calendar was in vogue shortly after, which moved his birthday up to the 22d, but the old friends clung to the old fashion, and so as long as he was with them his neighbors in the little city up river celebrated on the 11th.

His birthday was celebrated twice this year of 1799, the second time on the 22d, within the walls of his own home. There "Miss Custis was married ab^t Candle Light to Mr Law^e Lewis." Washington chronicled events in deceptively few words. The wedding was in fact a brilliant occasion and was the culmination of a romance which enlisted the General's most interested solicitude, for Nellie Custis was the object, next to his wife, of his tenderest affection. She came into his life at a time when it was apparent that his union would not be blessed with a child of his own. He adopted her and brought her to Mount Vernon, and she never knew any other father or any other home than his.

She was known and loved by every servant and slave on the place. To them as to all who came to Mount Vernon in the later years of Washington's life, she represented the youth of the place. They had seen her grow up and watched her romance, and sensed it and gossiped it possibly before she realized it herself; for it was wholly of Mount Vernon.

Lawrence Lewis was the General's nephew, son of his sister Betty, and a member of the household. He had, some time before, become a member of the family at the mansion for the purpose of assisting in the entertainment of the visitors, "particularly of nights," his uncle said, "as it is my inclination to retire (and unless prevented by very particular company, I always do retire) either to bed or to my study soon after candle light."

It was in the gardens, along the walks, and in the quiet corners of the old mansion that Lawrence and Nellie were drawn together, and love held them. He was offered another commission in the military service just before his marriage but he declined it, which caused the General to remark that his nephew had relinquished "the lapp of Mars for the Sports of Venus."

With the arrival of spring visiting abroad began. There were the races, dinners, and Independence Day celebration in Alexandria; visits to the homes of Mrs. Washington's granddaughters, Mrs. Law and Mrs. Peter, in Washington City and its suburb, Georgetown; tours afield to run surveys of his land about Four Mile Run between Alexandria and Washington City; and once faring forth as far as Difficult Run, some twenty miles northwest of his home—with one exception, farther than he had ventured from Mount Vernon after he retired from the public service. That exception was his visit to Philadelphia during the previous November and December, when war threat-

ened with France and he was again called to command
the armies of his country.

It was a gay summer at the mansion, if possible with
more guests than ever. Though when had it been
without guests? A short time before this the General had
written Lear that "Mrs. Washington & myself will
do what I believe has not been done within the last
twenty years by us,—that is set down to dinner by ourselves."

Small wonder he compared his house to "a well resorted tavern" and to the end of his life complained of
being poor. Hospitality did its share to beget many
a pinched pocketbook. Much less sought-after Virginians than Washington bent under the strain of
Virginia hospitality, the unending procession of visitors,
singly, by coach loads, and by whole families. It is said
of Henry Fitzhugh of Chatham, opposite Fredericksburg, that he found his whole substance was going
to the support of the public, and in sheer economy he
built Ravensworth in Fairfax County, some ten miles
northwest of Mount Vernon, to be away from the well-
travelled highways. Hospitality bankrupted General
Henry Lee.

Washington's wealth was never the production of
his Mount Vernon farms. A luxury they remained
to the end, a toy of his thoughts and plans and experiments. This year of '99 he completed an elaborate
system for the cultivation of his plantations, with
tables to govern his overseers in the rotation of the
crops. It covered thirty large pages closely written
by his own hand, and it remains one of the testimonials
to his genius for organization and detail, and the sound-

ness of his mind and the clearness of his perceptions in the sixty-seventh year of his life.

Mount Vernon now absorbed Washington more and more, to the exclusion of other interests, and the public life receded farther into the background of memory. Though to the neighbors he was by name "the old General," neighborly feeling eclipsed the significance of the title and to them he became merely a planter, "a clear-headed, sensible man, whose opinion was worth having, and who was well worth consulting in farming matters or on common business."

Their traditional picture of him was a rugged old gentleman, dressed in gray clothes, a broad-brimmed hat on his head, and an umbrella under his arm, sitting his horse like a centaur, and riding afield to the extremities of his estate, slipping out of the saddle on occasion to chat with his old legionaries—Jack of Jack's Mill, the Mill at Epsewasson of his third year above three-score years before, and Gray of Gray's Hill, on that ridge which includes Woodlawn, the land for which was his wedding present to Nellie and Lawrence, and was called by him "a most beautiful site for a Gentlemans seat."

When the Gentlemen of the Alexandria Assemblies sent their polite invitation to the General and his wife for their winter dances, he replied that his dancing days were over. But he drove up to town frequently for visits that included a duck dinner at mine host Gadsby's City Hotel, a review of Captain Piercy's Independent Blues, and the casting of his last vote. The polling place was up a flight of outside steps, so rickety that, when the huge form of the General approached their foot, the bystanders, apprehending danger to him, with silent and spontaneous accord braced the stairway with their shoulders as he mounted, and waited there until he descended.

November was a month of expectation and great preparation in the mansion. Nellie and Lawrence had been back some time since from their honeymoon. Finally their old friend Doctor Craik was summoned on the 27th, "came to Breakfast & stayed dinner," and during the forenoon Nellie's first child, a daughter, was born.

In the early autumn had come word of the General's brother Charles Washington's death. "I was the first, and am, now, the last of my father's children by the second marriage who remain," he said. "When I shall be *called upon to follow them*, is known only to the Giver of Life. When the summons comes I shall endeavor to obey it with a good grace." With that time in view he pointed out to Lawrence Lewis, in early December, where he intended to build a new burial vault to replace the old vault which had begun to weaken under the ferreting roots of the trees growing above it. He declared this would be the next improvement he would make, adding "for after all, I may require it before the rest."

On Saturday, the 7th of December, Washington drove up to Mount Eagle on Great Hunting Creek and dined with Bryan Fairfax and his family. When he returned home he did not leave Mount Vernon again. There was something of a family party over Sunday, the 8th, but on Monday Lawrence Lewis and Washington Custis set off for New Kent on the York, and another nephew, Howell Lewis, and his wife, departed for their home. On Wednesday he had quite a dinner party about him, including Bryan Fairfax, his son and daughter, Mrs. Warner Washington and her son Whiting, and Mr. John Herbert.

Washington was apparently in his usual health. Following his daily custom of riding over his farms between breakfast and dinner, he was, on Thursday, caught out in a storm of snow, hail, and sleet, and returned to the mansion through a settled cold rain. He believed his greatcoat had given him sufficent protection and sat down to dinner without changing his clothes.

He seemed none the worse for his experience on Friday, and during the afternoon he tramped through three inches of snow, marking trees which were to be cut down to improve the grounds between the house and the river. In the course of the day he wrote a letter of instructions to his manager, the last letter he is known to have written. And it is interesting to this chronicle that his last activities and his last written words should have been devoted, even as was his whole life, to the care of Mount Vernon.

He spent the evening with the family and appeared to be in a cheerful mood, though somewhat hoarse. The papers had been brought from the post-office and he read them aloud and commented on items of peculiar interest. Lear suggested a remedy for his cold as the General retired, but he refused it, as he never took anything for a cold, and preferred to "let it go as it came." And so upstairs to his bedroom at the south end of the house over the library.

GEORGE WASHINGTON'S BEDROOM

Showing the bed in which he died

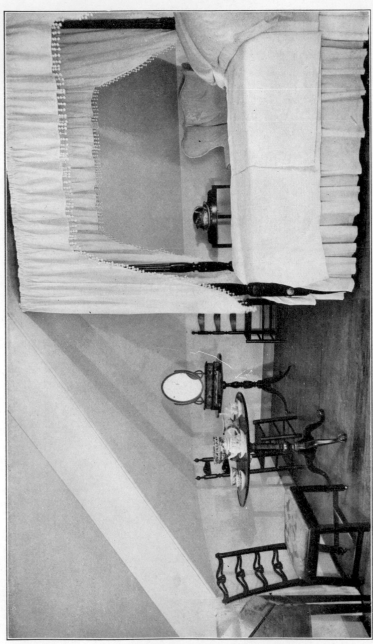

MARTHA WASHINGTON'S BEDROOM

This is the room above the General's bedroom to which Mrs. Washington moved after his death, and here she died May 22, 1802

From the dormer window on the left she looked out on his tomb

Between two and three o'clock in the morning (Saturday, December 14th) he wakened Mrs. Washington and confessed that he was very unwell. He would not let her get up to call assistance lest she take cold. When a servant appeared, however, Doctor Craik and Doctor Dick of Alexandria and Doctor Brown of Port Tobacco were sent for, and all arrived before four o'clock in the afternoon. They found the General suffering with a well-defined case of what was then called quinsy. Their ministrations gave no relief.

The General several times during the day expressed his belief that his end was near. "It is a debt we all must pay," he said, and faced the inevitable with perfect resignation. His wife, his old friend Doctor Craik, his faithful secretary Lear, and the domestic servants remained in the room with him continuously.

The day dragged itself into darkness. A fire flickered on the hearth opposite the foot of his bed. Candles spread a soft light. About ten o'clock he whispered some directions to Lear, and when assured he was understood, added: " 'Tis well." He did not speak again. Shortly afterward it was noticed that his breathing became much easier, and presently he felt his own pulse. In a few minutes, without struggle or pain, he breathed his last.

Riders were dispatched from Mount Vernon to the north and to the south, to notify the President of the United States, other officials, relatives and friends, of the death of General Washington.

The brick wall across the opening of the old vault above the river was torn away and the interior made ready. Mrs. Washington directed that a wooden door be built, for she said, "It will soon be necessary to open it again." Wednesday, December 18th, was fixed for the funeral.

The ceremonial was simple. His Masonic and military friends of Alexandria and his neighbors and relatives of the countryside nearby were the only ones present. The casket rested in the portico. A schooner in the river fired minute guns, beginning about three o'clock, as the procession moved down the slope toward the tomb.

The military led the way, the musicians playing a dirge with muffled drums, followed by the clergy; then the General's horse with his saddle, holsters, and pistols, led by two of his grooms; the body borne by Masonic and military officers; the relatives and intimate friends, Masons, the Corporation of Alexandria, and the people of the estate.

The Rev. Mr. Davis, rector of Christ Church, Alexandria, read the service and spoke briefly. The Masons then performed their ritual, after which the body was deposited in the tomb.

So with the simplicity he would have preferred, surrounded only by his friends and his neighbors, he was laid to rest where he had lived with the fullest happiness. Mount Vernon was his home; it now became the nation's shrine.

CHAPTER XVIII

Death Chamber Sealed—Washington's Will—Mount Vernon Bequeathed to Bushrod Washington—Other Bequests—The Inventory—The Slave Problem—Martha Washington's Last Days—Death—Family Matters—Pictures, Plate, Furnishings, and Souvenirs Dispersed—Sale of 1802—Bushrod Washington Takes Possession of Mount Vernon.

AFTER the General's death Mrs. Washington, following a custom then prevalent, closed his bedchamber and moved into another. She chose the room at the south end of the third floor, directly over the one she had occupied with the General, because from its solitary dormer window she could see her husband's tomb. She continued to occupy this room as long as she lived.

In the afternoon of his last day the General called his wife to his bedside and asked her to go below to his library and from his desk there bring his two wills. This she did. He examined them, declared one of them to be superseded by the other, and requested her to burn the earlier, which she did.

The destroyed will was probably the one drawn for Washington by his attorney, Edmund Pendleton, in Philadelphia, when he was commissioned Commander-in-Chief of the Revolutionary Army. In his letter to Mrs. Washington, telling her of the new military career he had then entered upon, he said:

"As life is always uncertain, and common prudence dictates to every man the necessity of settling his temporal concerns, while it is in his power, and while the mind is calm and undisturbed, I have, since I came to this place (for I had not time to do it before I left home) got Colonel Pendleton to draft a will for me, by the directions I gave him, which will I now enclose. The provision made for you in case of my death, will, I hope, be agreeable."

This was, in fact, probably the second will Washington had made at the time he caused it to be drawn. When in the late fifties he left for the western campaign and put John Augustine Washington in charge of his estate, he told his brother that if he fell in the war he would leave Mount Vernon to him. Washington was too methodical and thorough a man not to have embodied such a promise in a will, and no doubt he made his first will at this time.

The document which he finally ordered preserved, and by which the future proprietorship of Mount Vernon and of its furnishings and belongings was determined, was completed by him July 9, 1799. The concluding paragraph discloses four points of interest: he prepared the will without legal advice, he provided for arbitration in case of dispute, he omitted the final "9" in the dating, and he signed it without witnesses.

He bequeathed the whole of his Mount Vernon estate, real and personal, to his wife "for the term of her natural life." He gave her and her heirs "forever" all the household furniture of every kind, except that otherwise disposed of. To his nephew Bushrod Washington, who had risen to the distinction of a seat on the bench of the Supreme Court of the United States, he gave his library and all his papers relating to his civil and military administration of the affairs of the country. He directed the return of the Wallace Oak Box to the Earl of Buchan. The crabtree walking-stick with the gold head, which Benjamin Franklin bequeathed to him, he gave to his brother Charles Washington. Two other gold-headed canes engraved with the Washington arms, and two spyglasses used during the war, he gave "the friends and acquaintances of my juvenile years, Lawrence Washington and Robert Washington of Chotanck," to his "compatriot in arms and old and intimate friend," Doctor Craik, he gave his writing desk and chair; to Doctor David Stuart, his telescope and large shaving and dressing table; to Bryan Fairfax, a Bible in three large volumes; to General de LaFayette, "a pair of finely wrought steel pistols taken from the enemy in the Revolutionary war"; to Tobias Lear, the use, rent free, during the remainder of his life, of the farm where he lived about four miles east of Mount Vernon mansion; and, finally, "To each of my nephews William Augustine Washington, George Lewis, George Steptoe Washington, Bushrod Washington and Samuel Washington, I give one of the swords or *cutteaux* of which I may die possessed, and they are to *chuse* in the order they are named.—These swords are accompanied with an injunction not to unsheath them for the purpose of shedding blood except it be for self-defence, or in defence of their Country and it's rights, and in the latter case to keep them unsheathed, and prefer falling with them in their hands to the relinquishment thereof."

A natural pendant to the will of General Washington and of the most valued evidence in realizing the character of the furnishings of the mansion during his lifetime, is the inventory of his personal effects made by those charged with their final appraisement. If it makes no mention of some objects otherwise known to have been in the house, it does place many valuable and curious things in the rooms where Washington and his guests were accustomed to see them.

In the large room in the north end, variously styled the New Room, the New Dining Room and the Banquet Room—were twenty-seven mahogany chairs, two sideboards, and large looking-glasses, four silver-plated lamps, on each sideboard, "an Image and China flower Pot," two "Elegant Lustres," two candlestands, and two "Fire Skreens." On the walls hung the ornately framed engraving of Louis XVI sent by that monarch to the General, "2 large Gilt frame Pictures representing falls of Rivers, 4 do. representing water Courses, 1 do. Small 'Likeness of Gen. W——n,' 4 Small Prints (1 under each lamp), 1 Painting 'Moonlight,' 2 Prints 'Death of Montgomery,' 2 do. 'Battles of Bunker Hill,' 2 do 'Dead Soldier,' 1 likeness 'Saint John, and 1 do Virgin Mary.'"

In the little parlor on the east front were a looking-glass, a tea table, a settee, ten Windsor chairs, a "Likeness of Gen¹. Washington in an Ovolo frame, do. LaFayette, do. Dr. Franklin"; prints representing Storms at Sea, the naval battle between the *Bon Homme Richard* and the *Seraphis*, "the distressed situation of the Quebec &c.," the whale fishery at Davies Streights, another of the Greenland Streights, and nine gilt frames containing "the likenesses of a Deer," "Painted likeness of an Alloe," "wrought work cont^{g}. chickens in a basket," and six other different paintings.

In the front or west parlor were eleven mahogany chairs, a tea table, a "Sopha, 1 Elegant looking-glass," three lamps and two mirrors, five china flower pots, three portraits of the General, two of Mrs. Washington, other portraits of Mr. Law, Mrs. Lear, George Washington LaFayette, Nellie Custis, John and Martha Custis as children, Martha when grown, and one of LaFayette and his family, all in gilt frames.

Apart from the tea table, "2 dining tables," a mahogany sideboard, an Ovolo looking-glass, "1 large case" and "2 knife cases," and ten mahogany chairs, the Dining Room contained "1 large gilt frame print the death of the Earl of Chatham, 1 do. Genl. Woolfe, 1 do. Penns Treaty with Indians, 1 do. David Rittenhouse, 1 do Dr Franklin, 1 do Genl Washington, 1 do Gen'l Greene, 1 do America, 1 do Genl. Fayette on Closusion [Conclusion?] of the late war, 1 do Genl. Wayne, 1 do the Washington family of Mount Vernon, 1 do Alfred visiting his noblemen, and 1 do do dividing his loaf with the Pilgrim."

The room opposite the East Parlor was furnished as a bedroom with bedstead, small table, looking-glass, and four mahogany or walnut chairs. In a gilt frame on the wall hung "a battle fought by Cavalry."

There were fourteen mahogany chairs in the Passage, or Central Hall, an "Image" over the door into each of the four adjoining rooms, a "Spye Glass" through which the General and his guests observed the life on the Potomac, a thermometer which may have been the one recommended by "Doctor Priestly or Mr. Madison," the "Key of the Bastille with its Representation," and prints of Diana deceived by Venus, Dancing Shepherds, Morning, Evening, the River Po, Constantine's Arch, and the General himself. Along the wall of the stairway ascending to the second floor were other prints of Musical Shepherds, Moonlight, Thunderstorm, the Battle of Bunker Hill, and the Death of Montgomery. In the upper passage a looking-glass is the sole object enumerated.

The details of one bedroom, the General's, will serve for all: "Bed, Bedstead & Curtains," a looking-glass which was the least expensive in the house, dressing table, one writing table and chair, an easy chair, two other mahogany chairs, the only clock listed in the inventory, a chest of drawers, six paintings of the members of Mrs. Washington's family, five small drawings, pictures of the Countess of Huntington, General Knox, "A Parson," and five other small pictures. In the adjoining "closet" were one mahogany and two leather trunks and a washbasin valued at fifty cents.

There were carpets in all the rooms, likewise "Irons, Shovel, Tongs and Fender." In the passage outside the General's room there were "3 Pictures *nailed to the house*." In the "Garret" the inventory accounts for "two furnished bedrooms and the Lumber Rooms," in which were furniture, trunks, chests, pictures, fire screens, a side saddle, books, a warming pan, "2 Surveyors Machines," and "2 sets Platteaux" valued at one hundred dollars, probably the mirrors for the state dining table.

Among the interesting objects in the Study or Library were the General's Tambour secretary and its circular desk chair, two copying presses, numerous pistols, "7 Swords & 1 blade, 4 canes, 7 guns, 11 Spye Glasses, Trumbuls Prints, 1 Case Surveyors Instrum[ts]., 1 Traveling Ink Case, 1 Globe, 1 Chest of Tools, 1 Compass staff, 1 Case Dentists Instrum[ts]., 2 Setts money weights, 1 Telescope, 1 Box Paints," Houdon's bust of the General, a plaster profile, two seals with ivory handles, his Masonic emblems, additional surveying instruments, some Indian presents, and an iron chest containing securities, jewelry, medals, and a variety of other things, including a portrait of Lawrence Washington.

The inventory contains a list of the books in Washington's library, but it is full of inaccuracies. Moreover, it does not furnish satisfactory material for a study of Washington's taste in reading, for the books represent his selection only in part. Many were gifts, and some he subscribed to for various motives other than original interest in the subject matter. The list includes about eight hundred titles. It is interesting to observe that the books on all other than agricultural topics were in the cases behind glass. The books on farming, however, were "on the table," where the General could reach them handily. This subject formed the principal and almost the only topic of his reading.

Washington's letters to Lear disclosed the parlor as having been furnished in blue. An investigation* of the walls and woodwork of the passage and the upper rooms, made in 1897, revealed other interesting facts about the interior color scheme of the house. The side-

---

*Report of C. Mellon Rogers, Architect, of Philadelphia.

wall panels, the ceiling, and the stair-skirting were a
delicate French gray, almost a robin-egg blue. The
doors, trim, door-heads, chair rail, washboard, windows, stair-skirting battons, and cornice were painted
ivory white with a china gloss finish.

The wall of the stairway leading to the second floor
was made of "a buff or yellow mortar," in some places
white coated. The walls of the river bedroom on the
north side of the upper hall were originally gray with
mantel and other woodwork in white, which was also
the color treatment of the bedroom over the family
dining-room. The walls of the General's bedroom were
gray, the mantel was white, the washboard was stained
and varnished.

After the General's death Mrs. Washington found
herself confronted with a problem in the slaves on the
estate. They gave the gravest concern. Washington
would gladly have freed his slaves, but the situation
was complicated by their intermarriage with the dower
slaves whom he could not free. They came to Mount
Vernon by his marriage with the widow of Daniel
Parke Custis, to whose heirs they reverted by law. Re-
garding his slaves his will said:

"Upon the decease of wife it is my will and desire,
that all the slaves which I hold in *my own right* shall
receive their freedom—To emancipate them during her
life, would tho earnestly wished by me, be attended with
such insuperable difficulties, on account of their inter-
mixture by marriages with the Dower negroes as to
excite the most painful sensations,—if not disagreeable consequences from the latter while both descrip-

tions are in the occupancy of the same proprietor, it
not being in my power under the tenure by which the
dower Negroes are held to manumit them—— And
whereas among those who will receive freedom according to this devise there may be some who from old age,
or bodily infirmities & others who on account of their
infancy, that will be unable to support themselves, it is
my will and desire that all who come under the first
and second description shall be comfortably clothed
and fed by my heirs while they live and that such of the
latter description as have no parents living, or if living
are unable, or unwilling to provide for them, shall be
bound by the Court . . . taught to read and write
and to be brought up to some useful occupation."

Mrs. Washington's grandson, and a member of the
family at the time, says in his memoirs that "the slaves
were left to be emancipated at the death of Mrs. Washington; but it was found necessary (for *prudential*
reasons) to give them their freedom in one year after
the General's decease." Some light may be thrown on
this statement by the remarks of Edward Everett Hale,
who in his eightieth year, in 1902, said:

"I have been assured by gentlemen who lived in
northern Virginia that the universal impression there
was that the slaves of the Washington plantation hurried Martha Washington's death because their own
liberty was secured by Washington's will after her
death. I do not believe that this bad statement can
be authenticated, but there is no doubt, I believe, that
Madison made a similar will liberating his slaves after

attaches to the noticeable infrequency of the visits of Washington's next of kin to Mount Vernon, except on business, during Mrs. Washington's lifetime, and to the fact that not a single blood relative of Washington stood at his tomb when he was placed within.

By Lear's own account Mr. Law, Mr. Peter, and Dr. Stuart were notified by courier the evening the General died. Next day Lear enclosed notices to Judge Bushrod Washington and Colonel William Washington, under cover to Colonel Blackburn, "desiring him to forward them by express." A slave, Cæsar, was dispatched to New Kent to notify G. W. P. Custis and Lawrence Lewis. A letter was sent to the post-office to John Lewis, "desiring him to give information to his brothers George, Robert & Howell, & to Capt. Sam'l Washington." No other relatives were notified. The information sent in this way could not have found any of these except the first three in time for them to reach Mount Vernon for the funeral, which was fixed for the fourth day after the General's death.

Judge Bushrod Washington came to Mrs. Washington's funeral, but tradition says that Lawrence and Nellie Lewis did not invite him to remain for refreshment, and before leaving his estate he asked a slave to prepare dinner for him, which he ate in a cabin. It has long been said in the neighborhood that when Lawrence Lewis settled at Woodlawn, the mansion he built on the tract his uncle bequeathed him, the relations between that house and Mount Vernon were visibly strained.

The General, by his will, gave his widow a life interest in Mount Vernon and in everything that pertained to it. The only bequest that he made to "her and her heirs forever" was that of "the household and kitchen furniture of every sort and kind with the liquors and groceries which may be on hand at the time of my decease, to be used and disposed of as she may think proper." Mrs. Washington, during her widowhood, made frequent gifts to her relatives of objects from the mansion.

By her will she gave to her grandson, G. W. P. Custis, "all the silver plate of every kind, . . . together with the two large plated coolers, the four small plated coolers with the bottle castors, a pipe of wine if there be one in the house at the time of my death—also the set of Cincinnati tea and table china, the bowl that has a ship in it, the fine old china jars which usually stand on the chimney piece in the new room: also all the family pictures of every sort and the pictures painted by his sister, and two small skreens worked by his sister and the other a present from Miss Kitty Brown—also his choice of ———— prints—also the two girandoles and lustres that stand on them—also the new bedstead which I caused to be made in Philadelphia together with the bed, matrass bolsters and pillows and the white dimity curtains belonging thereto: also two other beds with bolsters and pillows and the white dimity window curtains in the new room—also the iron chest and the desk in my closet which belonged to my first husband; also all my books of every kind except the large bible and prayer book, also the set of tea china that was given me by Mr. Van Braam every piece having M W on it."

To Nellie Custis Lewis she gave "the large looking glass in the front Parlour and any other looking glass which she may choose—Also one of the new side board tables in the new room—also twelve chairs with green bottoms to be selected by herself also the marble table in the garret, also the two prints of the dead soldier, a print of the Washington family in a box in the Garret and the great chair standing in my chamber; also all the plated ware not herein otherwise bequeathed—" and many other domestic articles.

To her two other grandchildren she gave,—"my writing table and the seat to it standing in my chamber, also the print of Gen¹. Washington that hangs in the passage" to Mrs. Peter,—"the dressing table and glass that stands in the chamber called the yellow room, and Gen¹. Washington's picture painted by Trumbull" to Mrs. Law. "All the wine in bottles in the vaults" was ordered "equally divided between" her granddaughters and her grandson.

Everything else in the mansion not specified in her will was ordered to be sold by the executors "for ready money" for the education of three of her nephews. This sale took place July 20, 1802. Relatives of General Washington were extensive purchasers, and it was in this way that they obtained such relics of Mount Vernon as they afterward possessed.

When Bushrod Washington moved into the mansion he found it dismantled of all its objects which he did not buy in at the sale. No, there was one object which escaped bequest as well as sale. It had excited no one's interest. By some irony of fate this object was the sole and only portrait of the man who, in the uncertainty which surrounds the fact, is generally believed to have built Mount Vernon house, who bequeathed it to his

MOUNT VERNON MANSION AS IT APPEARED JUST BEFORE THE CIVIL WAR

From a photograph taken at that time

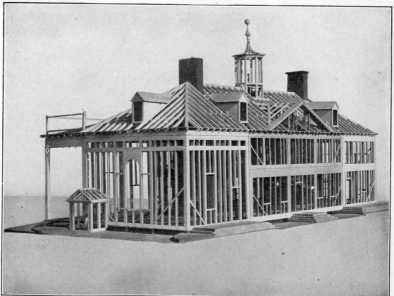

SKELETON MODEL OF MOUNT VERNON MANSION

In the National Museum at Washington
Above, the river front.   Below, the west front from the north

much-loved young brother George, and was thereby the
indirect instrument of its great fame.   It is not a great
work of art, but it has found appreciation since, and is
now treasured by another Lawrence Washington, great-
great-grandnephew of this one.

CHAPTER XIX

Career of Bushrod Washington—Justice of the Supreme Court of the United States—Estimates by Contemporaries—Mount Vernon and the English Fleet in 1814—Battle off Belvoir —Rev. Charles O'Neill—Return of LaFayette—Death of Justice Washington—The Two John Augustine Washingtons —New Tomb—Reëntombment of the General and Mrs. Washington—Other Burials—The Key Thrown into the Potomac.

BUSHROD WASHINGTON, third Washington to own and to live in Mount Vernon Mansion, was the second child of John Augustine Washington, who was a second younger brother of the General. He was born in Westmoreland County, Virginia, June 5, 1762.

He graduated from the College of William and Mary in 1778, later joined the army, and was a private soldier under Mercer at Yorktown. In his twenty-second year he accompanied the General on his tour of western Pennsylvania, when they rode six hundred and eighty miles in thirty-four days, and he afterward received substantial evidence that he was his Uncle George's favorite nephew. Bushrod chose the law as his profession and by the influence of his uncle he was admitted to study in the office of James Wilson of Philadelphia, later one of the Justices of the Supreme Court of the United States. He began to practise in his native Westmoreland, which he represented in the Virginia Assembly and also in the Virginia Convention which ratified the Constitution.

Bushrod married Anne, daughter of Colonel Thomas Blackburn of Rippon Lodge, Prince William County, about twelve miles from Mount Vernon. There was no issue. As his country practice did not thrive, he moved to Alexandria; perhaps also to be nearer the Mount Vernon influence. Indeed he wrote the General asking to be appointed an attorney in the Federal Court, but learned that "nepotism was not one of his uncle's redeeming vices." He next established himself in Richmond and almost immediately became one of the leading members of the Virginia bar. His wife was an invalid, however, and he led a retired life, devoting his leisure to editing the Reports of the Virginia Court of Appeals between 1790 and 1796.

When Justice Wilson died President Adams reduced his choice of a successor to John Marshall and Bushrod Washington. "Marshall is first in age, rank and public service, probably not second in talents," the President wrote Mr. Pickering, his Secretary of State. "The character, the merits and abilities of Mr. Washington are greatly respected, but I think General Marshall ought to be preferred; of the three envoys [to France] the conduct of Marshall alone has been entirely satisfactory, and ought to be marked by the most decided approbation of the public. He has raised the American people in their own esteem, and if the influence of truth and justice, reason and argument is not lost in Europe, he had raised the consideration of the United States in that quarter of the world. If Mr. Marshall should decline, I should next think of Mr. Washington." Marshall did decline, and Bushrod Washington became an Associate Justice of the Supreme Court, December 20,

1798, in his thirty-sixth year, succeeding his own learned preceptor.

Justice Washington is described as a small man, with an emaciated frame and a countenance like marble. Though his fame was overshadowed by his illustrious uncle, he was undoubtedly a man of parts. He specialized in commercial and *Nisi Prius* law, and Justice Binney said of him that he was "as accomplished a *Nisi Prius* judge as ever lived. I cannot conceive a better. . . . I do not believe that even he [Lord Mansfield] surpassed him." Judge Hopkinson and David Paul Brown made equal estimates of his abilities.

Justice Story reviewing the partiality shown Bushrod Washington by his uncle in bequeathing him Mount Vernon, his private and public letters and papers and his library, and in making him executor of his will, said: "Such marks of respect from such a man,—the wonder of his own age, and the model of all future ages,—would alone stamp a character of high merit, and solid distinction, upon any person. They would constitute a passport to public favour, and confer an enviable rank, far beyond the records of the herald's office, or the fugitive honors of a title. . . . He was as worthy an heir as ever claimed kindred with a worthy ancestor. . . . Few men indeed have possessed higher qualifications for the office, either natural or acquired. . . . His mind was solid, rather than brilliant; sagacious and searching, rather than quick or eager; steady, but not unyielding; comprehensive, and at the same time cautious; patient in inquiry, forcible in conception, clear in reasoning. He was, by original temperament, mild, conciliating, and candid; and yet he was remarkable for his uncompromising firmness."

He was a man of few activities apart from his attention to his duties on the Supreme Bench. He was, however, the first President of the American Colonization Society, which sought to transfer negroes from the United States to colonize the little Republic of Liberia, and in his later years he edited the Reports of the United States Circuit Court of the Third District, 1803 to 1827.

Justice Washington's enforced presence in Philadelphia, during many of the years of his ownership of Mount Vernon, afforded him brief intervals to retire to his estate. Whenever he was there he dispensed a modest and graceful hospitality to the great number of visitors who came to view the home and tomb of his uncle. Among the happy incidents of his occupancy of the mansion were the occasional dinners which he and his wife gave to the Chief Justice and his Associate Justices of the Supreme Court.

Apprehension for Mount Vernon again seized the people during the second war with Great Britain, when, on August 24, 1814, the British fleet sailed up the Potomac. Instead of attacking and destroying Mount Vernon, as anticipated, it is said Captain Gordon of the Royal Navy caused the seven vessels of his fleet to fire salutes as they came abreast. Almost immediately thereafter, and in sight of the mansion, Fort Washington, on the site of Mr. Digges' Warburton Manor lands, surrendered without a shot to the astonished English.

When the enemy returned from the plunder of Alexandria, however, they bore away a different tale of Mount Vernon neighborhood. Two batteries under Commodore David Porter and Commodore Oliver H. Perry engaged the retreating ships from the Virginia shore, following their passage down river. They crossed the western end of Mount Vernon estate and took up a position on Belvoir heights. As the English ships passed there was a spirited engagement. But this naval battle fought in sight of Mount Vernon was overwhelmingly onesided. The land batteries were of small calibre and the guns were outnumbered many times over by those on the ships.

Of a more peaceful nature were the visits to Mount Vernon of the Rev. Charles O'Neill, rector of rejuvenated Pohick Church, recounted by Bishop Meade, then rector of Christ Church, Alexandria, where Justice and Mrs. Washington worshipped: "The families at Mount Vernon and Rippon Lodge were fond of him. He always spent his Christmas at Mount Vernon, and on these occasions was dressed in a full suit of velvet, which General Washington left behind, and which had been given to Mr. O'Neill. But as General Washington was tall and well proportioned in all his parts, and Mr. O'Neill was peculiarly formed, being of uncommon length of body and brevity of legs, it was difficult to make the clothes of one even though altered sit well upon the other."

General the Marquis de LaFayette, accompanied by his son, George Washington LaFayette, crossed the Atlantic once more, in 1824, for a tour of America as the nation's guest, and he came again to Mount Vernon to refresh his souvenirs and lay his homage at the tomb of his chief and friend. It was a pilgrimage of much state though of simple ceremonial.

Bushrod Washington possessed Mount Vernon for twenty-seven years. The only impress of his ownership which survives on the mansion is the porch which he built on the southwest end outside the library windows. In erecting this porch he tore away the shelter over the steps descending into the cellar, similar to the shelter which survives at the northeast cellar door.

Justice Washington's health began to fail in the autumn of 1829, and he died while attending court in Philadelphia, November 26th, of that year. His wife died a few days later, of grief it is said. They were buried side by side in the family vault at Mount Vernon.

In his will Justice Washington divided that portion of the original estate which he had inherited from his uncle, the General, among his own nephews and a niece, Mary Lee Washington, daughter of his brother Corbin, who was married to Noblet Herbert in the mansion in 1819, and is buried within the vault. The mansion and a large tract surrounding, including the river front, he bequeathed to John Augustine Washington, third child of his brother Corbin.

This John Augustine Washington was born at Walnut Farm, in Westmoreland County, Virginia, about 1792. He married Jane Charlotte, daughter of Major Richard Scott Blackburn, of the United States Army, in 1814, and they lived at Blakeley, in Jefferson County, then Virginia, now West Virginia. There five children were born to them, of whom two died in infancy. On the death of his Uncle Bushrod, John Augustine moved with his family to Mount Vernon and proposed to make the cultivation and improvement of the estate his chief business in life. He died in 1832, however, and was buried in the vault, after only a little more than two years' ownership of the estate, which he bequeathed to his widow.

Jane Washington seems to have been a woman of character and resources. With such aid as she could command she kept her young family about her—her eldest son was only eleven years old—and applied herself to carry on her husband's work. What a burden it must have been to her can be little realized by those who have not staggered under the tax, in time and entertainment, of the proprietorship of one of the most-frequented patriotic shrines in the world.

John Augustine, Jane's eldest boy, was his mother's main dependence, and within a few years he is found shouldering responsibilities in the management of the place. Soon after Bushrod Washington's death the green-house next the flower gardens burned, which explains an allusion in a letter of November 10, 1837, to John Augustine from his mother: "The portico and pavement round the House at Mount Vernon should be immediately laid—many of the flagstones are broken and much defaced—there are more than eno' to replace them in the Burnt Hot house, the rubbish must be removed & have them carefully taken up."

Jane Washington lived at Mount Vernon until 1843. In February of that year John Augustine was married to Eleanor Love Selden of Exeter, Loudoun County, Virginia. His mother then retired to her other estate, Blakeley, in Jefferson County. She transferred Mount Vernon Mansion and about twelve hundred acres of

surrounding land to him by deed of gift in 1850, which
gift she confirmed in her will.

To this John Augustine, last Washington to own
Mount Vernon, and Eleanor his wife, were born seven
children: Louisa Fontaine, 19 February, 1844; Jane
Charlotte, 26 May, 1846; Eliza Selden, 17 July, 1848;
Anna Maria, 17 November, 1851; Lawrence, 14 January, 1854; Eleanor Love, 14 March, 1856; and George,
22 July, 1858. All were born in Mount Vernon Mansion except Eliza, and they were the last children born
there.

The years of Jane Washington's residence at Mount
Vernon made little history for the estate apart from
the notable events of 1831 and 1837, the years which
saw the realization of the General's wish expressed in
this item of his will:

"The family Vault at Mount Vernon requiring repairs, and being improperly situated besides, I desire
that a new one of Brick, and upon a larger scale, may
be built at the foot of what is commonly called the
vineyard enclosure,—on the ground which is marked
out.—In which my remains, with those of my deceased
relatives (now in the Old Vault) and such others of
my family as may *chuse* to be entombed there, may be
deposited."

In the thirty-odd years since his death, the proposal
to move his remains from Mount Vernon to Washington City was twice agitated. During Martha Washington's widowhood President Adams requested that
her husband's ashes might be brought to the national
Capital. She consented, but the project was not pursued. Again in 1832, when the nation celebrated the

centennial of Washington's birth, Congress renewed the request to the Washington family and a platform was prepared for his sarcophagus in the crypt underneath the centre of the dome of the Capitol of the United States. But it remains untenanted to-day, and the General reposes in the quiet of his beloved Mount Vernon, as his relatives refused to give a permission contrary to the desire expressed in his will.

It was a vandal's effort, happily futile, to steal the body of Washington from the old tomb, which stirred Lawrence Lewis and G. W. P. Custis, surviving executors under the General's will, to fulfil his desire. This was about 1830. Already the damp condition of the old tomb, smothered under the dense foliage of trees which grew above it and shot their destructive roots through its roof and walls, had three times destroyed the wooden casings of the General's leaden casket. In 1831 the new tomb was completed and into it all the remains of the deceased members of the Washington family in the old vault were at once moved.

When, the next year, the proposal to remove Washington and his wife to the United States Capitol was agitated, John Struthers, of Philadelphia, asked and received permission to present sarcophagi for their bodies, which he proceeded to chisel from solid blocks of marble. When the effort was finally abandoned and it became certain that Washington's wish to remain at Mount Vernon would be respected, Mr. Struthers presented the sarcophagi to the Washington family for use in the family vault.

Attention was called to the fact that the marble would discolor and perhaps decay in the damp and darkness behind the iron door of the vault. It was then decided to build the vestibule that the marble caskets might have air and light. This was completed in 1837, when the remains of George and Martha Washington were sealed in the marble sarcophagi in the places where they have since rested in the open vestibule before the vault.

On this occasion a delegation headed by Henry Clay drove to Mount Vernon from the Capital and joined Lawrence Lewis, his son Lorenzo Lewis, John Augustine Washington, his mother Jane Washington, the Reverend Mr. Johnson and his wife, and others in the informal but solemn ceremonial of reëntombment.

A circumstantial story has been published that the leaden casket was opened, that Washington's face was looked upon by those present, and that his features were little changed. "I believe this to be untrue," said Mr. Lawrence Washington to the writer. "The late Mr. Richard B. Washington told me that the leaden casket was not opened. He was present and about fifteen years old. He said there was a small circular hole immediately over the face, through which several persons attempted to look on Washington's face, and some of them claimed that they saw it, but that he on attempting to look through the hole could see nothing. I am aware that Strickland's account is very circumstantial, but my uncle did not hesitate to denounce it as false."

The marble receptacles are severely plain. That of Washington has on its upper surface a sculptured device in high relief representing the eagle above the American shield against a drapery of the Flag of the

Union. Beneath this is the single word "Washington." Martha's has carved on its upper surface the words, "Martha, Consort of Washington," and, on the upright surface at the end, "Died May 21, 1801, aged 71 years." This is obviously erroneous. Martha Washington died the 22d day of May, in the year 1802.*

After the entombment in 1837 there were seven other burials at Mount Vernon—four within the vault and three in the ground on the southeast side. The first of these was Lawrence Lewis. After Martha Washington's death, Lawrence and Nellie built Woodlawn Mansion, three miles northwest of Mount Vernon house, on the superb site which the General bequeathed his nephew. It is one of the stateliest houses in Virginia, built of brick throughout, in the Georgian style, and its pillared portico overlooks the Potomac down the length of Dogue Creek, all of the original acres of Mount Vernon, and a long stretch of lovely valley to the north. The Lewises continued to live at Woodlawn until the early thirties, when they moved to Audley, another estate of theirs in Clarke County, near the Shenandoah. Lawrence died November 20, 1839, and is buried in the vault at Mount Vernon. Their daughter Angela, Mrs. Conrad, died at Pass Christian, Mississippi, in 1839, according to the shaft above her grave, and John Augustine Washington's diary says that on July 10, 1843, her body "and that of her child were buried near the new vault." Mrs. Lewis survived her husband thirteen years. She died at Audley, July 15, 1852, and was brought to Mount Vernon and buried near her

---

* Since the text above was written the date on Martha Washington's sarcophagus has been corrected.

daughter and granddaughter at the side of the vault. Her brother, G. W. P. Custis, died October 10, 1857, and is buried at Arlington. Of two of the others to be admitted to the vault at Mount Vernon one was Mary Lee Washington Herbert, who died in 1852. Mr. Washington's diary records the other burial there on April 16, 1842: "Reverend Mr. Johnson had the body of his child placed in the vault." The father of this child was the Rev. W. P. C. Johnson, who married a Miss Washington of Mount Zephyr.

Jane, mother of the last Washington to own Mount Vernon, passed away at Blakeley, her home in Jefferson County, in the year 1855. She was brought to Mount Vernon and placed near her husband in the vault.

On that occasion John Augustine Washington entered in his diary, under date of September 10, 1855, these invaluable memoranda (see next page) of the positions of the persons buried in the vault, omitting unfortunately to indicate the bodies marked C, D, E, and F in his diagram, though sequence would seem to determine them:

"We buried my mother *in the vault* at Mount Vernon —as she desired, at my father's feet. The bodies buried there lie as follows. The first body inside the door of the inner vault is Major Lawrence Lewis (marked A. in the subjoined diagram). The second B. is my mother. Then at right angles to these with their feet to them are Judge Bushrod Washington marked [blank]. His wife Ann Washington My father John Augustine Washington marked [blank] and his sister Mary Lee Herbert marked [blank]"

A tradition has lingered about Mount Vernon that,

We buried my Mother in the vault at Mount Vernon - as she desired, at my Father's feet - The bodies buried there lie as follows. The first body inside the door of the inner vault is Major Lawrence Lewis (marked A. in the subjoined diagram) The second B. is my Mother - Then at right angles to these with their feet to them are Judge B.H. Bushrod Washington marked   . His wife Ann Washington

My Father John Augustine Washington marked and his sister Mary Lee Herbert marked

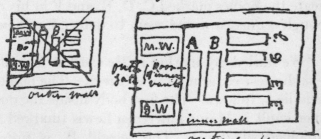

I make this rough diagram that no mistake may hereafter be made as to the position of the bodies —

Extract from the Diary of John Augustine Washington, last private owner of
Mount Vernon, under date of September 10, 1855

after the burial of Mrs. Jane Washington, the tomb was locked, the keyhole sealed with the little metal plate which obscures it to-day, and the key was thrown into the Potomac. There seems to be no written history to corroborate this. However, oral confirmation is furnished by Thomas W. Buckey, a connection by marriage with John Augustine Washington's brother Richard, from whom he had these facts.

One evening shortly after the burial of Jane Washington a number of the Washington family were gathered in Mount Vernon Mansion, and talk turned on the crowded condition of the family vault. The discussion of what other members of the family should enjoy the distinction of burial in the historic tomb disclosed so many claims that it was decided then and there that no one else should be buried therein, and to prevent it to throw the key into the river. To avoid responsibility for this radical act it was decided to draw lots. The obligation fell to Richard Washington, who at once took the key, went down the hill in the darkness, and with all his strength hurled the key far out into the Potomac.

When this was repeated to Lawrence Washington, nephew of Richard Washington, he told the writer he had never heard it before, but added: "If Uncle Dick said so you can depend on it."

John Augustine's ownership was notable in its termination which saw the home of Washington pass from the precarious ownership of an individual to the more comprehensive and efficient care of a zealous national organization which sprang into being for this patriotic purpose.

CHAPTER XX

Mount Vernon Lands Diminish—Burden of a National Shrine—Neglect and Decay—Speculators—Vain Appeal for Government Purchase—Ann Pamela Cunningham Organizes the Mount Vernon Ladies' Association of the Union—Contract for Purchase—Campaign for Funds—Edward Everett's Work—Possession Given—Restoration Begun—During the War—Regents, Superintendents, and Other Officials.

THE maintenance of Mount Vernon on the scale established by General Washington was only possible for a man of his other resources. When he died he owned, besides the eight thousand acres on or near Dogue Creek and Little Hunting Creek, other land and chattels which he estimated to be worth five hundred and thirty thousand dollars. He directed that these possessions be sold and the proceeds be divided in twenty-three parts. His will named twenty-three or more of his sister's and brothers' children, and the four grandchildren of Mrs. Washington, who received each at most one twenty-third part. This bequest, generous as it was, made none of the recipients wealthy.

When Mount Vernon passed to Bushrod Washington its yielding acres were diminished more than two-thirds. The owner was wholly without the western landed domain of his uncle from which strip after strip had been sold to realize the capital needed to support his seat on the Potomac. Each subsequent transfer of Mount Vernon saw the boundary lines draw in. The last private owner, John Augustine Washington, had about twelve hundred acres. As the owners of the mansion saw their lands diminish, they saw the obligations attached to its ownership increase by leaps and bounds. Fifty years after his death Washington's fame and the patriotic curiosity to see his home and tomb had grown to such proportions that it was not possible any longer for the owners to live there with privacy or without bankruptcy. In spite of their devotion to the sacred spot it became a burden they could not any longer bear.

Year after year saw the place fall farther and farther into neglect and decay. Justice Washington was absent on the bench nearly all the twenty-seven years of his ownership. His nephew and heir, John Augustine, survived him less than three years. The widow of John Augustine struggled bravely with the heavy burden, and finally, when her eldest son, John Augustine, married in his twenty-second year, she handed the estate over to him and fled with relief to a remote home in the mountains on the western edge of the state.

In addition to tourists from Europe and all parts of the world, every one in public life in Washington City felt privileged to come and to send his friends and visiting constituents with letters of introduction. Among his father's and grandmother's papers the surviving son of the last owner has an astonishing number of letters from members of the antebellum Senate, House, Supreme Court, and Cabinets asking attention for the bearers. Hospitality directed that they have not merely the liberty of the house and grounds, but substantial entertainment as well. It was not then an easy hour's ride on the wings of electricity. The journey was made in a primitive slow river steamer or in carriages over precarious roads.

Bushrod's heir foresaw that Mount Vernon would eventually ruin any member of the family who undertook to wring a living from its well-worn acres and remained to meet the tide of visitors with open house and open-handed hospitality, which is the tradition of the planters. In his will he wisely included permission for his heirs to sell to the national government. The mansion and estate reached his son in a depleted and ruined state. Had he the means to restore it to its original condition it would have required an annual fortune to keep it in repair, under the normal wear and tear of pilgrims, and to maintain a corps of guards against the idle, conscienceless visitors who not merely stole but destroyed to bear away souvenirs of the great shrine.

As early as 1848 speculators were keen to acquire the home and tomb of the first President. His great-grandnephew knew better than any one else how many and how keen they were, and he refused at great sacrifice to allow the estate to drift into speculative hands. At one time he was offered three hundred thousand dollars for the house and one thousand acres. At another time he refused two hundred and fifty thousand dollars for the house and two hundred and fifty acres. Mr. Washington was not holding Mount Vernon primarily for a high price. He had a proper sense of its speculative value but he had also a proper and a higher sense of its patriotic national quality, and for this reason he withheld it that the United States Government or the State of Virginia might own and care for it.

At one time he offered to let either the state or the national government take Mount Vernon at its own price. Both refused. So far as governmental appreciation, national or state, were concerned, the home of the immortal First Citizen went begging.

Mount Vernon seemed doomed to decay and perhaps to disappear. That fate overtook many of the famed mansions intimately associated with Washington's life, which their builders raised, not as he did in perishable wood, but in enduring brick. Mount Vernon survived Wakefield, where Washington was born; Greenaway Court about which as a young man he made his early surveys under the friendly eye of old Lord Fairfax; the White House, scene of his wedding festivities; Mr. Digges' Warburton Manor, and the Fairfaxs' Belvoir in sight of his own front door; nearby Hollin Hall of another neighbor, Thomson Mason; and Councillor Carter's Nomini Hall where he was a frequent visitor.

But, more enduring than the work of man's hand was custom, the work of his heart. By day and by night, as the boats sped along the Potomac past the tomb of Washington, their bells tolled in memory of the departed liberator who lay asleep beneath the trees on the hillside. Many heard but only one responded. Journeying up the river one night in the year 1853, a South Carolina woman was moved by the solemnity of the tolling bell, by the decay she knew of in spite of the softening moonlight and by the tales of the neglect of government, to a plan for the salvation of Mount Vernon. Her inspiration was to place the work of rescue in the hands of the women of America. This was a bolder proj-

ect then than now.   Feminine activity was undignified
not to say unorganized.   She confided the idea to her
daughter, who seized it and became its standard-bearer.
This was Ann Pamela Cunningham, founder and first
Regent of the Mount Vernon Ladies' Association of the
Union.

Miss Cunningham possessed a strong will and in-
domitable purpose in a frail body.   But even when
invalidism kept her off her feet she planned and wrote
and exhorted in a truly remarkable manner.   She
began her crusade for funds to purchase Mount Vernon
in December, 1853.   For three years, though she was
breaking the way, there was little tangible result.   The
organization was unincorporated and though some
money was coming in it was inconsiderable in proportion to the effort or to the whole amount required.

At first Miss Cunningham reported that Mr. Washington's reception of her plan was not wholly cordial,
and this was wholly natural.   The day of feminine
efficiency had not arrived.   Even Miss Cunningham
operated under an incognito, as "The Southern Ma-
tron," and was horrified when her own name appeared
in an obscure journal.   Moreover, the fact that she
was an invalid did not inspire confidence in her ability
to accomplish such a prodigious work.   Her prop-
osition to Mr. Washington was based on hope, expectation perhaps, and promise; all at the time without substance.

The idea had taken form, however, and the patriotic
fervor of Miss Cunningham and her growing group of
workers began to achieve results.   The Assembly of
the State of Virginia granted a charter to the Mount

Vernon Ladies' Association of the Union on the seventeenth day of March, 1856, which it revised by a further act of March, 1858.

The governing body of the Association thereby consists of a Regent and the Grand Council made up of the Vice-Regents, who are appointed from each state in the Union. They serve without pay. By this charter it is provided that, should the Association fail in its work, Mount Vernon Mansion and land shall be taken over by the State of Virginia and held sacred to the purposes for which it was purchased from the Washington family. The work of the ladies is surveyed once a year by a Board of Visitors appointed by the Governor and reporting to him. Mount Vernon is exempt from taxation, and the sum saved thereby is in effect Virginia's annual contribution to the work.

On the incorporation of the Association Mr. Washington at once entered into a contract with it for the sale of the mansion and two hundred and two acres of land immediately surrounding it for two hundred thousand dollars, giving four years during which to complete the payment.

The agreement with the Washington heirs specified that they "shall at all times have and enjoy the right to inter the remains of such persons whose remains are in the vault at Mount Vernon as are not now interred, and to place the said vault in such a secure and permanent condition as he or they shall see fit, and to enclose the same so as not to include more than a half-acre of land, and the said vault, the remains in and around it, and the enclosure shall never be removed or disturbed, and that no other person hereafter shall ever

be interred or entombed within the said vault or enclosure."

The campaign for funds was organized on the plan of
dollar contributions, and every state responded to the
call. The most notable individual assistance given
the Association in its campaign for the purchase money
came from the Honorable Edward Everett of Massachusetts. For four years he travelled from New
England to the Mississippi and south into Georgia
delivering his oration on the character of Washington
and devoting the proceeds to the purchase fund. In
addition he accepted the proposal of the editor of the
New York *Ledger* to write one article each week for
one year, for which ten thousand dollars was paid to
the fund. In all, Mr. Everett, by tongue and pen,
earned and donated to the purchase money needed to
redeem Mount Vernon the sum of $68,294.54, more
than one-third of the whole amount.

The final payment on the purchase contract was made
in December, 1859, and formal possession was given
February 22, 1860. On the outbreak of the Civil
War John Augustine Washington joined the Confed-
erate Army and was given a commission as aide on
General Robert E. Lee's staff, with the rank of Colonel.
He was killed September 13, 1861, at Cheat Mountain,
and was buried in a family burying ground at Charles-
town, West Virginia.

In the mansion at this time the only objects associated with the General's life there were the Key of the
Bastille, the clay bust of Washington which Houdon modelled from life, a plaster bust of LaFayette, the old globe
in the library, and some camp equipment. The owner

said that aside from papers, these were the only things which he possessed which had belonged to the General, and he presented them to the Association.

Upton H. Herbert was the first resident superintendent for the Association, and the estate was placed under his care, and he began restorations a few months before possession was given. The mansion received first attention. The crumbling portico, whose roof was at the time supported in places by masts from the sailboats of the river fishermen, offered the most compelling opportunity; the tottering colonnades were strengthened and these and the mansion received the needed protection of paint. All the outbuildings near the house had survived but were in bad condition. They were all roofed in 1860. The walks and drives were cleared, the wharf was made practical, and a small steamer, the *Thomas Collyer*, was purchased and put in commission to carry visitors between Washington City and Mount Vernon. From this source the Association received its first revenue. The work began to march, when suddenly the Civil War broke out, the steamer was confiscated for army transport service, interest in Washington's home was deflected, and revenue was almost totally cut off.

There followed dark days for the courageous women who had undertaken the salvation of Washington's home, but they did not falter even in the face of war; they maintained the work, and improvements progressed, though only by many individual sacrifices and contributions from the members' private savings, which some of them were little able to give. The pioneers remember with especial gratitude the substantial assistance given in these days by George W. Riggs of Washington, for many years treasurer of the Association, who financed many an emergency.

During the Civil War Mount Vernon was by spontaneous consent of those on both sides of the great contest the only neutral ground in the country. Soldiers were requested to leave their arms outside the gates, which they did, and men in blue and men in gray met fraternally before the tomb of the Father of their divided country. Mr. Herbert remained on the estate throughout the war and at its end said: "There was no effort to disturb the tomb or the place by troops on either side during that period." Which admits the inference that it was a civilian relic hunter who passed the iron barrier before Washington's sarcophagus and broke off one of the talons of the eagle sculptured on its top, for this bit of vandalism was committed at this time.

After the war the Association was so poor that it was unable to pay a superintendent's salary, and Miss Cunningham came in 1868 and lived at Mount Vernon and directed operations until her frail health broke down entirely in 1872. J. M. Hollingsworth then took up the work as resident secretary and superintendent. He remained in charge until May 30, 1885, and was succeeded by Harrison Howell Dodge who has held this same post more than forty-five years. James Young came to assist Mr. Dodge as clerk in 1886, but he has been assistant superintendent continuously since 1890, which was the year in which this office was created.

Since the death of the Founder of the Mount Vernon Ladies' Association it has had four Regents: Mrs. Lily

M. Berghman of Pennsylvania, who presided in council
from 1873 until her death in 1891; Mrs. Justine Van
Rensselaer Townsend of New York, who held the
presiding office until 1909; Miss Harriet C. Comegys
of Delaware, who presided until 1927; and Mrs. Alice
H. Richards of Maine, who has held the office of Regent
since that date.

Miss Cunningham died May 1, 1875, at her home at
Laurens, South Carolina, a little over one year after resign-
ing the office of Regent, which she had held from the birth
of the Association. In her letter of resignation to the
Council of Vice-Regents she left this declaration of
purpose: "Ladies, the Home of Washington is in your
charge; see to it that you keep it the Home of Washington. Let no irreverent hand change it; no vandal
hands desecrate it with the fingers of progress! Those
who go to the Home where he lived and died, wish to
see in what he lived and died! Let one spot in this
grand country of ours be saved from change! Upon
you rests this duty."

CHAPTER XXI

Remaking the Home of George Washington—The Summer House—The Old Tomb—Deer Park—Gifts of Protective Lands—North Lodge Gates—Sea Wall—Garden, Screen, and Ha-Ha Walls—A Colonial Ruin Bought to Get Colonial Brick—Tunnelling to Prevent Mount Vernon from Slipping—Earliest Shingles Still Shelter the Mansion—Flagging from St. Bees—Precautions Extraordinary—If Mount Vernon Were Destroyed—Historic Relics—When Naval Vessels Pass the Tomb of the Father of His Country—A Symbol—The End.

THERE have been two grand divisions in the life of Mount Vernon since the passing of the man who made it and made it famous. For sixty years it declined and decayed. Cedar and scrub pine possessed the neglected fields. The unregenerate honeysuckle caressed and then strangled everything its tentacles touched. Drives and paths lost their gravelled surface under matted wire grass. The unprotected palings of the garden fences rotted to the core, literally lost their heart, and tottered. Roof and column succumbed to the corrosion of time and the elements; the dampened plaster lost its grasp and fell; and paradoxically the heavy feet and meddling fingers of the thousands of pilgrims were hastening the disintegration of the shrine to which they came with worshipful patriotism. Once flames raised their tongues and licked out one of the buildings, mercifully detached. Only by a seeming miracle has the frail old mansion, whose

timber is tinder, been preserved from the annihilation
by fire.

Then came the patriotic women who took up the
work government had repudiated, and the mantle of
a new life spread over the place. For another period of
sixty odd years restoration has been re-creating the
home of Washington as he established and held it and
loved it.

The rooms of the mansion, the various outbuildings,
and the special phases of work about the estate were
apportioned among the Vice-Regents. Each had her
share of the whole work of restoration which became her
obligation and for which she gathered the funds.

The efforts of the pioneer Regents had overmatched
their first need, and when Mount Vernon was paid for
there remained a balance of above twenty thousand
dollars. This enabled them to begin repairs which
would forestall disintegration, and to buy the steamer
which would furnish further funds. At the end of the
war which had deprived them of this revenue they
fought for an indemnity, and a cautious Congress
allowed them seven thousand dollars and directed its
expenditure under army engineers. The sum went into
a new wharf and into the digging of a channel for a
larger boat.

For the first twenty years after the war revenue was
slight and the improvements were maintained in a large
measure by contributions from the private purses of the
ladies of the Association or by funds raised by their
efforts. Indeed, until 1886, there was a desperate
struggle to preserve rather than to restore. At the end
of that period the mansion and outbuildings were placed

beyond the probability of destructive decay, and order was restored in the environing grounds.

The summer house on the brow of the hill to the south of the mansion was rebuilt in 1886 with contributions from the school children of Louisiana.   From this point Washington watched the schooners load and unload at his wharf, and here hung a bell which regulated the hours of labor on the estate.   The deep cellar underneath was intended by the General for an ice-house, but it was abandoned for another in a more convenient locality north of the mansion.

From the time that the bodies of Washington and other members of his family were removed in 1831 the old tomb was abandoned and allowed to decay.   This spot so precious in association was reclaimed in 1887, by contributions from the State of Michigan, and restored as nearly as possible to the condition in which Washington put it when he built it in pious fulfillment of his brother Lawrence's will.   The capstone, inscribed "Washington Family," had been removed and was lost sight of for many years,   It was discovered at Woodlawn Mansion, worn by service as a carriage block, and was replaced in its ancient position.

At the same time the smothered bluff before the mansion was cleared, the rotted palings of the deer-park stockade were removed, and an iron fence replaced them and the enclosure was again stocked with deer, by the generosity of the sons of Mrs. Robert Cambell of Missouri.

The amusement speculator was for many years a continual menace to Mount Vernon.   The rising ground on the north side of the mansion became the basis of a plan, in anticipation of the coming of the electric-car service to the estate, to establish a public resort there. In 1887 Jay Gould of New York visited the national shrine and heard of this scheme. His sense of propriety as well as his sense of proportion grasped how essential this piece of land was to the ideal of those preserving Washington's home, and he bought thirty-three and a half protective acres and added them to the Association's holdings. Another gift of two acres on the west river front came from Christian Hcurich of Washington City, in 1893, when an unhealthy swamp near the wharf was converted into a fertile meadow. This brought the landed holdings of the Association up to two hundred and thirty-seven and a half acres.

The Masons and other patriotic citizens of Texas provided the means to erect the North Lodge Gates when, in 1892, the electric railway established its terminus here. They are wholly new, but in spirit and architectural detail repeat bits from the General's own designs for other buildings on his estate. Another new feature, unknown there before, is the sea wall, extending along the river front, provided as "a necessary protection to the wooded shore against the wave wash during storms." It was built in the nineties and was the gift, as was the wharf-house erected in 1891, of Mrs. Phoebe A. Hearst of California. The old wharf of pilings after generations of repairs was replaced in 1913 by the present permanent structure of cement.

When Washington completed his comprehensive scheme of landscape gardening after the Revolution he used brick walls with liberality and with decided effect. They were of three kinds: the garden walls, the screen walls, and the ha-ha walls. The first was a formal part of the plan of his buildings and grounds. They have withstood the wear of all the intervening years since. Even the decorative palings of the fences they support are in large part original.

There is a different story to tell of the screen and ha-ha walls. The former were wholly utilitarian and masked the buildings north and south of the mansion from the lawn. They were in ruins and had in part disappeared when the restoration was undertaken in 1910. The ha-ha walls, so intimately a part of the grounds as to be invisible from the mansion, had almost disappeared. The north ha-ha wall was replaced in 1896, the south in 1910, and the west in 1915. In these works it was thought wise not to depend on the skill of modern brickmakers to imitate the effect of a century of wear and weather, so the bricks were bought and brought from the ruins of Thatcher Thornton's splendid old colonial mansion, Society Hill, at the head of Upper Machodac Creek, an inlet on the Westmoreland shore of the Potomac, and they contributed harmoniously to the mellow tones of the original brick. The walls at Mount Vernon are reproduced to-day exactly as Washington planned and left them, except the boundary wall at the North Lodge Gate, which, though harmonious in design, is newly made necessary by conditions which the General did not anticipate.

Washington declared the old tomb to be "improperly situated." The reasons thereof were the springs which, on an extensive stratum on the Virginia side of the Potomac, render the adjoining banks liable to slides. Mount Vernon Mansion and the old tomb stand on a height which has been peculiarly susceptible to danger from this source. Minor slides occurred at intervals. To forestall further danger the hill was, in 1904, tunnelled by Jas. Archer's suggestion and under his direction, and is now drained of twenty thousand gallons of water a day, an engineering feat as unique as it was successful in its preservative effect.

In another way nature acts in time continually to change the conditions created and intended by Washington. His plans for trees and vistas were precise as they were extensive. He left a mass of information in his diary and letters by which to re-create and preserve the arboreal environment he prepared. These have been followed in discounting the changing aspects of growth, but this problem was less difficult than to restore the destructive influences of storm, insects, and decay. Washington built and planted with an eye to the vistas with which his estate naturally abounds. The weed trees which grew up and obscured these outlooks have been given the consideration which they merit, for the custodians of Mount Vernon subscribe to the landscape artist's axiom that a view is more valuable than a tree. The custom of planting memorial trees near the tomb has been discontinued.

The mansion was reshingled in 1913, for the first time in fifty-two years. This was a great event. The business of the repairs was approached as usual with an eye to preserving the identity of every detail. The old shingles were duplicated in North Carolina cypress from Lake Waccamaw, and hewed to the old samples. Tarpaulins were made to fit the roof, and their safe anchorage planned against high winds. As small a space as possible was opened at one time. Every night,

and during the day at any sign of "weather," the tarpaulins were battened down tight. When the house
was re-covered a stain reproduced the age and original
tones of the old roof.

In prying loose the shingles along the line where the
portico's roof reaches up on to the mansion Mr. Dodge
discovered that a whole section of shingles had been left
in place underneath when the portico was restored in
1860, a steeper pitch being given its roof at that time by
extending it back on to the roof of the mansion to the
sills of the dormer windows. Among these hidden
shingles there proved to be valiant survivors of the
course laid on when the mansion was first built. The
elements had etched evidence on their sides which
showed that they had been turned and twice exposed.
Some of the original shingles were used when the mansion was enlarged and re-roofed during the Revolution.
It is authentic later tradition that the roof had not been
touched since the old General's death until 1860. At
that time the old shingles were left before the east dormer
windows on that portion of the roof over which the
portico roof extended. Hence it is an interesting fact
that among the shingles on Mount Vernon to-day there
are some which were placed there when the original
villa was built.

Another result of Mr. Dodge's research was the dis-
covery of the quarry from which were cut the stone
flaggings in the great portico pavement. The originals
there have thinned nearly to the vanishing point. Frost
destroyed the edging course of the flags first laid there
by Lund Washington when the portico was erected
during the Revolution, and the General included the re-

paving of his portico among his repairs after the war. After many disappointments the sandstone blocks which he placed there were matched by stones from the ancient quarries whence he derived the original on the estate of Lord Lonsdale, at St. Bees Head, on the west coast of England near Whitehaven. A supply was then ordered in excess of that needed to repave the portico, and the reserve stock will be available should the source of these paving stones become exhausted.

The interior of the mansion has known radical repair only in two instances. It is true that the underpinnings have been made more nearly equal to the increased strain of the growing procession of visitors and that minor visible discrepancies have been corrected with finished skill, but the West Parlor and the Banquet Hall have demanded and received the more ambitious treatment. The harmonious condition of the panelling in the former room was the work of repair in 1879. The ceiling in this room remained intact as late as 1878 when it gave signs of loosening the hold it had kept for a full century. The design was drawn to scale, each of the twenty-eight hundred leaves radiating about the great circle were removed, a new ceiling laid on, and the decorations were reproduced in the original material.

Foresight was less acute in the case of the ceiling in the Banquet Hall. It cracked and pieces fell in 1880. At that time it was merely patched. But the accident was repeated in 1884, and the year following saw the entire ceiling made new in detail identical with the original, the devices of husbandry therein being repeated in the decorative effects of the capitals over the doors.

No fire, for either light or heat, is permitted in the mansion. Visitors are admitted only during the hours of daylight. At five o'clock in summer and at four o'clock in winter the house is closed. During the winter months heat is of course necessary for the comfort of visitors. It is furnished by hot water brought from boilers detached and distant from the big house and is introduced in such an adroit manner as to make the means practically invisible. The fireplaces continue to give out heat as in the olden time, but from the unseen coils in the gratings below the fire baskets. The hall or passage is heated by pipes concealed under the perforated supports of the stair treads. To these and other ingenious extremes does the care of Washington's home extend in the effort to preserve not merely its very existence, but its spirit as well, from modern device.

There is but one recorded instance that the mansion has been threatened by fire. In his diary Washington wrote on January 5, 1788: "About Eight o'clock in the evening we were alarmed, and the house a good deal endangered by the soot of one of the Chimneys taking fire & burning furiously, discharging great flakes of fire on the Roof but happily by having aid at hand and proper exertion no damage ensued."

Shortly after the death of Bushrod Washington fire destroyed the greenhouse and "Quarters" on the north side of the formal gardens, and they were restored between 1894 and 1896.* A complete fire department

* The West Quarters, adjoining the Conservatory, were restored by penny contributions, aggregating over one thousand dollars, from the school children of Kansas. The East Quarters were rebuilt with funds raised by the Vice-Regent for the State of New York.

was installed in 1892. Fire drills are frequent and the various apparatus are subject to frequent inspection. In unison with the intention to disturb none of the colonial harmonies, the fire-fighting forces remain out of sight. A steam engine is kept at some distance from the buildings, but the main batteries of hose and the chemical engine are close at hand in a sunken well in the centre of the circle before the great front door. As an added precaution smoking is not allowed on the estate. Watchmen and guards patrol the big house and all the grounds by night as well as by day.

If, in the last emergency, Mount Vernon were destroyed, its replica would rise in its place. Safely stored in fireproof vaults in the National Capital are architectural drawings of every building, with every conceivable detail of structure and decoration. With these are a great number of photographs of every aspect, inside and out, of the big house and its nest of buildings.

It has been seen how General Washington's personal belongings and the contents of his home were dispersed, first by his will, which removed only a few objects from Mount Vernon, then by Mrs. Washington's gifts, and later her will, by which her grandchildren came into possession of most of the furnishings of value, and finally after her death by the sale, in 1802, when the General's kinsmen bought many souvenirs of his home life. In 1848 Bushrod Washington's heirs offered for sale the bulk of their grand-uncle's library. When it appeared probable that this library would find an English purchaser and be removed from the country, a group of patriotic Americans arose in Massachusetts and paid a price which insured the sale to them. The books were presented to the Boston Atheneum, where nearly all the original Mount Vernon library may be found to-day.

The treasures which Martha Washington gave her grandson, George Washington Parke Custis of Arlington, and which adorned that mansion for over half a century, had many vicissitudes on the outbreak of the war. When Arlington was taken by the Federal troops some of the Washington relics had been removed to Ravensworth, to the northwest in Fairfax County; others, left in the house, were removed to the Capital, where they were placed on exhibition. The national government after the war restored these articles to Mr. Custis' descendants, who have made some of the most valued contributions to the reassembling of the original furnishings of the historic mansion.

Many other Mount Vernon treasures, in particular those which passed from Mrs. Washington through her granddaughter, Nellie Custis Lewis, to the Lewis family, and valued Washington documents and letters in the hands of the Washington co-lateral descendants of the General, were offered at public sales in Philadelphia in the early nineties of the last century. It is from the purchasers at these sales that the Mount Vernon Ladies' Association obtained by purchase, gift, and loan others of the relics which are again in their original positions.

The articles already mentioned as left in the house when the Washington family sold and gave possession of it were the nucleus of the later collection. Among them the most valuable treasure is the Houdon bust of Washington, made in the house and never removed therefrom. Perhaps because it is clay instead of marble, it seems to have excited no cupidity during the early distributions.

Of highest historic interest is the bed on which Washington died, which is in its original position in his bedroom over the library. Here, too, are the mahogany shaving-stand presented to the General by the first French Minister to this country; his military trunk quaintly curved and studded with brass nails, and a chair which stood in the room the night of his death.

The "tambour desk" and chair which were bequeathed to Dr. Craik are again in the library, with his silver inkstand, snuffers and tray; and here is the Washington family Bible containing the record of George Washington's birth and christening. A few books of the original library are back in place by the sides of many volumes which merely duplicate the originals.

Four of the General's swords are home again, and after an absence of over a century the old crystal and wrought-iron lantern which Admiral Vernon sent Lawrence Washington hangs once more in the hall. Nearby is the veritable deed given by Lord Culpepper to Nicholas Spencer and John Washington for the tract on which Mount Vernon was later built.

The one complete group in the mansion is that associated with the Vaughan mantel in the Banquet Hall. Here are the identical firedogs presented by LaFayette, the original rosewood pedestals, clock, candlesticks, vases, and wall lamps. Elsewhere in this room are the model of the Bastille which the Polish Gentleman found in the portico exposed to the elements and the vandal fingers of playful children; a mirror plateau imported by Washington to adorn his dining table; a painting of the Great Falls of the Potomac; his gold watch, knee and shoe buckles, silver toilet articles, silver spectacles, needle book used at Valley Forge, spoons, punch bowl, champagne and other glasses, and additional souvenirs not only of the master of Mount Vernon but of its mistress and of Nellie Custis. In an adjoining parlor is the harpsichord which Washington imported from abroad for Nellie and over which her stern grandmother kept her so many hours at tearful practice.

In the dining-room are the sideboard, a sixteen-gallon wine chest and four wine decanters, a pair of pitchers, and the portrait of David Rittenhouse, which were all there in the General's day. Elsewhere are tables and chairs which Washington placed in the house and some of the identical pictures. But where the originals either of pictures or furniture could not be found or, being found, could not be secured, duplicates have as far as possible been installed, awaiting the proper means or the generous impulses which will restore the identical articles which Washington knew and used in his home.

The whole aspect of the house is simple without severity and elegant without ostentation, representative of the taste, dignity, and eminence of the great man whose environment has been reconstructed. The same is true of the exterior of the mansion and of the grounds. There is perhaps a trimness to the walks and a smartness to the cropped lawns and an absence of littered corners which even the old General could not have wrung from his shiftless slave labor. The young trees he planted and watched are now veteran giants, many with the deep scars of time and storms bound up in sustaining cement. But if the General were to return he would find surprisingly few changes, in the spirit of the place least of all.

The ideal sought by the zealous patriots who have the custody of Washington's home is to maintain the environment which he created in the eighteenth century. So the restoration of Mount Vernon may be said to progress backward. But the cycle of fashion has played a paradoxical trick on the old place by making the new fashions in domestic landscape and architecture those of the days when old Mount Vernon was new.

Though it is the tomb of Washington, the place is instinct with life. The house is kept with the nice domestic simplicity that suggests the personal presence of the master and mistress. The solemnity of death is only sensed when one stands uncovered beneath the open sky among the trees before the reliquary of all that is mortal of the immortal Washington, or not less poignantly when upon the broad Potomac one hears the unfailing requiem of the bell of passing vessels.

There is an order in the United States Navy by which, when ships of the service pass Mount Vernon between sunrise and sunset, a full guard and band is paraded, the bell is tolled, the colors are dropped to half-mast, the bugle sounds taps, the guard presents arms, and officers and men on deck stand at attention and salute as the ship passes the hallowed spot.

This is but a symbol of the emotion which Mount

Vernon raises in the heart of every American, commanding the attention and the salute of all lovers of liberty. It is not merely the home of Washington, living and dead, but it focusses our ideals, and our glory as a people, in our first national shrine.

THE END

APPENDIX

A—The Title to Mount Vernon.

B—Table of General Washington's Visits to Mount Vernon While President.

C—Tables of Those Born, Married, and Buried at Mount Vernon.

D—Regents and Vice-Regents of the Mount Vernon Ladies' Association of the Union, Since Its Organization.

APPENDIX A

The Title to Mount Vernon

I.—Lord Culpepper to John Washington and Nicholas Spencer, 1674, 5,000 acres, "in the ffreshes of Pottomeek River and neare opposite to Piscataway, Indian towne of Mariland," in Stafford County, Virginia. Later divisions of Stafford County placed this land in Fairfax County. The original document hangs in the hall at Mount Vernon.

II.—George H. Jeffers to Nicholas Spencer and John Washington, 1679, 5,000 acres. Grant, on record in Richmond.

III.—John Washington bequeathed his half of the above land to his son, Lawrence Washington, by his will, 1677; recorded in Westmoreland County.

IV.—A division of the above tract in 1690, recorded in Stafford County, by which Lawrence Washington received 2,500 acres, his half lying to the north and east on the river and Hunting Creek.

V.—Lawrence Washington to his daughter Mildred, 2,500 acres as above, by his will, 1697; recorded in Westmoreland County. Mildred Washington married Roger Gregory.

VI.—Mildred and Roger Gregory to her brother Augustine Washington, 2,500 acres as above, by deed, May 26, 1726; recorded in Westmoreland County

VII.—Augustine Washington to his son Lawrence Washington, 2,500 acres as above; deed recorded at a session of the General Court of Virginia, Williamsburg, October 28, 1740.

VIII.—Augustine Washington confirmed above grant to his son Lawrence Washington in his will, 1743; recorded in King George County.

IX.—Lawrence Washington to his brother George Washington, all his real estate in Virginia, by his will, 1752; recorded in Fairfax County. Lawrence and George Washington both added lands to the tract devised by their father, but Mount Vernon Mansion and present surrounding land is included in the 2,500 acres above.

X.—George Washington to his nephew Bushrod Washington, Mount Vernon Mansion and 4,000 acres, by his will, 1799; recorded in Fairfax County.

XI.—Bushrod Washington to his nephew John Augustine Washington, Mount Vernon Mansion and 1,225 acres, by his will, 1829; recorded in Fairfax County.

XII.—John Augustine Washington to his wife Jane C. Washington, all his property, with power to devise it as she pleased among her children, by his will, 1832; recorded in Jefferson County, West Virginia.

XIII.—Jane C. Washington to her oldest son, John Augustine Washington, Mount Vernon Mansion and 1,225 acres, deed, 1850; recorded in Fairfax County.

XIV.—Jane C. Washington to John Augustine Washington, by her will, 1855, confirms above deed; recorded in Jefferson County, West Virginia.

XV.—A Contract between John Augustine Washington and the Mount Vernon Ladies' Association of the Union, for the purchase of Mount Vernon Mansion and surrounding buildings and the tomb and 202 acres of land; recorded in Fairfax County, April 6, 1858.

XVI.—W. A. Taylor, Commissioner, and the heirs of John Augustine Washington to the Mount Vernon Ladies' Association of the Union, deed confirming above contract, November 12, 1868, recorded in Fairfax County.

XVII.—Two simultaneous deeds, Lawrence Washington and wife to Jay Gould, and Jay Gould and wife to the Mount Vernon Ladies' Association of the Union, thirty-three and one-half acres northeast of the mansion, July 23, 1887; recorded in Fairfax County.

XVIII.—Christian Heurich and wife to the Mount Vernon Ladies' Association of the Union, deed for two acres on the southwest side of their original tract, November 13, 1893; recorded in Fairfax County.

APPENDIX B

TABLE OF GENERAL WASHINGTON'S VISITS TO MOUNT VERNON
WHILE PRESIDENT

Dates and duration of General Washington's visits to Mount
Vernon during his two terms as President of the United States,
April 30, 1789 to March 4, 1797.

(The dates in italics are estimated from relative evidence in
letters, diary, newspapers, etc., in the absence of direct evidence
of the exact date, from which they are believed to be not more
than one day removed.)

1789, April   16. . . . Left for New York.
1790, Sept.   11. . . . Arrived at Mount Vernon.
      Nov.   22. . . . Left for Philadelphia. 71 days.
1791, March   30. . . . Arrived at Mount Vernon.
      April   7. . . . Left on Southern Tour. 8 days.
      June   12. . . . Arrived at Mount Vernon.
      June   27. . . . Left for Philadelphia. 15 days.
      Sept.   20. . . . Arrived at Mount Vernon.
      Oct.   17. . . . Left for Philadelphia. 27 days.
1792, May   15. . . . Arrived at Mount Vernon.
      May   24. . . . Left for Philadelphia. 9 days.
      July   16. . . . Arrived at Mount Vernon.
      Oct.   8. . . . Left for Philadelphia. 84 days.
1793, *April*   1. . . . Arrived at Mount Vernon.
      April   13. . . . Left for Philadelphia. 12 days.
      June   27. . . . Arrived at Mount Vernon.
      July   6. . . . Left for Philadelphia. 9 days.
      Sept.   14. . . . Arrived at Mount Vernon.
      Oct.   28. . . . Left for Philadelphia. 44 days.
1794, *June*   22. . . . Arrived at Mount Vernon.
      July   3. . . . Left for Philadelphia. 11 days.
1795, April   19. . . . Arrived at Mount Vernon.
      April   26. . . . Left for Philadelphia. 7 days.
      July   20. . . . Arrived at Mount Vernon.
      Aug.   6. . . . Left for Philadelphia. 17 days.
      Sept.   13. . . . Arrived at Mount Vernon.
      Oct.   12. . . . Left for Philadelphia. 29 days.
1796, June   20. . . . Arrived at Mount Vernon.
      Aug.   17. . . . Left for Philadelphia. 58 days.
      Sept.   23. . . . Arrived at Mount Vernon.
      Oct.   26. . . . Left for Philadelphia. 33 days.
1797, March   15. . . . Arrived at Mount Vernon.

APPENDIX C

TABLES OF THOSE BORN, MARRIED, AND BURIED AT MOUNT VERNON

BORN IN MOUNT VERNON MANSION

To Lawrence and Anne (Fairfax) Washington, four children, born between 1743 and 1751 inclusive. Lawrence mentions his three deceased children and his surviving daughter, Sarah, in his will.

To George Augustine and Frances (Bassett) Washington, four children born between 1787 and 1791 inclusive, while he resided at Mount Vernon in charge of the estate during his uncle's absence at the seat of government as President. (Welles' "History and Geneology of the Washington Family," page 187.)

To Lawrence and Nellie (Custis) Lewis, two children. Washington records in his diary the birth of the first, December 1, 1799. The second was born "about 1801" while Mr. and Mrs. Lewis made their home in the mansion with Mrs. Lewis' widowed grandmother, Mrs. Martha Washington.

To John Augustine and Eleanor Love (Selden) Washington, six children born between 1844 and 1858 inclusive. Welles in his "History of the Washington Family" records, pages 255 and 256, the births of seven children. Lawrence Washington, one of these and the last surviving male child born in Mount Vernon Mansion, confirms Welles except as to Eliza, who was not born there.

MARRIED IN MOUNT VERNON MANSION

George Augustine Washington, nephew of George Washington, to Frances Bassett, niece of Mrs. George Washington, October 15, 1785. Recorded by General Washington in his diary under that date.

Lawrence Lewis, nephew of George Washington, and Eleanor Parke Custis, granddaughter of Mrs. George Washington, February 22, 1799. Recorded by General Washington in his diary under that date.

Noblet Herbert to Mary Lee Washington, granddaughter of General Washington's brother, John Augustine Washington, 1819.

(Welles' "History and Geneology of the Washington Family," page 216.)

BURIED AT MOUNT VERNON

Lawrence Washington, who died at Mount Vernon, 1752, and his three children, who died at Mount Vernon before this date, and were buried in the first or old vault as soon as it was completed by George Washington.

Sarah Washington, infant daughter of Lawrence and Anne Washington, died at Mount Vernon in 1752 and was buried in the first vault.

Martha Parke Custis, daughter of Mrs. George Washington, died at Mount Vernon, June 19, 1773, and was buried in the first vault.

George Washington, died at Mount Vernon, December 14, 1799, and was buried in the first vault. Reëntombed 1831 in the second or new vault.

Daughter of Mr. & Mrs. T. Peter, age five, died August, 1800, at Georgetown, D. C., and interred at Mount Vernon, September 1, 1800. (Diary of Mrs. Thornton, in "Records of Columbia Historical Society," volume 10, page 186.)

Martha Washington, wife of George Washington, died at Mount Vernon, May 22, 1802, and was buried in the first vault. Reentombed in the new vault in 1831.

William Augustine Washington, nephew of George Washington, and one of the executors of his will, died at Georgetown, D. C., October, 1810, and "was buried at Mount Vernon." (Welles' "Pedigree and History of the Washington Family," page 174.)

Bushrod Washington, nephew of George Washington, executor of his will and heir to Mount Vernon, died in Philadelphia, November 26, 1829. His remains are in the second or new vault. (Diary of John Augustine Washington, September 10, 1855.)

Ann Washington, wife of Bushrod Washington above, died a few days after her husband, November, 1829. Her remains are in the new vault. (Diary of John Augustine Washington, September 10, 1810.)

Bushrod Washington, fourth child of William Augustine Washington above, "died at Mount Zephyr, in 1830, and was interred in the vault at Mount Vernon." (Welles' "Washington Family," page 196.) Not mentioned in John Augustine Washington's diary.

Ann Aylette Washington, daughter of William Augustine Washington, was "born at Haywood, Westmoreland County, Virginia, about 1787. Died and was buried at Mount Vernon." (Welles'

Washington Family," page 196.) Not mentioned in John Augustine Washington's diary.

John Augustine Washington, grand-nephew of the General, died at Mount Vernon in June, 1832, and his remains are in the new vault. (Diary of his son, John Augustine Washington, September 10, 1855.)

Lawrence Lewis, nephew of the General, died November 20, 1839, and his remains are in the new vault. (Diary of John Augustine Washington, September 10, 1855.)

A Child of the Reverend W. P. C. Johnson, placed in the new vault, April 16, 1842. (Diary of John Augustine Washington, April 16, 1842.)

Mrs. M. E. A. Conrad, daughter of Lawrence and Eleanor Custis Lewis, died September 21, 1839, at Pass Christian, Mississippi. Her body "and that of her child were buried near the new vault," July 10, 1843. (Diary of John Augustine Washington, July 10, 1843.)

Eleanor Parke Custis Lewis, granddaughter of Mrs. George Washington, died at Audley in Clarke County, Virginia, July 13, 1852. Buried outside the new vault beside her daughter and granddaughter. A marble shaft marks the spot.

Mary Lee Washington Herbert died 1852 and her remains were placed in the new vault. (Diary of John Augustine Washington, September 10, 1855.)

Jane C. Washington, wife of John Augustine Washington who died at Mount Vernon in 1832, and mother of John Augustine Washington last private owner of Mount Vernon, died at Blakeley, Jefferson County (now West Virginia), 1855. Her body was placed in the new vault September 10, 1855, after which none other has been admitted. (Diary of John Augustine Washington, September 10, 1855.)

APPENDIX D

THE REGENTS AND VICE-REGENTS OF THE MOUNT VERNON LA-
DIES' ASSOCIATION OF THE UNION SINCE ITS ORGANIZA-
TION WITH THE DATES OF THEIR APPOINTMENT

MISS ANN PAMELA CUNNINGHAM, *Regent*, 1853-1873
(Resigned, 1873; Died, May 1, 1875)

VICE-REGENTS

1858

1	Mrs. Anna C. O. Ritchie . .	resigned	1866	Virginia
2	Mrs. Alice H. Dickinson . .	resigned	1859	North Carolina
3	Mrs. Philoclea E. Eve . . .	. died	1889	Georgia
4	Mrs. Octavia Walton LeVert .	. died	1877	Alabama
5	Mrs. Catharine A. MacWillie .	. died	1872	Mississippi
6	Mrs. Margaretta S. Morse .	. resigned	1872	Louisiana
7	Mrs. Mary Rutledge Fogg . .	. died	1872	Tennessee
8	Mrs. Elizabeth M. Walton	. resigned	1858	Missouri
9	Miss Mary Morris Hamilton .	resigned	1866	New York
10	Mrs. Louisa I. Greenough . .	resigned	1865	Massachusetts
11	Mrs. Abba Isabella Little . .	resigned	1866	Maine
12	Mrs. Catharine Willis Murat .	. died	1867	Florida
13	Mrs. Mary Bootes Goodrich .	resigned	1864	Connecticut
14	Miss Phebe Ann Ogden . .	. died	1867	New Jersey
15	Mrs. Alice Key Pendleton . .	{ resigned	1863	Ohio
		{ died	1885	
16	Mrs. Abby Wheaton Chase .	. died	1892	Rhode Island
17	Mrs. Jane Maria Van Antwerp .	died		Iowa
18	Mrs. Margaret A. Comegys .	. died	1888	Delaware
19	Mrs. Hannah B. Farnsworth .	. died	1879	Michigan
20	Mrs. Sarah King Hale . . .	resigned	1861	New Hampshire
21	Mrs. Martha Mitchell . . .	. died	1902	Wisconsin
22	Mrs. Rosa V. J. Jeffreys . .	. died	1894	Kentucky
	Mrs. Janet M. C. Riggs, *Acting Vice-Regent*			Dist. of Colum.

1859

23	Mrs. Elizabeth W. Barry . .	. died	1883	Illinois
24	Mrs. Sarah J. Sibley . . .	. died	1869	Minnesota
25	Mrs. Mary P. J. Cutts . .	. resigned	1878	Vermont
26	Miss Lily Lytle Macalester .	. died	1891	Pennsylvania
27	Mrs. Magdalen G. Blanding .	resigned	1884	California
28	Mrs. Harriet B. Fitch . . .	. died	1880	Indiana

29	Mrs. Sarah H. Johnson . . .	died	1866	Arkansas
30	Mrs. Letitia Harper Walker . .	died	1908	North Carolina

1860

31	Mrs. Ann Lucas Hunt	died	1878	Missouri
32	Mrs. Mary Chestnut	died	1867	South Carolina

1866

33	Mrs. Margaret J. M. Sweat . .	died	1908	Maine
34	Miss Emily L. Harper	died	1891	Maryland
35	Mrs. Lucy H. Pickens	died	1899	South Carolina
36	Mrs. M. E. Hickman . . .	resigned	1874	Nevada
37	Mrs. M. A. Sterns	resigned	1873	New Hampshire
38	Mrs. Emily R. M. Hewson .	resigned	1872	Ohio
39	Miss Ella Hutchins. . . .	resigned	1872	Texas

1867

40	Mrs. Janet M. C. Riggs . .	{ resigned	1868	
		died	1871	Dist. of Colum.
41	Mrs. Maria Brooks. . . .	resigned	1876	New York
42	Mrs. Matilda W. Emory . .	resigned	1873	Dist. of Colum.

1868

43	Mrs. Nancy Wade Halsted . .	died	1891	New Jersey
44	Mrs. Nannie C. Yulee	died	1884	Florida

1870

45	Mrs. Susan E. J. Hudson . . .	died	1913	Connecticut
46	Mrs. Ella B. Washington . . .	died	1898	West Virginia

1872

47	Mrs. Betsy C. Mason	died	1873	Virginia
48	Mrs. A. P. Dillon	{ resigned	1873	
		died	1898	Iowa
49	Mrs. C. L. Scott	resigned	1878	Arkansas

1873

50	Mrs. William Balfour . . .	resigned	1875	Mississippi
51	Mrs. Mary T. Barnes	died	1912	Dist. of Colum.
52	Mrs. David Urquehart. . .	resigned	1876	Louisiana
53	Miss M. E. Maverick . .	resigned	1873	Texas

MRS. LILY M. BERGHMAN, *Second Regent*
(Made Acting Regent, 1873; Regent, June, 1874; Died, 1891)

1874

54	Mrs. Emma Reed Ball			Virginia
55	Mrs. Aaron V. Brown	died	1889	Tennessee

1875

56	Mrs. Lily L. Broadwell . . .	died	1889	Ohio
57	Mrs. John P. Jones. . . .	resigned	1876	Nevada

1876

58 Mrs. Jennie Meeker Ward . . . died 1910 Kansas
59 Mrs. Justine Van Rensselaer
    Townsend . . . . . died 1912 New York

1878

60 Mrs. J. Gregory Smith . . . resigned 1884 Vermont

1879

61 Miss Alice Longfellow . . . . Massachusetts
62 Mrs. Robert Campbell . . . . died 1882 Missouri

1880

63 Mrs. Ida A. Richardson . . . died 1910 Louisiana

1882

64 Mrs. Ella S. Herbert . . . . died 1884 Alabama

1885

65 Mrs. E. B. A. Rathbone . . . died 1923 Michigan
66 Mrs. Mary T. Leiter . . . . died 1913 Illinois
67 Mrs. Janet Dekay King . . . died 1896 Vermont
68 Mrs. Elizabeth Woodward . . . died 1897 Kentucky

1888

69 Miss Harriet C. Comegys . . . died 1927 Delaware
70 Mrs. Fannie Gilchrist Baker . . died 1901 Florida

1889

71 Mrs. Alice Hill . . . . . . died 1908 Colorado
72 Mrs. Rebecca B. Flandrau . . . died 1912 Minnesota
73 Mrs. Phoebe A. Hearst . . . died 1919 California

1890

74 Mrs. A. R. Winder . . . . . died 1906 New Hampshire

1891

75 Mrs. Georgia Page Wilder . . . died 1914 Georgia

MRS. JUSTINE V. R. TOWNSEND, *Third Regent*
(Elected Temporary Regent, December, 1891; Regent, June, 1892;
Died, 1912)

1893

76 Mrs. Geo. R. Goldsborough . { resigned 1904
                                   died 1906 Maryland
77 Mrs. J. Dundas Lippincott . . died 1894 Pennsylvania
78 Miss Mary L. Pendleton . . resigned 1897 Ohio
79 Mrs. Philip Schuyler . . . resigned 1894 New York
80 Mrs. Christine B. Graham . . . died 1915 Missouri

81 Mrs. Francis S. Conover . . . . died 1914 New Jersey
82 Mrs. Mary P. Yeatman Webb . . died 1917 Tennessee

1894
83 Miss Lelia Herbert . . . . . died 1897 Alabama

1895
84 Mrs. Robert H. Clarkson . { resigned 1900
                              { died 1902 Nebraska
85 Mrs. William Ames . . . . . died 1904 Rhode Island
86 Miss Amy Townsend . . . . . died 1920 New York

1896
87 Mrs. Chas. C. Harrison . . . . died 1922 Pennsylvania
88 Mrs. Thomas S. Maxey . . . . Texas

1897
89 Mrs. James E. Campbell. . . resigned 1902 Ohio

1900
90 Mrs. Robert D. Johnston . . . . . . Alabama
91 Mrs. C. F. Manderson . . . . died 1916 Nebraska
92 Mrs. Eugene Van Rensselaer . . died 1923 West Virginia

1901
93 Mrs. J. J. Pringle . . . . . . died 1921 South Carolina
94 Mrs. Wm. F. Barret . . . . . died 1920 Kentucky
95 Mrs. Chas. Denby. . . . . . died 1906 Indiana

1905
96 Mrs. Henry W. Rogers . . . . Maryland

1907
97 Mrs. Lewis Irwin . . . . . . died 1916 Ohio
98 Miss Mary F. Failing . . . . Oregon
99 Mrs. Eliza F. Leary . . . . Washington
100 Mrs. Frances J. Ricks . . . resigned 1914 Mississippi
101 Mrs. J. Carter Brown . . . . Rhode Island

1909
102 Mrs. A. B. Andrews . . . . . died 1915 North Carolina

MISS HARRIET CLAYTON COMEGYS, *Fourth Regent*
(Elected May, 1909; resigned May, 1927; died July, 1927)

1911
103 Mrs. Alice H. Richards . . . . Maine
104 Miss Mary Evarts, resigned 1923, reappointed, 1924 Vermont
105 Mrs. Antoine Lentilhon Foster . . . . . . Delaware

106 Miss Annie Ragan King . . . . Louisiana
107 Miss Jane A. Riggs . . . . . died 1930 Dist. of Colum.

1913

108 Mrs. Horace Mann Towner . . . . Iowa
109 Mrs. Thomas P. Denham . . . . Florida

1914

110 Miss Harriet L. Huntress. . . . died 1922 New Hampshire
111 Mrs. Charles E. Furness . . . . Minnesota
112 Mrs. Benjamin D. Walcott . . . . . . Indiana
113 Mrs. Louis Hanks . . . . Wisconsin

1915

114 Miss Annie B. Jennings . . . . Connecticut
115 Mrs. W. H. Bradford . . . . New Jersey

1916

116 Mrs. Anne Shepley Nagle . . . . . . Missouri
117 Mrs. Harriet Isham Carpenter . . . . . Illinois
118 Miss Mary Govan Billups . . . . . . Mississippi
119 Mrs. John V. Abrahams . . resigned 1921 Kansas

1919

120 Mrs. Margaret Finley Busbee Shipp . . . . North Carolina
121 Mrs. Horton Pope. . . . . Colorado
122 Mrs. Charles J. Livingood . . . . . . Ohio
123 Mrs. Jefferson Randolph Anderson . . . . . Georgia
124 Mrs. Celsus Price Perrie . . . resigned 1922 Arkansas

1920

125 Mrs. Horace Van Deventer . . . . Tennessee
126 Mrs. Charles Stetson Wheeler . . . . . California

1921

127 Mrs. William Ruffin Cox . . . died 1925 Virginia

1922

128 Mrs. Henry Gold Danforth . . . . New York

1923

129 Miss Mary Mason Scott . . . . Kentucky
130 Mrs. Alexander C. Troup . . . . Nebraska
131 Mrs. John R. Shelton . . . resigned 1930 Kansas
132 Mrs. Edward H. Parker . . . died 1924 Michigan

1924

133 Miss Virginia Leigh Porcher . . . . . . South Carolina
134 Mrs. Wm. R. Mercer . . . resigned 1928 Pennsylvania

135 Miss Constance Lee Peterkin . . . . . . West Virginia
136 Miss Mary Evarts . . . . . died 1928 Vermont

1925

137 Mrs. Benjamin S. Warren . . . . Michigan

Mrs. Alice H. Richards, *Fifth Regent*
(Elected May, 1927)

1927

138 Mrs. Fairfax Harrison . . . . Virginia

1928

139 Mrs. Gordon Woodbury . . . . New Hampshire
140 Mrs. Benj. Franklin Pepper . . . . Pennsylvania

1930

141 Mrs. Harold Lee Berry . . . . Maine
142 Mrs. Nathaniel Thayer . . . . Massachusetts
143 Mrs. Horace Brown . . . . Vermont
144 Mrs. Earl King Lord . . . . Kansas

INDEX

293